Explore
QUEENSLAND

Explore
QUEENSLAND

Bruce Elder

NH
NEW
HOLLAND

First published in 1997 by
New Holland (Publishers) Ltd
London • Cape Town • Sydney • Singapore

Produced and published in Australia by
New Holland Publishers (Australia)

3/2 Aquatic Drive, Frenchs Forest, NSW 2086, Australia

24 Nutford Place, London W1H 6DQ, United Kingdom

80 McKenzie Street, Cape Town 8001, South Africa

ISBN 1 86436 200 6

Publishing Manager: **Mariëlle Renssen**
Managing Editors: **Averill Chase, Sally Bird**
Editors: **Thea Grobbelaar, Jacquie Brown**
Designer: **Mandy Moss**
DTP Cartographer: **John Loubser**
Picture Researchers: **Vicki Hastrich, Bronwyn Rennex**
Proofreader: **Anouska Good**
Reproduction by Unifoto (Pty) Ltd, Cape Town
Printed and bound by Tien Wah Press (Pte) Ltd, Singapore

PHOTOGRAPHIC CREDITS

ECOPIX (Wayne Lawler) (Compliments of **Redcliffe City Council**): p. 19; **Bruce Elder:** pp. 17, 26, 27, 28 (right), 29, 40, 41, 45, 46,
47, 48, 49, 50, 51 (centre, bottom), 58, 59, 65 (centre right, bottom right), 71 (top right, bottom right), 72, 91, 92, 93 (top right,
bottom right), 96 (left), 97, 98, 99 (top right), 102, 103, 115 (bottom left), 125 (top, centre), 128, 129 (bottom), 140 (left), 146, 152,
166; **Tom & Pam Gardner:** p. 25 (centre, bottom); **Richard I'Anson:** pp. 37 (bottom left), 73 (top left, top right); **T Lindsey:** p. 129
(top left); **News Limited:** p. 23 (top); **NHIL:** pp. 15, 18, 33 (top right), 39 (top), 51 (top), 115 (top, bottom right), 116, 117 (top left,
bottom left), 142, 143, 161 (top right); **NHIL (Shaen Adey):** front cover (top left and right, bottom left and right), spine, half title, title page,
pp. 5, 6, 28 (left), 32, 33 (top left, bottom left, bottom right), 34, 35, 37 (top, bottom right), 38, 39 (bottom), 42/43, 53, 54, 55, 56, 57,
60/61, 62, 63, 65 (top, bottom left), 66, 67, 68, 69 (top left, bottom), 71 (top left, bottom left), 75, 76/77, 78, 79, 80, 81 (bottom),
83, 84, 85, 87, 88, 89 (top left, bottom left), 93 (left), 99 (top left, bottom left), 104/105, 107, 108, 109, 110, 111, 112, 113, 118, 119,
120/121, 122, 123, 124, 125 (bottom), 127, 130, 131, 132/133, 134, 135, 136, 137, 139, 140 (right), 141, 144/145, 147, 148, 149, 150,
151, 153 (top), 154/155, 156 (right), 157, 158 (top left, bottom left), 161 (top left, bottom left, bottom right), 162 (bottom), 163 (top left,
top right), 165, 167 (bottom), 168, 169, 170, 171, 172, 173 (bottom); **NHIL (Bruce Elder):** 81 (top, centre), 82, 89 (top right, bottom right),
94/95, 96 (right), 100, 101, 153 (bottom), 173 (top left, top right, centre left, centre right); **NHIL (Denise Greig):** p. 129 (top right);
NHIL (Anthony Johnson): cover (main picture), back cover, pp. 10/11, 13, 30/31, 156 (left), 158 (right), 159, 162 (top), 163 (bottom), 167
(top); **Joe Shemesh:** p. 117 (right); **SPLB (J Cook):** pp. 23 (bottom), 25 (top), 73 (bottom); **SPLB (D Kelly):** p. 24; **SPLB (W Long):** p. 21;
SPLB (H Plowman): p. 20; **SPLB (P Vines):** p. 74; SuperBee (compliments of **SuperBee Honey Factory**): p. 69 (top right).

The following abbreviations have been used:
NHIL New Holland Image Library
SPLB Stills Photo Library Brisbane

Copyright is held by agents or photographers in **bold type**

INTRODUCTION

Queensland's fame for diversity is clearly evident in its range of landscapes: the impcnetrable rainforest of Cape York and the endless plains of the outback; the ribbon of high-rise apartments along the Gold Coast and the sleepy towns of Thargomindah and Quilpie; the unspoilt beauty of the Great Barrier Reef off Cairns and the Whitsunday Islands; and the bustling urban sprawls of Brisbane, Bundaberg, Rockhampton, Mackay, Townsville and Cairns.

Given the number of major tourist attractions it offers, it is hardly surprising that a recent survey among overseas visitors found that more than 60 per cent nominated Queensland as their primary destination in Australia. Nowhere else in the world is there a reef formation over 1000 kilometres long, tropical beaches only moments away from modern urban society, and the opportunity to view Aboriginal actors and dancers re-enacting the stories of their Dreaming. It is also seldom that one can drive for hours across an ancient seabed seeing only the occasional emu and forlorn mobs of sheep.

This book provides the traveller to Queensland with 71 self-contained round-trips. While most of them are planned to be completed in a day, the distances involved might tempt the traveller to stop, and, particularly in the case of the larger towns, a single day would never do justice to the richness of their history.

It is important to remember that beyond the coast Queensland is a region of truly daunting distances. Travelling up the Matilda Highway – which starts in the outback town of Cunnamulla and does not stop until it reaches the shores of the Gulf of Carpentaria – it is common to travel more than 100 kilometres without passing through a town. In some instances – most notably the stretch between Winton and Cloncurry which is a distance of some 348 kilometres – the two towns on the way are little more than a petrol station, a pub, a general store and a few lonely buildings.

Equally the density of settlement along the coast, particularly in areas which have become popular tourist destinations, can mean that a journey of only 50 kilometres can pass through literally dozens of thriving communities.

The aim of this book is to provide travellers in Queensland with a rich cross-section of tours. While the vast majority of these journeys can be done on good sealed roads in a conventional vehicle, there are many which require specialist forms of transport. In the case of Fraser Island, for example, the two journeys most commonly available from the marina at Hervey Bay and the ecotourism-orientated Kingfisher Bay Resort are discussed. In the case of the cruises to the Outer Reef at Cairns–Port Douglas and in the Whitsundays, journeys made by the author with commercial operators are described. There are also other operators working in these popular destinations and the reader should not assume that these journeys are the only ones available.

All travellers should be aware that Queensland is subject to cyclonic weather during the summer months. This, combined with the presence of sharks, stingers and crocodiles in the waters of the far north, means simply that summer travel should be undertaken with caution and with the awareness that you may end up staying in a destination for a few days while rivers subside and the weather improves.

Queensland is one of Australia's truly wonderful regions. Its breathtaking beauty – the rainforest, the coastal beaches and the seemingly infinite plains of the outback – remains in the memory of travellers long after their journey is over.

CHAPTER 1
BRISBANE AND ENVIRONS

1 HISTORIC BRISBANE

■ WALKING TOUR ■ 5 KM ■ 4 HOURS ■ A WALK INTO BRISBANE'S HISTORIC PAST

This tour, which is best done on foot, begins at St John's Cathedral, takes in some of Brisbane's most gracious and impressive historic buildings, and ends at the Queensland Maritime Museum.

*B*risbane has long had a tradition of 'newness' and there are relatively few genuinely old public buildings. This can in part be explained by the city's history of using timber for the construction of its buildings, and the fact that an 1864 fire destroyed many of the finest early structures.

The city experienced three major periods of building during the 19th century. The first occurred between 1824 and 1839 when Brisbane was a closed penal colony. It was during this time that the 1828 Observatory (or 'Old Windmill') and the Old Commissariat Store (1829) were constructed using convict labour. Brisbane was opened to free settlement in 1842 and became a separate colony on 10 December 1859. In spite of an active building program during that period, only two buildings survive – old St Stephen's Church and The Deanery of St John's Cathedral. The last building boom was between 1860 and 1880 when an impressive array of public buildings, including Government House and Parliament House, both symbols of the city's new affluence and independence, were built.

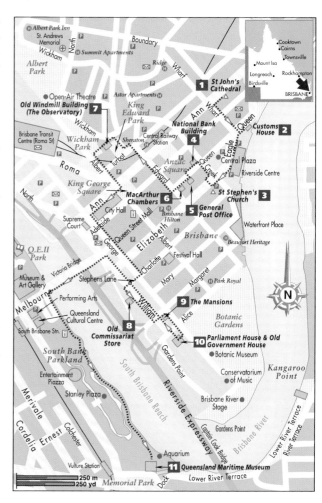

1 ST JOHN'S CATHEDRAL AND THE DEANERY

St John's Cathedral (at 417 Ann Street) could well lay claim to being Australia's oldest uncompleted building. This handsome Gothic cathedral, constructed of brick, Helidon sandstone and Brisbane porphyry stone, was started in 1901 and, even today, the western section remains unfinished.

John Loughborough Pearson was the architect chosen to design the building. Unfortunately, he died before the work was completed and his son took over. The interior of this Gothic Revival cathedral is laid out in the form of a crucifix, with some particularly impressive flying buttresses and rose windows.

The construction of the cathedral has been a never-ending saga. The foundation stone was laid in 1901, the first stage consecrated in 1910, the second stage was consecrated in 1958 and new bays were completed in 1968. Still to be completed is the whole of the western end, which includes a central tower with two matching towers. A model of how the cathedral will eventually look is located inside the church.

Next door is The Deanery, a gracious, two-storeyed porphyry-stone residence designed by Andrew Petrie and built for Dr William Hobbs in 1853. It is one of the few remaining buildings constructed between 1842 and 1859 and it served as the Governor's residence (1859–1862) while Government House was being built. Perhaps The Deanery's finest secular moment came in 1859, when the proclamation separating Queensland from New South Wales was read from the building's east balcony.

2 CUSTOMS HOUSE

Walk to the south down Ann St towards the river for about 100m and turn left at Wharf St. Follow it for two blocks (250m) until you reach Queen St. Cross the road and turn left up Queen St. The Customs House is less than 100m up the road, just before you reach Patrick Lane.

With its solid Corinthian columns and greenish copper dome, the Customs House stands beside the Brisbane River like a great Victorian matriach. Its position and prominence make it one of Brisbane's most impressive landmarks. It was built by John Petrie between 1886 and 1889 and features twin pediments with heraldic shields and the words 'Advance Australia'. A noble thought, although at the time of its construction 'Australia' as such did not exist.

3 ST STEPHEN'S CHURCH

Walk back down Queen St to Wharf St (100m) and head south along Eagle St until it meets Elizabeth St (150m). Proceed south along Elizabeth, past Creek St and 80m down on the left is St Stephen's Church.

Located in Elizabeth Street, St Stephen's Church, sometimes known as Pugin's Chapel, is the city's oldest church. Built in 1850 and attributed to the English architect Augustus Welby Pugin, it is a simple Gothic sandstone structure. It is superseded by St Stephen's Cathedral, which stands next to the old building, in 1874. The 'new' cathedral was built between 1863 and 1874 to a design by Benjamin Backhouse.

4 NATIONAL BANK BUILDING

Walk back up Elizabeth St to Creek St, turn left into Creek St, walk to the intersection with Queen St (80m), cross the road, and on the corner of Queen and Creek sts is the National Bank Building.

Located at 308–322 Queen Street, this large and gracious structure is regarded as one of Australia's finest Classical Revival buildings. The National Trust's description notes:

Constructed from Murphy's Creek sandstone with columns and carved work in New Zealand Omaru limestone … Its opulent yet precise composition features two major facades rising through three spacious levels, dominated by tall Corinthian columns … The interior features a large banking chamber which is lit naturally by means of a leaded glass dome and approached via a corridor with a coffer-ceiling. Fine cedar joinery and plaster work, largely intact and beautifully preserved, are evident throughout … The fireplaces are in Italian marble.

The Mansions on William Street.

5 GENERAL POST OFFICE

Head 70m down Queen St in the direction of Edward St, and on the opposite side of the road, but in the same block, is the GPO.

The GPO is located on the site of the city's original female convict barracks. Construction was started in 1871 and completed in 1879, and it is recognised as a fine example of a late-Victorian Classical Revival building. When the Central Railway Station was built in Ann Street at the end of the 19th century, the architects quite consciously placed its tower in the centre of the block so that the towers of the GPO and the railway station were aligned.

Although the project had started 59 years earlier, it wasn't until 1930, with the creation of Anzac Square, that the entire streetscape was completed. As if to establish the perfect symmetry of the precinct, the War Memorial Shrine and the bronze equine statue commemorating the Boer War were aligned with the post office and railway station towers. On the first floor is the GPO Museum, which is open from 10:00–15:00 on Tuesdays, Wednesdays and Thursdays.

6 MACARTHUR CHAMBERS

Continuing 80m to the south along Queen St, on the same side of the road and at the next intersection (on the corner of Queen and Edward sts) you will find MacArthur Chambers.

This building became important during the latter half of World War II when General Douglas MacArthur, the Commander-in-Chief of the South-West Pacific area, used the building as his headquarters. MacArthur Chambers is open for inspection from 9:00–17:00 Monday to Friday.

7 OLD WINDMILL BUILDING (THE OBSERVATORY)

Head three blocks west along Edward St until you reach Turbot St (300m). Across the road and slightly to your left is King Edward Park. If you cut through the park to Wickham Terrace, turn left and walk 80m, you will see the Observatory on your left.

One of only two structures in Brisbane remaining from the city's convict era, this rendered stone and brick building, located on Wickham Terrace, dates back to 1828. The Old Windmill has played many varied parts in its time, including a starring role in Australia's very first television transmission in the 1930s.

While originally constructed as a windmill (the colony's first industrial building), it was soon converted to a treadmill, with convicts rather than the wind driving the machinery. The site of at least one hanging, the building was also used as a signal station and a fire lookout at various times. By the end of the 19th century an observation platform and cabin had been added, and the building became known locally as 'the Observatory'.

8 OLD COMMISSARIAT STORE

Cut back through Wickham Park to Albert St. Turn left heading east until Albert terminates in Ann St and King George Square. Turn right and head south for 220m past City Hall until you reach George St. Turn left and follow George St to Charlotte St (450m), and on the right-hand side of the road is Stephens Lane. Cut through the lane to William St.

Brisbane's other remaining convict-era building is the Old Commissariat Store at 111 William Street. Built by convicts when Brisbane was a closed penal colony, this is now the headquarters of the Royal Historical Society of Queensland.

Reputed to be the state's first stone building, it was constructed with walls ranging in thickness from 60cm to 1.2m. The first building was completed in 1829 as a two-storeyed structure, but during the period 1886–1926 it was expanded to three storeys.

9 THE MANSIONS

Continue east along William St to the next main intersection at Margaret St (250m). Cross the road and turn left up Margaret St. Continue on Margaret St to George St. The Mansions are on the corner.

A really superb example of 19th-century ornateness in the Free Classical style, The Mansions were erected as six elegant townhouses in the 1890s. The deep arcaded verandahs on both floors give the building a very distinctive appearance. The Mansions now contain a number of up-market shops – including a restaurant, an antiquarian print gallery, a bookshop, an antique shop and the National Trust of Queensland Gift Shop.

10 PARLIAMENT HOUSE AND OLD GOVERNMENT HOUSE

Turn right and head south-east down George St until you reach Alice St. The Parliament House and Old Government House complex is across the road, adjoining the Botanic Gardens.

Soon after Queensland was declared a separate colony in 1859, construction of the Parliament House building began on the hill above the Botanic Gardens.

The colonial architect Charles Tiffin was awarded the commission to build Parliament House after he had won a countrywide competition with his unusual imitation of the French Renaissance style. The building was started in 1865, first occupied in 1868, and finally completed in 1889. It is characterised by solid colonnades that keep the building cool in summer, some truly magnificent timberwork executed in local Queensland timbers, and an elegant interior.

Located between the Queensland Institute of Technology and the Brisbane River, Old Government House was built in 1862. This Classical Revival building was designed by Charles Tiffin, built of porphyry and sandstone, and constructed between 1860 and 1862. Old Government House remained the Governor's official residence until 1910, after which it was used as the first building of the University of Queensland. It currently houses the offices of the National Trust of Queensland.

11 QUEENSLAND MARITIME MUSEUM

Walk up William St to Victoria Bridge (500m), cross the bridge and walk south-east through the South Bank complex, along Riverside Promenade, for 1.2km.

The Queensland Maritime Museum is situated on the river at the end of Dock Street, almost directly opposite the Queensland Institute of Technology. With an interesting display of charts, model ships, engines and memorabilia, combined with 'on-the-water' displays of a World War II frigate and an old steam tug, the museum will keep any nautical enthusiast interested for hours.

The Old Windmill on Wickham Terrace.

Parliament House, Alice & George streets.

2 BRISBANE – GARDENS AND CULTURE SPOTS

■ DRIVING TOUR ■ 40KM ■ 1 DAY ■ ESCAPING TO TRANQUILLITY AND BEAUTY

This tour includes a selection of Brisbane's places of cultural interest and visits some of its 200 parks and reserves, ranging from Mount Coot-tha Reserve to small city parks.

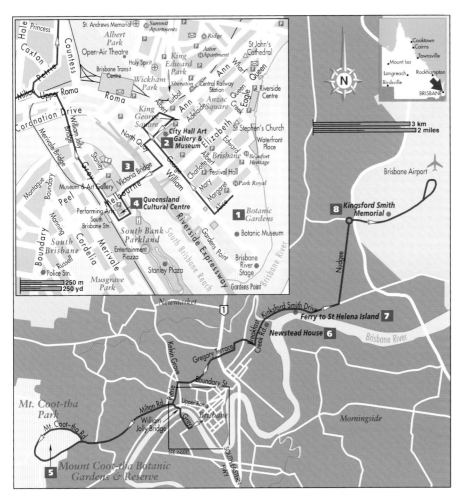

1 BOTANIC GARDENS

Located on the northern bank of the Brisbane River, Brisbane's Botanic Gardens lie on the gentle slope between Parliament House and the river.

The City Botanic Gardens cover over 20ha of land and are one of Brisbane's show-pieces. Beautifully located on the banks of the Brisbane River and spreading over the gentle slopes and undulations below Parliament House and Old Government House, the gardens are a peaceful respite from the bustle of the Central Business District. They date back to the earliest years of European settlement. Long before 1855, when they were formally laid out by Walter Hill, the first Gardens Director, the area had been used as a vegetable garden. It was Hill who planted rows of bunya pines and intro-duced plants such as the poinciana and jacaranda. He also built a fountain in 1867 and planted a row of weeping figs.

The subtropical climate, combined with the rich soils of the river bank, ensure a per-manent display of spectacular colours and the heady fragrances of frangipanis, orchids, oleanders, flame trees, bougainvilleas and jacarandas. A walk through the gardens, particularly one along the river bank, is a must for every visitor to the city.

2 CITY HALL ART GALLERY AND MUSEUM

Heading down Alice St, turn right into George St, con-tinue through Margaret, Mary, Charlotte, Elizabeth, Queen, Adelaide and Ann sts and turn right up Turbot St. Taking the right ramp, which leads into Roma St, turn right again and you will see the entrance to the King George Square Car Park.

One of historic Brisbane's most significant landmarks, the City Hall Art Gallery and Museum complex, combines King George Square, the Brisbane Administration Centre and the City Plaza Shopping Centre.

The City Hall itself is an interesting example of an attempt to use English neo-classical architecture in a modern building. It uses Queensland brown-tinted freestone, marble, sandstone and timbers. The scale is impressive and full of old-world charm. The main foyer inside King George Square, for example, makes use of ornate high-vaulted ceilings, floor mosaics, and crafted timber and plasterwork to great effect. There is also a huge 16m sculpture depicting Queensland protecting her citizens.

The City Hall Art Gallery and Museum was opened by Queen Elizabeth II in 1977 and contains extensive displays of paintings, ceramics and photographs. The clock tower, an amazing Italian Renaissance structure which rises 91m above the City Plaza, pro-vides excellent panoramic views of the city.

3 VICTORIA BRIDGE

Head south down Ann St, cross George St, and take the next sharp left turn into North Quay. Victoria Bridge is your first right-hand turn.

Although it is not the oldest bridge across the Brisbane River (the William Jolly Bridge can claim that distinction) the Victoria Bridge does have a couple of predecessors. It is the third bridge to be built on a site which was used as the earliest European crossing point.

A pylon from the second bridge (1897) has been retained as a monument and is now listed on the National Estate. On the pylon is a plaque to a Greek boy who was killed during the World War I victory cele-brations in 1918.

The Victoria Bridge runs from the Central Business District across the Brisbane River to the Performing Arts Complex and the Queensland Cultural Centre.

4 QUEENSLAND CULTURAL CENTRE

Turn left immediately after crossing the bridge and watch for the signposted car parking stations within the Cultural Complex.

If the essence of modern Brisbane is a new sense of sophistication, the Queensland Cultural Centre in some ways sums up the city's current aspirations.

Brisbane does not enjoy a reputation as an important home of the arts. It may be a reac-tion to this criticism which led the city to construct Australia's finest cultural complex, opened to coincide with the Brisbane World Expo in 1988. This superb complex now includes the Queensland Art Gallery, the Performing Arts Complex, the Queensland Museum and the State Library. It was designed by the local architect Robin Gibson and has successfully drawn together, on the banks of the Brisbane River, most of the city's major cultural activities.

Surrounded by lush subtropical gardens, the complex consists of the State Library (which houses the country's most important

A view of Parliament House from the City Botanic Gardens.

collection of books and papers relating to the history of Queensland), the Queensland Museum with its 2 million exhibits including the tiny 'Avian Cirrus' aeroplane in which Bert Hinkler made the first solo flight from England to Australia in 1928, a number of restaurants, and the Performing Arts Complex with its Lyric Theatre, Concert Hall and Cremorne Studio Theatre.

The Art Gallery, in which the State's extensive collection is housed, is open from 10:00–13:00 every day of the week.

5 MOUNT COOT-THA BOTANIC GARDENS AND RESERVE

Access Grey St from the Cultural Complex and head north across the river over the William Jolly Bridge. Take the left-hand fork along the short Skew St and turn left as it terminates in Upper Roma St. Take the first right-hand turn and then turn left immediately and you are in Milton Rd (Route 32). Follow this main road for about 3.5km and turn right into Mt Coot-tha Rd (watch for the signs – the turn is not easy). The Botanic Gardens are on your left. Continue until you see the signs for the car parking area.

In recent times a second, and equally spectacular botanic garden has been opened on Mount Coot-tha Road. Located in Toowong, only ten minutes' drive from the city centre, the Mount Coot-tha Gardens are reputed to contain Australia's largest display of subtropical flora. They cover an area of 57ha in which plants are set against an environment of lakes, ponds and streams. There are literally thousands of tropical plants housed in the unusual Tropical Dome indoor display. Of particular interest are the Japanese Gardens, a delightful and quiet retreat. Nearby is the Exotic Rainforest and beyond it are the sections of Bunya Forest, Bougainvilleas, Australian Rainforest, Open Eucalypt Forest, Melaleuca Wetlands and a section devoted to Western Australian Flora. Mount Coot-tha also contains a Planetarium and at the top of the hill there is an impressive lookout with panoramic views over the city. It would be very easy to spend a whole day wandering around the Gardens.

6 NEWSTEAD HOUSE

Return towards the city centre along Milton Rd. Turn left into Petrie Terrace, follow it to where it ends at a major intersection (about 800m) and take a right-hand turn into College Rd. Continue for about 400m. The road branches right and left. Keep left and turn into Gregory Terrace (Route 10). After about 2km this road finishes at Brooks St. Turn left into Brooks St, which curves right and becomes Hamilton Place, then take a hard right-hand turn into Campbell St. Follow Campbell St into Cowlishaw St until you reach Wickham St (Route 25). Turn left into Breakfast Creek Rd. Newstead House is located just before the bridge and is clearly signposted.

One of the many superb buildings in suburban Brisbane, Newstead House (located on the riverside at Breakfast Creek Road, Newstead) was built in 1846 for the pastoralist Patrick Leslie. It became the residence of Captain Wickham from 1847–1859. The most intriguing feature of the building is that it is actually a two-storeyed dwelling masquerading as a single-storeyed house. It was Captain Wickham who built the verandah around the house and extended and raised the ground level. Today Newstead House is recognised as one of Brisbane's oldest and most impressive residences. It is open from 11:00–15:00 Mondays to Thursdays and also from 14:00–17:00 on Sundays.

7 ST HELENA ISLAND

Continue along Breakfast Creek Road for a short distance. It becomes Kingsford Smith Dve. From the BP Marina at 101 Kingsford Smith Dve, Breakfast Creek, you can take a cruise with Adai Cruises along the river out to St Helena Island. The alternative is to drive to Manly or Wynnum and catch a ferry.

Now owned and run by the Queensland National Parks and Wildlife Service, St Helena Island contains the ruins of one of Queensland's major prisons. The oldest ruins on the island date from 1866 when a quarantine station was constructed, using a combination of locally hewn stones and handmade bricks. Within a year the building had been converted to a prison. At its peak

St Helena Prison held 300 prisoners. It was downgraded to a prison farm in 1921 and finally abandoned in 1933.

8 KINGSFORD SMITH MEMORIAL

Continue for 2km along Kingsford Smith Dve and turn left into Nudgee Rd. After 3km you will reach the roundabout which joins Airport Dve. Drive towards the airport until you see the Kingsford Smith Memorial on your left.

Just 10km from the city centre on Airport Drive near the new Brisbane Airport is the famous *Southern Cross* which Charles Kingsford Smith flew in the epic first crossing of the Pacific Ocean. The plane was built by Fokker in Holland in 1926 and later modified by the Douglas Aircraft Company in America. It made the Pacific crossing in terrible weather, stopping at Fiji and arriving in Brisbane on 8 June 1928. In 1929 it was involved in the famous, or 'infamous', attempt to fly to England which resulted in Kingsford Smith and his crew being forced to land on the coast of Western Australia. At the time there was much controversy as some suggested that the forced landing had been nothing more than a publicity stunt. It then completed the journey to London in 12 days and 18 hours and, after being rebuilt by Fokker, flew across the Atlantic, thus completing an around-the-world journey. It was bought by the Federal Government for £3000 in 1935 and then found a permanent home at Brisbane Airport.

The Tropical Dome at Mount Coot-tha.

The drawing room, Newstead House.

3 BRISBANE'S SUMMER DAYTRIP

■ DRIVING TOUR ■ 167KM ■ 1 DAY ■ A TIME FOR FISHING AND BEACHCOMBING

Among the variety of daytrips Brisbane offers, one of the most popular retreats is largely unspoilt Bribie Island and the peaceful coastal beaches of Beachmere, Woorim and Banksia.

*I*n his book Portrait of Brisbane, *the passionate Queenslander Bill Scott described the city's informality and uniqueness when he wrote: 'Brisbane is a lazy town with its sleeves rolled up, casually sprawling across its thirty-seven hills. The hills are patterned with paling fences, mango trees, high-stepping weather-board houses, and a tangle of overhead wires like the web of a demented spider.'*

Similarly, the novelist Thea Astley, in a lecture she gave called 'Being a Queenslander', described the city: 'Growing up in Brisbane in the thirties and forties meant alignment with a shabby town, a sprawling timber settlement on a lazy river; meant heat and dust and the benefits of the sub-tropics – brighter trees, tougher sunlight, slower-moving people and a delicious tendency to procrastinate. I think it was the weather.'

Brisbane is Australia's fourth-largest city. Its climate is subtropical with an average annual rainfall of 1090mm (most of which falls between December and March), an average of over seven hours of sunshine each day, a humidity level that hovers around 50 per cent all year, and a temperature range from 10°C in winter to 30°C in summer. Despite the sometimes oppressive summer heat, the locals will happily tell you that Brisbane is the only Australian capital city to enjoy a perfect climate.

Brisbane, like so many early settlements along the coast of eastern Australia, started life as a penal colony. It is thought that the Ngundanbi and Yagara Aborigines lived along the banks of the river before Europeans settled the area.

In September 1822 the British government instructed the Governor of the Colony of New South Wales, the Scottish astronomer and administrator Sir Thomas Brisbane, to send out exploration parties to Moreton Bay, Port Curtis and Port Bowen with a view to finding a suitable place for a new penal colony.

In November 1823 the explorer John Oxley reached the waters of Brisbane's Moreton Bay. Within days of his arrival he chanced upon three escaped convicts – Thomas Pamphlett, Richard Parsons and John Finnegan. The convicts claimed that, while on a woodcutting expedition, they had been swept out to sea. Their small vessel had floated north and eventually been washed up onto the lonely sands of Moreton Island. They were found by the local Aborigines, who showed them their source of fresh water. The convicts duly revealed it to Oxley, who named it the Brisbane River after the Governor. Oxley immediately returned to Sydney Cove with news of the discovery.

The next year Governor Brisbane sent the explorer back to Moreton Bay accompanied by 29 convicts, 14 soldiers, the botanist Allan Cunningham, a surgeon and storekeeper named Walter Scott, and the new settlement's first military commandant, Lieutenant Henry Miller. Before the small sailing ship Amity *left Sydney Cove, Brisbane told Oxley: 'The* Amity *is placed under orders for the purpose of crowning your late discovery of a large river flowing into Moreton Bay with the formation of a new settlement in its vicinity. The spot which you select must contain three hundred acres of land, and be in the neighbourhood of fresh water. It should lay in the direct course to the mouth of the river, be easily seen from the offing of ready access. To difficulty of attack by the natives, it ought to join difficulty of escape for the convicts.'*

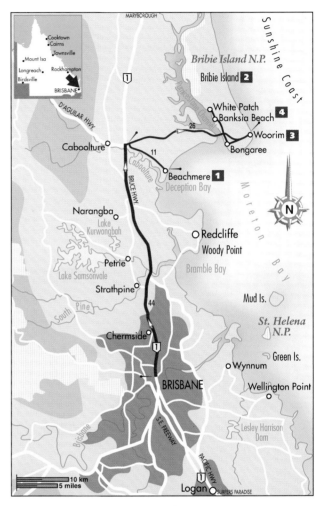

1 BEACHMERE

Starting from the intersection of Queen and Edward sts, at the north-eastern end of the Queen Street Mall, turn into Queen St and drive away from the Mall. The road gradually bends to the left, cutting back across Adelaide and Ann sts. Continue across Boundary St, with Centenary Place on your right. Now on Wickham St, drive across Gipps St and turn left at the next inter-section, into Brunswick St. This leads directly on to Bowen Bridge Rd, which becomes the Bruce Highway (Route 1). This route heads north out of the city. Some 44km out of Brisbane, the Bruce Highway intersects with the D'Aguilar Highway, which leads west to Caboolture. Head in the opposite direction, however, turning right onto the signposted Bribie Island road. Less than 1km along this route, another road branches off to the south – headed to Beachmere, which is 11km away.

Located on the northern shores of Deception Bay, the village of Beachmere has grown up along the coast near Brisbane and has been largely ignored by the tourist industry. This is one of those secrets that only locals and a few others enjoy. There is a good beach here, and the area's fishing is considered to be outstanding. The quietness of the Beachmere region has been a magnet for people interested in fishing and sailing, and also those who wish to escape from the more developed areas of the coast. Accommodation is limited, but there is a caravan park.

2 BRIBIE ISLAND

Return for 11km along the northern road, then turn right, heading east. After 19km you will come to the bridge across Pumicestone Channel leading to Bribie Island. Take the immediate sharp right turn, travel along Welsby Parade, which follows the shoreline for 2.5km, and then turn left into First Ave.

Bribie Island is an interesting combination of retirement location, fun-packed destination for daytrippers, family holiday retreat, and haven for fishermen, sporting people (there's an excellent golf course on the island) and sunlovers.

The first European to visit Bribie Island was explorer Matthew Flinders. He arrived here in 1799 and reputedly saw his first dugong, also making contact with some distinctly unfriendly local Aborigines. It is said that the island township of Bongaree was named after Flinders' Aboriginal companion. John Oxley landed on the island in 1823, meeting the shipwrecked convicts who showed him the entrance to the Brisbane River, thus leading to the subsequent settlement of the area.

The first European to live here was a convict from the Moreton Bay penal colony. Apparently convict Bribie, after whom the island is named, had been most successful at catching mud crabs for the officers at Moreton Bay and was rewarded with his freedom. He departed for Bribie Island with an Aboriginal woman and the two of them lived here until Bribie's death.

Development of the island was slow. A short-lived fish cannery was established in the late 19th century, a jetty was built in 1912, and a car was shipped over to the

A bridge across Pumicestone Channel connects Bribie Island with the mainland.

island in 1919. However, it wasn't until 1953 that the island was connected to the mainland's electricity supply.

Bribie Island's great transformation occurred in 1963, when the bridge was built. Since the 1960s, the island has become an increasingly popular tourist and retirement destination. Its close proximity to Brisbane has been a distinct advantage and it now has a population of over 7000.

Interestingly, although on weekends and during school holidays people pour onto the island (both from Brisbane and from further afield), it has never consciously sought to develop its tourist potential.

Perhaps the most impressive example of the island's commitment to retirement living is the remarkable development behind the Bribie Waterways Motel. Here, the developer has created a series of waterfront blocks of land by building a canal above the high-tide level. Entry into this exclusive little watery cul-de-sac is by a lock which only the residents can operate.

Settlement has been restricted to the southern tip, with the balance of 30km-long Bribie Island being maintained as a flora and fauna sanctuary.

3 WOORIM

Bribie Island's main township of Bongaree is located directly across the Pumicestone Channel (or Passage) from the mainland. This settlement offers all the necessary facilities for a stay on the island. Either Welsby Parade or Goodwin Dve will take you to First Ave. Woorim is situated 3.5km along this road.

Woorim is an attractive beach township that attracts both surfers and sun-lovers. Like the rest of Bribie Island it has remained relatively underdeveloped, preferring to promote itself as a contrast to the over-developed beaches of the Sunshine Coast and Gold Coast. The town has a licensed hotel/motel and a caravan park, and there are some good walks along the beaches to the north and south.

The eastern coastline of Bribie Island is characterised by low-lying barrier dunes: the beaches are beautifully white, and the sense of peacefulness that pervades the area continues to entice Brisbane residents looking for a city escape. One of the great attractions here is the fishing, and it is possible to catch whiting off Woorim Beach.

4 BANKSIA BEACH AND WHITE PATCH

Head back along First Ave and turn right into Goodwin Dve. After nearly 3km, before the roundabout, turn right into Verdoni St. After a bend to the right, this becomes Sunderland Dve, which will take you straight out to Banksia Beach.

For those people eager to escape even further from 'civilisation', the dirt roads on the Pumicestone Channel side of the island lead to the small, peaceful beaches of Banksia Beach and White Patch. The Channel is noted for the mangroves that grow at the water's edge – this area is rich in mangrove wildlife and one of the major attractions is to explore the waterfront, as well as to wander through the island's sandy interior. The Channel is ideal for sailing, canoeing, sailboarding and fishing – an accomplished angler can expect to catch fish such as flathead, whiting and tailor here.

Head back along Sunderland Dve to the junction of Verdoni St and Goodwin Dve and then turn right. This road leads to a roundabout, back across the bridge, and on to the Bribie Island–Caboolture Rd. After 19km head south, and travel 44km back along the Bruce Highway to Brisbane.

Fishing trawlers at Bribie Island.

4 BEACHSIDE HISTORY AT REDCLIFFE

■ DRIVING TOUR ■ 70KM ■ 1 DAY ■ QUEENSLAND'S FIRST EUROPEAN SETTLEMENT

Redcliffe proudly describes itself as 'the first white settlement in Queensland', which is not entirely correct, as Cooktown holds that honour. Redcliffe, however, is also steeped in history.

Redcliffe, once a small seaside retreat 40km north of Brisbane, is now, thanks to the construction of the Hornibrook and Houghton highways, an outer-northern suburb only 35km from Greater Brisbane.

The area was first visited by Matthew Flinders in July 1799. He spent 15 days in Moreton Bay, landed and, noting the redness of the cliffs in the area, named Red Cliff Point on 17 July. It was not until 1823 that John Oxley, on instructions from Governor Brisbane to find a suitable place for a northern convict outpost, visited Moreton Bay. It was on Oxley's recommendation that Red Cliff Point was chosen for the penal colony.

On 24 September that same year the brig Amity brought officials, soldiers, their wives and children, and 29 convicts to Redcliffe. Two children, the first European children born in Queensland, were born in September and November 1824.

The settlement was short-lived. Three weeks after the establishment of the outpost two convicts and a soldier were speared to death by the local Aborigines and this event, combined with the prevalence of fever and poor anchorage facilities, led to the settlement being moved to the banks of the Brisbane River in the middle of 1825.

A few of the buildings were left standing at Redcliffe and it is claimed that the local Aborigines, with a rather nice sense of irony, called the houses 'oompie bong', meaning 'dead house'. The name stuck and the anglicised 'humpybong' was applied to the whole of the Redcliffe Peninsula.

During the short life of the outpost, a store, prisoners' barracks, kitchen, well, whipping post (no good convict settlement could be without one), gaol, guardroom, brick kiln, soldiers' barracks and commandant's house were all constructed. The stores and the main landing place were located where the Redcliffe Jetty now juts out into Moreton Bay.

It was not until the late 1860s that the Redcliffe area was opened up for agricultural purposes. Over the next 70 years it grew slowly. The first school was opened in 1876, hotels were built at Woody Point, Redcliffe and Scarborough in the 1880s, the Woody Point Jetty was completed in 1881, the Redcliffe Jetty and Post Office were built in 1885 and Garnet & Natone's steamer from Brisbane started a regular service in the 1880s.

In 1908 a publication, the Souvenir of Humpybong (it can be obtained from the Redcliffe Historical Society), sang the praises of the peninsula: 'The exhilarating climatic conditions of Redcliffe, Woody Point and Scarborough cannot be too highly praised.

'Excellent as summer resorts, their chief attractions are their beautiful mild winter … This little book, it is hoped, will be the means of inducing those who desire a change of scene and who are in search of health and renewed youth to visit Humpybong and sojourn there at all seasons of the year.'

Redcliffe remained an isolated retreat until 1935 when the construction of the Hornibrook Highway linked Redcliffe to Brisbane and, particularly after World War II, was instrumental in the rapid growth of the Redcliffe area.

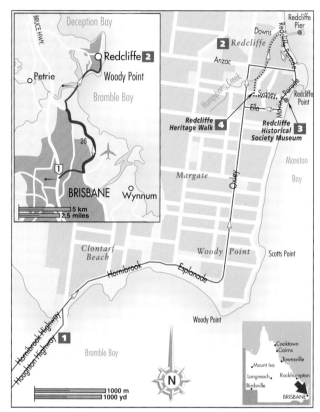

Redcliffe, an outer-northern suburb of Brisbane.

1 HORNIBROOK AND HOUGHTON HIGHWAYS

Leave the city centre via Queen, Adelaide or Turbot St, heading north-east. All three streets join Wharf St. Turn left into Wharf St and follow it until it terminates in Leichhardt St. Turn right, cross over Boundary St, and continue along what is now St Paul's Terrace. After 1.4km this terrace crosses Brooks St and becomes Markwell St. After the next major intersection it becomes Abbotsford Rd. This route (Highway 26) leads out to Scarborough via Redcliffe. It becomes Sandgate Rd after the suburb of Albion, and Deagon Deviation once past the suburb of Deagon. Some 26km out of the city, the road crosses a bridge over Bramble Bay.

The problem with Redcliffe was always the difficulty of crossing the shallow Hayes Inlet and mouth of the Pine River. Access to Brisbane was limited by this major obstacle until the Hornibrook Highway was opened in 1935. It operated as a toll bridge until 1975. As the 'suburb' expanded, the pressure of transport on the Hornibrook Highway became such that another bridge was required. In 1974 it was decided to build a second bridge which was completed in 1979. By 1979 some 20 300 vehicles were using the bridge daily and with a single lane either way just one breakdown caused chaos. The new bridge has 99 spans and a total of 400 beams. The longest pile was driven 38m deep before reaching sandstone.

2 REDCLIFFE

Head north-east along Hornibrook Esplanade which eventually turns north into Oxley Ave and continues into the heart of Redcliffe. Continue along Oxley Ave and turn right into Anzac Ave. Anzac Ave reaches Moreton Bay just to the north of Redcliffe Point and at the southern end of Queens Beach. Drive north along Redcliffe Parade. Redcliffe Jetty (also known as Redcliffe Pier) is 500m north of Redcliffe Point.

Today Redcliffe is one of the popular outer city beachside retreats for Brisbane residents. It is a pleasant and thriving centre which officially became a city in 1959.

3 REDCLIFFE HISTORICAL SOCIETY MUSEUM

Turn south from Redcliffe Pier and continue along Redcliffe Parade past Redcliffe Point. At Anzac Ave the name changes to Marine Parade. About 300m to the south of Redcliffe Point is the Old Bathing Pavilion which is currently being used as the Redcliffe Historical Society Museum.

Central to any understanding of the peninsula is a visit to the Redcliffe Historical Society Museum which is located in the Old Bathing Pavilion at Suttons Beach, south of Redcliffe Point. It is open on Tuesdays from 10:00–15:00 and also on Sundays from 13:00–16:00. For further information, contact Patricia Fairhall at (07) 3284 4412. The Museum, which moved to the Pavilion in 1975, contains a fascinating collection of memorabilia and photographs which reflect the changing history of the peninsula.

The Historical Society has made a serious and successful attempt to record the history of the area through the collection of documents and personal narratives. An excellent interpretative booklet which looks at the

Scarborough, one of the many beaches on the Redcliffe peninsula.

underlying politics of the establishment of the penal colony at Redcliffe, titled *Redcliffe's Origins*, is also available from the Historical Society.

More details on the early history of the settlement are contained in the excellent *Redcliffe 1824* and *Matthew Flinders in Moreton Bay 1799*, both of which are available from the Redcliffe Museum.

4 REDCLIFFE HERITAGE WALK

The Redcliffe Historical Society has also developed an excellent 'Heritage Walk' which starts at the Museum and includes a number of interesting buildings (such as Sutton House, the Redcliffe Jetty and the old Redcliffe Hotel – now the Ambassador Hotel) as well as some of the sites of the original penal colony. The walk starts at the Museum (the Old Bathing Pavilion which was built in 1937 and converted into a museum in 1970). Across Marine Parade is Sutton House where the first Church of England service was held in 1886. The walk then moves to the west along Sydney Street and north to Humpybong Creek, which was

chosen as the site for the original settlement because of its fresh water supply.

Walking north along the creek's banks, you will pass the site where convicts built a weir. At the location of the mini-golf course, a brick kiln was built by convicts and across the road is the site where the prefabricated Commandant's House once stood. When the settlement moved to modern-day Brisbane, the house was removed and rebuilt. Further north, where the creek meets Downs Street, are the sites of the convicts' vegetable garden and the Commissariat Store. Although these places have all since disappeared, it is still fascinating to stand where a few soldiers and convicts once attempted to establish a new settlement, and marvel at everything that has occurred in the past 170 years.

At the mouth of the creek is Redcliffe Jetty, which was originally constructed in 1885. A more modern jetty was constructed in 1922. Walking back along the seafront in Redcliffe Parade, the visitor passes the Ambassador Hotel which was once the site of the convicts' kitchen and the Prisoners' Barracks.

Redcliffe's Hornibrook Bridge, built in 1935.

5 A DAY ON MORETON ISLAND

■ FERRY TOUR ■ ABOUT 60KM ■ 1 DAY ■ THE BEAUTIES OF AN UNSPOILT SAND ISLAND

The Brisbane River estuary is protected from the Pacific by Moreton Island and North Stradbroke Island. Three delightful daytrips can be taken to Moreton Island by ferry or barge.

To the east of Brisbane lies Moreton Bay which Captain James Cook, when sailing up the coast in 1770, named after James Douglas, the Earl of Morton. After receiving the honour of having a bay named after him, the earl had to live with the cruel irony that 'Morton' had ended up as 'Moreton'. A spelling error in the Hawkesworth edition of Cook's Journal *was never changed*, and thus it became the accepted spelling of the bay. The error was compounded in 1799 when Matthew Flinders decided to name the island to the east of the bay Moreton Island. It was Flinders who established that Moreton and Stradbroke islands were separated from the mainland (Cook had believed that they were both part of the coastline).

The name of the bay persisted and so, when a penal colony was established at Red Cliff Point in 1824, it became known as Moreton Bay. It wasn't until the establishment of the colony of Queensland in 1859 that Moreton Bay, as a description of the whole district, began to change to Brisbane.

Moreton Island became important to shipping in the area when a pilot station was established at its northern end in 1848. Less than a decade later the lighthouse, designed by the famous colonial architect Edmund Blacket, was built at the northern tip of the island. It was the first lighthouse built in Queensland. For some time the island was a whaling station and it later became a tourist resort which was finally closed in the 1960s.

Today Moreton Island is of considerable environmental interest. A huge 192 600ha wilderness, it is virtually untouched. It has typical sand island features including aeolian landforms, perched lakes, wetlands, and Mount Tempest which is reputed to be the highest permanent sand dune in the world.

There are no established roads on Moreton Island. However, 4WD vehicles can be driven along the tracks which run beside the 40km beach. Because it is a sand island it is very important to stay on recognised tracks at all times and to drive according to the Beach Driving Rules.

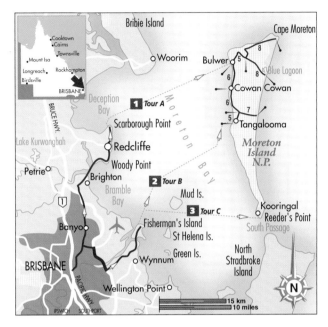

Moreton Island, the second-largest sand island in the world.

1 REDCLIFFE TO BULWER, CAPE MORETON AND NORTH POINT (TOUR A)

Leave Brisbane city centre via Queen, Adelaide or Turbot sts, heading north-east. All three streets join Wharf St. Turn left into Wharf St and follow it until it ends in Leichhardt St. Turn right, cross over Boundary St, and continue along what is now St Paul's Terrace. After 1.4km this terrace crosses Brooks St and becomes Markwell St. After the next major intersection it becomes Abbotsford Rd. This route (Highway 26) leads out to Scarborough via Redcliffe. It becomes Sandgate Rd after the suburb of Albion, and Deagon Deviation once past the suburb of Deagon. Some 26km out of the city the road crosses a bridge over Bramble Bay. Head north along Elizabeth Ave for 4km then turn right into Anzac Ave. After 1.7km , turn left into Scarborough Rd and follow it for about 3.5km, turning left into Jeays St. Follow this road to the end and turn right at the T-junction, with the water to the left. After 50–70m there is a left-hand turn into Thurecht Parade and the Boat Harbour. This is the mooring site for the Combie Trader, a vehicular ferry travelling between the mainland and Bulwer on Moreton Island. The ferry trip takes two hours. Contact tel: (07) 3203 6300 to find out departure times.

There are two major tracks from Bulwer. Both of these head east from the village for 5km. The northern track, which is 8km long, leads out to Cape Moreton and North Point.

The southern track heads east from the village for 5km and then south-east for 8km until it reaches the beach, passing the Blue Lagoon. It is possible to drive along the beach either to Cape Moreton in the north or to the south where a road south of Eagers Creek heads west for 7km and joins the road from Tangalooma (see Tour B below). It also goes north for 12km past Cowan Cowan point and back to Bulwer.

The ferry from Scarborough to Bulwer is an ideal way of experiencing the delights of the northern half of Moreton Island. Bulwer is a tiny village which is really geared to serve the travellers who arrive on the island and require food, bait and supplies.

Moreton Island is the second-largest sand island in the world (second only to Fraser Island) and is very similar in its attractions. It has numerous great 4WD routes. From Bulwer the most popular are to North Point and across to the island's eastern beaches. The roads pass through the thick forests of the Moreton Island National Park and at various points it is possible to stop and admire the island's large dunes and fresh-water lakes (Lake Jabiru – the largest on the island – is located to the south of the Bulwer–Cape Moreton track and Blue Lagoon is inland from the beach, near the south-eastern road from Bulwer).

The major structure of interest in this area is the lighthouse which was built at Cape Moreton in 1857. The Cape Moreton light-house was a vital aid to shipping trying to enter the shallow and complex waters of Moreton Bay.

Drive south along the beach from the lighthouse to join the other major road from Bulwer south of the Blue Lagoon.

2 BRISBANE ESTUARY TO TANGALOOMA (TOUR B)

Leave the city via Alice St and head across the Captain Cook Bridge. Take the left lane exit into Stanley St and turn right. Follow it until it terminates in Vulture St and turn right again. After 1.4km turn left into Wellington Rd. Take a right after 650m into Shafston Ave; Raymond Park is on the left and Waterloo St on the right. Pass Mowbray Park on the left. A little over 100m past the park turn to the left, into Wynnum Rd. After approximately 3.5km make a left-hand turn into Junction Rd. After 1.3km this road joins with Lytton Rd (Route 24). Follow Lytton Rd which, after about 2.5km, passes the road out to the Gateway Arterial Bridge. Continue along this road for another 10km behind the Ampol Refinery and Fort Lytton. Take the last left turn which crosses the mouth of the Brisbane River to Fisherman's Island, into Howard Smith Dve. The second building is the ferry terminus for the Moreton Island Venturer. Services run to both Tangalooma and Kooringal on Moreton Island. The trip takes around two hours. A 4WD vehicle is a must although many journeys to Kooringal at the southern end of the island are for fishing. Contact tel: (07) 3895 1000 for ferry departure details.

Tangalooma was originally established as a whaling station. It closed down as recently as 1962 and even more recently has become the location of the one major resort on Moreton Island. Like Bulwer in the north, the main attractions of Tangalooma are the scenic drives heading out of the small village and across Moreton Island to the eastern beach and north along the coast to Bulwer. For useful information on the Beach Driving Rules, contact the Ranger, Moreton Island National Park, at tel: (07) 3408 2710. There is a common track for about 5km to the north of Tangalooma. The route then turns either north or east. Approximately 7km to

Thick forest fringes much of Moreton Island's coastline.

the east is the island's main beach and it is possible to drive north to Eagers Creek and Mount Tempest.

Alternatively travellers can continue north to the tiny settlement of Cowan Cowan and drive along the island's western coast until they reach Bulwer.

Tangalooma's greatest attraction is the beautifully coloured sand desert which lies inland from the small settlement. Ask for directions at the jetty.

3 BRISBANE ESTUARY TO KOORINGAL (TOUR C)

The departure point for the Moreton Island Venturer is the same as for Tour B. The trip to Kooringal takes around two hours.

There are no recognised roads out of Kooringal although there is a route up the eastern beaches. Like the island's other settlements, Kooringal is a tiny village which provides for bushwalkers and visitors with 4WD vehicles.

6 NORTH STRADBROKE AND COOCHIEMUDLO

■ FERRY TOUR ■ ABOUT 30KM ■ 1 DAY ■ ESCAPE THE CITY FOR PEACE AND ISOLATION

North Stradbroke and Coochiemudlo islands are both easily reached by ferry and water taxi and offer excellent beaches, good surfing and a wide range of tourist facilities.

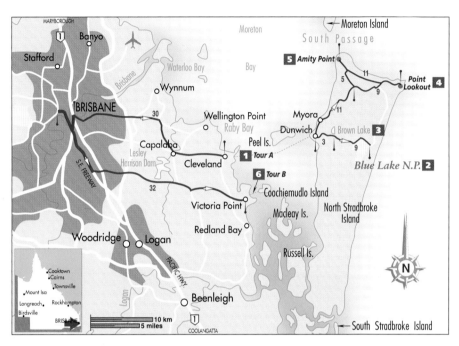

*L*ocated 30km south-east of Brisbane, North and South Stradbroke islands and the historic settlements at Dunwich and Amity Point have become popular holiday destinations and the ideal locations for Brisbane daytrippers wanting to escape from the city. The islands, which were separated by a storm in 1892, are only 13km from the seaside suburbs of Cleveland and Redland Bay when one uses the regular ferry services.

North Stradbroke Island is about 38km long and 11km wide while South Stradbroke is smaller, being only 22km long and about 2.5km wide.

Although the islands (at the time it was just one island) were sighted by both Captain James Cook and Matthew Flinders, it wasn't until 1827 that the name Stradbroke, after the then Earl of Stradbroke, was given to the island by his son, Captain H. J. Rous, the commander of the HMS Rainbow.

That same year there was a proposal to move the convict settlement in Moreton Bay out to the island. The argument was that mooring was difficult in the bay and that the island would provide better facilities. This was not entirely correct. The settlement, which saw the construction of the historic township of Dunwich, was abandoned in 1831 partly because of the difficulty experienced when unloading supplies in rough weather. Hostile local Aborigines and an unsatisfactory water supply compounded the problems.

Today North Stradbroke Island is a paradise only a few hours from central Brisbane. It is predominantly sand, although it is not a true sand island like Fraser and Moreton islands. It is noted for the long, clean white beaches of its eastern coastline, the rich diversity of its flora which includes wild orchids, and its isolation and peacefulness. The natural heritage of the area is impressive and is one of the many drawcards of this superb destination.

The appeal of North and South Stradbroke islands is that despite their easy accessibility from Brisbane, they have remained largely untouched by the city. The islands are ideal destinations for bushwalkers and surfers, and the family seeking a secluded picnic in an unspoilt area will find few more attractive places so close to the centre of Brisbane.

1 CLEVELAND TO DUNWICH ON NORTH STRADBROKE ISLAND (TOUR A)

Leave Brisbane city via the Victoria Bridge over the Brisbane River. Continue along Melbourne St until it terminates in Boundary St and turn left. After 400m the road intersects with Vulture St. Turn left and drive for 2.4km. Turn right into Main St and, at the next intersection, cross Stanley St and take the diagonal left into Logan Rd (Highway 1 to the Gold Coast). Approximately 1.5km along this route take the left-hand turn along Old Cleveland Rd (Highway 22) and it will lead, after 22km, directly through Capalaba and Cleveland and out along Shore St to Cleveland Point. A ferry departs from here to Dunwich on North Stradbroke Island. Within Queensland it is possible to call transport enquiries at tel: (13 1230) in order to ascertain departure times and other information.

The ferries, barges and water taxis from the mainland arrive at Dunwich on the western side of North Stradbroke Island. This old settlement was first established in 1827 as a convict out-station. The shallow waters of Moreton Bay made shipping goods up the Brisbane River difficult and ships arriving (most of them from Sydney) would off-load their supplies at Dunwich. In turn the goods would be ferried across to the mainland and up the Brisbane River in vessels with shallow draughts. In these early days the township of Dunwich was no more than a large warehouse with quarters for the convicts employed to load and unload the produce. It is possible to see the old stone wall of the original jetty on the northern side of the modern barge ramp.

One of the most interesting areas of Dunwich is the cemetery (listed by the National Trust) which has graves dating from as early as 1847. It was the burial site for the 42 typhus victims who arrived aboard the *Emigrant* in 1849 and were quarantined on the island. The graves include those of both Dr George Mitchell and Dr David Bellow, the ship's doctor and the local surgeon. The cemetery is now one of the few reminders of the early settlement which was established at Dunwich. The cemetery also offers visitors a very fine view over Moreton Bay towards the city.

For over a century Dunwich was the site for medical isolation facilities. At various times it was home to a quarantine station, an infectious diseases hospital and an asylum. A Benevolent Asylum operated from 1864–1947. Visitors interested in pursuing this history should visit the Historical Museum in Welsby Street where photographs and artefacts recall the island's colourful history. There is also a record of the shipwrecks which have occurred along the island's coast.

2 BLUE LAKE NATIONAL PARK

The Blue Lake can be reached by taking a 2.5km walk from the Trans-Island Road. If this walk is done either in the early morning or late afternoon, visitors are likely to see the fauna of the area.

Today North Stradbroke Island's greatest attractions are undoubtedly its natural assets. The beautiful 445ha Blue Lake National Park, located 10km to the east of Dunwich, has an unusual freshwater watertable lake set in sand dunes. The lake itself covers 7.3ha, is 9.4m at its greatest depth and is incredibly blue. The fauna in the park includes swamp wallabies, skinks, ospreys and the mottled tree frog, and the flora ranges from dry sclerophyll forest through heath, swamps, marshes and scrub. It is possible, although rare, to see golden wallabies in the area.

3 BROWN LAKE

Brown Lake is only five minutes' drive from Dunwich. It can be reached by taking a short gravel road which turns off the main Trans-Island Road.

Brown Lake is also a national park and Eighteen Mile Swamp supports a rich variety of native fauna.

There are very good picnic and barbecue facilities around the lake's edges and the lake itself offers excellent freshwater swimming. Walking trails lead around the edge of the lake and it is possible to see a range of orchids growing wild.

4 POINT LOOKOUT

Take the road north from Dunwich through Myora and continue along this road for about 25km across the island to Point Lookout. Do not take the turn-off to Amity Point which heads north from the road about 12km from Dunwich.

Point Lookout is Queensland's most easterly point. Many people tend to think that the coast turns eastward north of Brisbane but in fact North Stradbroke Island is the state's most easterly island. In recent times, with whale-watching becoming one of Queensland's major attractions, Point Lookout has become a popular destination. Its steep cliffs afford an excellent vantage point between June and September when the humpback whales make their way past the island en route to the breeding grounds further to the north. There are a number of excellent walking tracks in the area.

South of Point Lookout is Twenty-Two Mile Beach with its extensive Aboriginal middens of shells where, long before the arrival of Europeans, Aborigines feasted on the molluscs they collected in the area.

5 AMITY POINT

Take the road north from Dunwich through Myora, continue for about 12km across the island and take the turn-off to Amity Point. The total distance from Dunwich to Amity Point is about 20km.

The island's northernmost tip is called Amity Point. The first settlement of this important location occurred in 1825 when a pilot station was built to help shipping into Moreton Bay and the Brisbane River. By the 1950s Amity Point was the main access to the island and visitors would arrive and then make their way to Point Lookout, usually on the island's only bus.

Amity Point's critical location means that it is quite vulnerable to tidal action. A number of houses and a kiosk have suffered the consequences of beach erosion in recent times. The township has a particularly delightful park which is not only ideal for picnics but also provides excellent views over Moreton Bay.

Amity Point, now a popular tourist destination (although hardly in the same class as the Gold and Sunshine coasts) offers activities such as swimming and fishing.

6 BRISBANE TO COOCHIEMUDLO ISLAND (TOUR B)

To get to Coochiemudlo Island, make your way onto the F3 Expressway and cross the Brisbane River via the Captain Cook Bridge. It can be reached by various means. Start from Alice St, adjacent to the Botanic Gardens, head towards the river and this will lead you to the Expressway. Once on the freeway, continue south for about 13km and then turn left, headed east on Mt Gravatt Rd (Route 21). The turn-off comes after Toohey Forest Park and Mt Gravatt Cemetery on your right. After 8km take the branch to the right along Mt Cotton Rd (Route 21) instead of continuing on Mt Gravatt Rd, then take the left branch along Boundary Rd (still Route 21) instead of following Mt Cotton Rd. After a further 8km, as the road ends in Redland Bay Rd, turn right and head south for half a kilometre and then turn left into Cloburn Ave, which will take you out to Victoria Point. Island Link Ferries will take you from there to Coochiemudlo Island. Contact tel: (07) 3207 8960. It is only a ten-minute trip by barge.

Coochiemudlo Island, known affectionately as 'Coochie', was discovered by Matthew Flinders in 1799 and has remained largely

STRADBROKE'S POET

Stradbroke Island's most famous recent resident was Kath Walker (Oodgeroo Noonuccal), the highly regarded Aboriginal poet, who was born on North Stradbroke, established the Noonuccal Nughie Education and Cultural Centre on the island, and who has been at the forefront of attempts to curb the large-scale sandmining which has occurred here. When she died she was recognised as one of the most significant Aboriginal activists of her generation.

untouched since then. Only 130ha in area, it is still a haven for birdlife and exotic tropical plants including wildflowers, freesias, casuarinas and palm trees.

One of Coochiemudlo Island's major attractions is the beautiful Aminya Gardens Restaurant. It is housed in a superb two-storeyed colonial mansion surrounded by subtropical gardens which are home to a rich variety of birdlife.

North Stradbroke's Main Beach is some 35km long.

7 BRISBANE'S FOREST DRIVE

■ DRIVING TOUR ■ 83KM ■ 1 DAY ■ A COOL AND LEAFY RETREAT

Beyond Brisbane's urban sprawl, there are large areas of untouched forest where lakes, bushwalks and quiet picnic spots offer a welcome break from the bustle of the city.

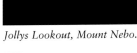

Jollys Lookout, Mount Nebo.

1 BELLBIRD GROVE

To embark on this route it is necessary to travel out of Brisbane proper and onto Musgrave Rd which is also known as Route 31. The best way out of the city is to drive north-west along George St until you reach the Brisbane Transit Centre. Deviate to the left into Roma St and follow this street until you cross the railway line and can turn right into Petrie Terrace. Follow Petrie Terrace to the north past Victoria Barracks and Hargrave Park and then turn left into Musgrave Rd. From here it is simply a question of following Musgrave Rd through Ashgrove and The Gap until it becomes Mt Nebo Rd. Continue along Mt Nebo Rd until, after approximately 12km, you reach the Brisbane Forest Park Information Centre. Stop at the centre and collect all the up-to-date information which will assist you on this trip. Approximately 3km further on you will reach the signs pointing towards Bellbird Grove. Travel up the road for a further 2km until you reach the Bellbird Grove Recreation Area.

Bellbird Grove is located in Camp Mountain State Forest Park which is part of the Brisbane Forest Park. This is primarily a destination for people wanting to have a picnic and go for short walks in the surrounding area. There are remnants of old gold mines in the vicinity but it is really the well-appointed adventure playground (ideal for the children) and the large and very comfortable picnic ground which are the major attractions. The whole area is well provided with shelter sheds (in case of rain or to keep out of the sun), picnic tables, drinking water and barbecue facilities. There is a short walking track for those people who feel they need some exercise after lunch.

2 CAMP MOUNTAIN STATE FOREST PARK

Drive back to Mt Nebo Rd and continue heading west until you see a sign pointing up a short road on the right to the Camp Mountain State Forest Park. Continue up the gravel road until you reach the parking and picnic area.

The great appeal of Camp Mountain State Forest Park is that it offers some of the best views available over Samford Valley. The elevation is such that it looks out over the whole of Brisbane city as well as providing an excellent opportunity to survey the city's suburban sprawl, the high-rise modernity of the city centre and the rich farmlands which lie at the foot of the D'Aguilar Range. The park, which is controlled by the Department of Forestry, is rich in a variety of wildlife and towering eucalypts. There is a good walking trail from the recreation area. This area is provided with shelter sheds, tables, running water, barbecue facilities and toilets. It is important when visiting state forests such as Camp Mountain to respect the rules of the Department of Forestry. It is necessary to stay on the gravel roads, to keep well away if there is a bushfire in the area, to protect all the flora and fauna and, particularly in summer, to be careful with barbecues and fires. These are high-risk areas and any fires that are not properly extinguished are potentially dangerous. It is also very important to recognise that it is not permitted to take domestic pets – particularly dogs and cats – into these areas. The State Forest Parks are intended for recreation and their protection ensures their continued use by the public.

3 MOUNT NEBO

Continue on Mt Nebo Rd, stopping at the numerous lookouts which provide excellent views across the city. The best known of the lookouts are McAfee and Jollys. Both provide views across Greater Brisbane. About 34km from the city centre is the small township of Mt Nebo.

Mount Nebo is a pretty township in the heart of the Brisbane Forest Park. In recent times it has become a centre of gift shops, cafes and picnic areas. It is an ideal stopover on the scenic journey through the Forest Park. The most appealing quality of Mount Nebo is its location.

5 KILCOY'S YOWIE

Drive through the town. There is a pleasant picnic area at the eastern end of the town. Pass this, continue up the hill, turn left and drive down the D'Aguilar Highway. When you reach the T-junction you will notice a park in front of you which has a Tourist Information Office (they sell gifts and have a small brochure on the area) and a little further along is a large statue of a yowie.

The shire's tourist brochure describes the yowie with a nice mixture of fact and humour (you can choose which is which):

Reputed to be half-man, half-beast, the yowie is Australia's equivalent of the Himalayan yeti or America's Big Foot and it appears in Aboriginal folklore dating back thousands of years. Official statistics show that over 3000 sightings were reported throughout Australia between 1975 and 1979. Print and electronic media made much of the latest reported sighting in Kilcoy in December 1979. Two Brisbane schoolboys claim the monster stood just 20m from them while they were on a pig-shooting expedition 4km north of the town.

They described the beast as being about 3m tall with a 'Kangaroo appearance' and covered in chocolate-coloured hair. They said it took giant 'thumping' strides which could be heard for hundreds of metres.

Following this incident the Shire Council commissioned a Birchwood statue to be carved and the artist's interpretation of the boy's description now stands tall in all his naked masculinity in Yowie Park beside the D'Aguilar Highway in Kilcoy.

6 SOMERSET DAM

Drive west from Kilcoy for 3km on the D'Aguilar Highway and take the road heading south to the Somerset Dam. The most popular picnic spot beside the dam is 9km from the town.

To the south of Kilcoy is the Somerset Dam, the construction of which was started in 1935. It was first used in 1943 to supplement Brisbane's water supply and it was completed in 1959. It has a catchment area of $340km^2$ and an area of 8100ha. It extends 56km upstream from the dam wall. The drive from Kilcoy to Esk around the foreshores of Lake Somerset is really delightful. There are many excellent viewing points and picnic areas around the edge of the dam.

7 LAKE WIVENHOE AND WIVENHOE DAM

Drive 15km south from the picnic site to the Somerset Dam wall and cross the valley, heading south towards Fernvale and Ipswich. The road travels along the eastern side of Lake Wivenhoe for 39km until it reaches the Brisbane Valley Highway. Turn north and continue for 4km to the main dam wall of Lake Wivenhoe.

A vital part of Brisbane's water supply, Lake Wivenhoe is capable of storing 1.15 million megalitres of water. The lake itself stretches back from the dam wall for 40km and at its widest point is 5km wide. Near the dam wall is an inlet named Cormorant Bay where there is a picnic area and restaurant, a great place to rest after a journey from Brisbane.

THE YOWIE STATUE

Kilcoy's rather dubious major attraction is a crude wooden statue of a very well-endowed male yowie. There is an on-going problem with 'the endowment'. It seems that the original statue has been vandalised on a fairly regular basis by someone who feels that naked male yowies – even if they are only statues – should not show their masculinity to the world. Thus the penis regularly gets knocked off.

8 FERNVALE

From the dam wall drive 9km south along the Brisbane Valley Highway to the tiny township of Fernvale.

This is a tiny little settlement and can quite easily be overlooked. The only real attraction here is the Wivenhoe Craft Gallery which offers visitors an interesting variety of locally made arts and crafts.

Lake Wivenhoe, a vital source of Brisbane's water supply.

CHAPTER 2
THE GOLD COAST

10 ALONG THE BEACHES OF THE GOLD COAST

■ DRIVING TOUR ■ 60KM ■ 1 DAY ■ PARADISE FOR SURFERS AND HOLIDAY-MAKERS

Australia's most popular stretch of holiday beaches combines seemingly endless vistas of high-rise apartments, motels and hotels with beautiful beaches, quiet parklands and excellent restaurants.

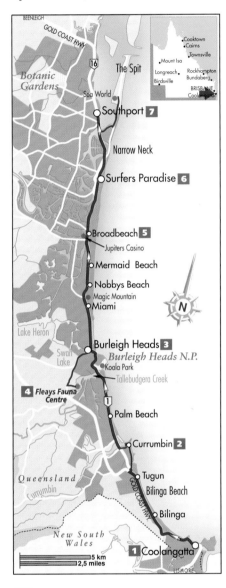

Surfers Paradise, with its seemingly endless oceanfront of high-rise development.

1 COOLANGATTA

Starting from the New South Wales border, turn east into Boundary St and continue until you come to the end of the road. In front of you the headland drops into the sea.

Coolangatta is the most southerly of the holiday destinations on the Gold Coast. It is, realistically speaking, a twin town with Tweed Heads. The border between New South Wales and Queensland is so blurred at this point that people pass from one state to the next barely knowing that they are crossing a border.

While it is true that Captain James Cook sailed up the Gold Coast in 1770, there are few points where he felt compelled to give the coastline a name. One of the places recorded by Cook is Point Danger which

was aptly named and subsequently had a lighthouse erected to warn ships of the treacherous coast. The lighthouse is now a memorial to Cook. It lays claim to being the first lighthouse in the world to experiment with laser technology, but the experiment was unsuccessful and it returned to the more conventional mirrors, magnifying glass and powerful electric lamps.

The town was actually named after the ship *Coolangatta* which was wrecked on the coast in the 1840s. It is said that this was an anglicised Aboriginal word meaning 'beautiful place'.

By the 1880s the beauty of the region had been recognised and people started acquiring holiday cottages, with the inevitable small number of people moving there permanently. Unlike Surfers Paradise (which also predates the postwar boom), Coolangatta has not really been radically modernised. It is therefore still a resort geared towards family holidays rather than the gaudy 'sophistication' of the destinations further to the north.

2 CURRUMBIN

Travel north from Point Danger past the rock pool and Snapper Rocks. Leave Coolangatta, heading to the north along Marine Parade, turn right into Musgrave St and continue north for approximately 1km to join the Gold Coast Highway. Pass Coolangatta Airport on your left and proceed through Bilinga and Tugun to reach Currumbin. Cross Flat Rock Creek and then turn right into Tomewin St.

Currumbin has become famous because of the excellent Currumbin Sanctuary (situated in Tomewin Street), noted for the rainbow

lorikeets which flock there at feeding time. Over the years this simple bird sanctuary has grown so that it now includes a wildlife reserve which houses kangaroos, wallabies, koalas and emus. There is also a range of tourist attractions including glass-blowing and a miniature railway. In many ways the Currumbin Sanctuary is one of the most impressive attractions on the Gold Coast.

3 BURLEIGH HEADS

Continue north from Currumbin along the Gold Coast Highway, passing through Palm Beach. Cross Tallebudgera Creek where the highway becomes Tweed St and turn right into Goodwin Terrace to reach Burleigh Heads and the Burleigh Heads National Park.

The Burleigh Heads National Park, comprising 24ha between Tallebudgera Creek and Burleigh Heads, is actually an isolated extension of an enormous volcano which was centred at Mount Warning 22 million years ago. Despite the development that has gone on around it, the park has managed to preserve a small area of coastal rainforest and heathlands. There is a short, well-maintained 3km track which offers superb views of the coast. The park is a habitat for wallabies, koalas and bandicoots.

4 FLEAYS FAUNA CENTRE

Return to the Gold Coast Highway via Goodwin Terrace. Travel 300m, then turn west into West Burleigh Rd and continue along it for 2km until you reach Fleays Fauna Centre which is located on the southern side of the road.

A few kilometres west of the coast on West Burleigh Road is Fleays Fauna Centre, which provides an opportunity to observe the native fauna of the region in its natural habitat. The fauna centre is home to crocodiles, cassowaries and brolgas. There is a special area for children. For more information, contact Fleays at tel: (07) 5576 2411.

5 BROADBEACH

Turn east into West Burleigh Rd and return to Burleigh Heads shopping centre. Turn left and continue north along the Gold Coast Highway through Miami, Nobbys Beach and Mermaid Beach to Broadbeach. The turn-off to Jupiters Casino is found on the left.

A few kilometres to the south of Surfers Paradise lies Broadbeach (it is now just part of the urban sprawl of the Gold Coast) which boasts the A$185 million Conrad International Hotel and Jupiter Casino complex with its gaming rooms, swimming pools, tennis courts and jogging tracks. Opened in 1986, it has over 600 guestrooms and is the only casino on the Gold Coast. Rare among casinos, it operates 24 hours a day, allowing the gambler to lose money as easily at 5am as at 5pm.

6 SURFERS PARADISE

Head north along the Gold Coast Highway for 3km to the centre of Surfers Paradise.

Surfers Paradise is the town and beach which symbolises the lifestyle and the aspirations of the people who come here either on holiday or to live. These people are not coming to a 'paradise for surfers'. The history of Surfers Paradise is fascinating. It seems that the Aborigines knew of the delights of the region long before Europeans arrived. The area around Surfers (as it is commonly known) was renowned for its excellent fishing grounds.

Development began in the late 19th century when a small group of fishermen and holiday-makers realised the delights of the area and started to move in. There was a hotel in the region by 1888 but the only access from the north was by ferry across the Nerang River at Southport. In 1925 a wooden bridge was built and this was upgraded in 1966. The place was known as Elston until the locals, encouraged by the success of the Surfers Paradise Hotel, named the area after the hotel.

The origins of the modern town really date to 1923 when James Cavill paid £40 for a block of land and proceeded to build his famous Surfers Paradise Hotel. Two years later the bridge across the Nerang River was built, giving access to the hotel which boasted a small zoo and excellent gardens.

A great change occurred in the 1950s. The Surfers Paradise Hotel had been used during World War II by convalescing soldiers who now returned with their wives and families to enjoy the beach and the excellent climate. This influx of tourists happened to coincide with an easing of building regulations which resulted in an ocean front of endless high-rise apartment blocks.

More recently, the nature of Surfers Paradise has changed again. It is now a place for young people. The hordes of students who arrive from New South Wales and Victoria after the completion of examinations, and the surfers who mooch around the promenade waiting for a good wave, are today's clientele. The families have moved on. Surfers Paradise, however, does still have the greatest concentration of five-star hotels in Queensland outside Brisbane.

7 SOUTHPORT

Leave Surfers Paradise heading north via the Gold Coast Highway, cross the Nerang River and proceed into Southport proper. To reach The Spit area (home of Sea World) from Surfers Paradise, travel north along Main Beach Parade, continue north into Main Beach Dve and then to Sea World Dve.

Southport is the newest and most expensive region of the Gold Coast. Out on the area known as The Spit or The Broadwater there is a superb new marina, Sea World and the Sheraton Mirage Hotel.

Southport was surveyed and named in 1874. It grew in the 1870s and 1880s and the Southport Hotel was built in 1876. A

The Rainbow Lorikeet, Currumbin Sanctuary.

pier was constructed in 1880 and the area known as Main Beach (where the Sheraton Mirage is located) was sold in 1885.

Since World War I development has been continuous. The bridge over the Nerang River was completed in 1925, giving easy access to the area. Prior to that the only way to reach the Broadwater had been by ferry. The old wooden bridge was eventually replaced by a concrete structure in 1966 so that now visitors barely notice the fact that they are crossing the river.

Today Southport concentrates entirely on tourism. Old historic buildings have been brushed aside by progress and the desire to convert the whole area into a modern holiday town. If you feel nostalgic, go to the Sundale Shopping Centre and try to imagine that the old Southport Hotel (1876) once stood on the site.

In sharp contrast, there is Sea World on The Broadwater across the river from the township (see Tour 11).

Interior of the Mirage Hotel, Southport.

The eye-catching Marina Mirage, Southport.

Boats moored near Fisherman's Wharf, Southport.

11 GOLD COAST ATTRACTIONS

■ DRIVING TOUR ■ 208KM ■ 1 DAY ■ BEING SEDUCED BY TOURIST ATTRACTIONS

The Gold Coast is as close as Australia gets to Disneyland and Florida: Movie World, Sea World and Wet'n'Wild are all ideal for a daytrip from Brisbane.

1 DREAMWORLD

Travel south from Brisbane along the Pacific Highway for 56km. Like all the attractions mentioned here, Dreamworld is well signposted from the highway and easy to find.

The tiny town of Coomera is known for its two tourist attractions – Dreamworld and Koala Town.

Dreamworld is an Australian version of Disneyland with a variety of rides and entertainments to occupy children and adults for an entire day. The characters are all Australian. There are Cooee and Kenny Koala (suitable replacements for Donald Duck and Mickey Mouse), a Main Street, the Thunderbolt Roller-coaster, the Cannonball Express, Goldrush Country, Koala Country, and a paddle-steamer called *Captain Sturt*. The theme park also has one of the few Imax Theatres in Australia. This remarkable movie technology provides a screen so large that it is quite impossible to sit in the audience and not be totally involved in the experience.

Like most of the attractions on the Gold Coast it has a single entry fee and, once inside, nearly every ride is free. For more information, contact tel: (07) 5588 1111.

2 KOALA TOWN

Less than 1km further south on the Pacific Highway and on the western side of the road is Koala Town. It is clearly signposted.

Koala Town has a wide range of Australian animals including, of course, koalas. The great appeal of a place like this is that although koalas keep themselves well away from human beings in the bush, visitors may come into close contact with the animals in a koala sanctuary. The park used to promote itself with the slogan 'Cuddle a koala, snuggle a snake and shear a sheep'. There is a strong emphasis on participation.

3 SANCTUARY COVE

From Koala Town, drive south for about 2km to the Oxenford turn-off where the Pacific Highway meets the Oxenford–Southport Rd. Follow the Oxenford–Southport Rd east to the roundabout at Santa Barbara Dve which heads north. Take the first turn right into Caseys Rd which runs beside the Pines Golf Course. At the roundabout turn north onto The Parkway and drive to Sanctuary Cove.

Sanctuary Cove was one of the dubious ideas of the 1980s. Created by Queensland entrepreneur Mike Gore (he became synonymous with the term 'the white shoe brigade' which was used to describe developers and entrepeneurs), it was opened by Frank Sinatra. It has since grown to consist of a shopping centre called Marine Village which has more than 75 shops ranging from gift shops to restaurants, cafes and bars, some very expensive housing designed for retired millionaires, and two excellent golf courses. Much of the development has been carved out of the shores of the Coomera River. While the design is clearly artificial, it still looks remarkably luxurious.

4 WARNER BROS MOVIE WORLD

Return to the Pacific Highway, retracing the route taken to get to Sanctuary Cove. The distance is about 7km. From the intersection of the Oxenford–Southport Rd and the Pacific Highway head south. Leave the Highway at the next junction. On the western side of the road there are large signs announcing the Movie World Theme Park, the Movie World Film Studios and Cades County Water Park (Wet'n'Wild).

Movie World is a working studio combined with a fun park. Designed as a studio with a number of large stages and an extensive range of state-of-the-art equipment, Movie World manages to combine a day out with a wide variety of activities. The combination of studio and fun park means that most of the park's attendants are young actors hoping for work, and their first big break, in the studios next door.

Warner Bros Movie World is basically a combination of Disneyland and Universal Studios. It celebrates the fun and excitement of movies, offering entertainments ranging from impromptu street events to a daily stunt show which re-enacts a *Police Academy*-style hold-up. The *Police Academy* show has as much to do with the *Keystone Cops* as it does with *Police Academy* and is typical of the kind of show offered by the complex. The set can accommodate over 500 people. The action includes

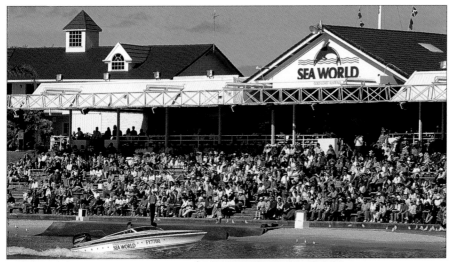

Waterskiing displays entrance spectators at Sea World on The Broadwater.

the mine. Walk the trails through the rainforest to rock pools, or through wildlife reserves and an animal nursery.' The mine also claims to have Australia's largest amethyst collection.

6 CEDAR CREEK FALLS

Continue further down the hill until you see the signs to the Cedar Creek National Park. Although travellers are invited to enter the national park through Thunderbird Park, there is a route to Cedar Creek from exterior roads.

One of the most delightful walks in the whole Tamborine area is the short walk down to Cedar Creek Falls in the Cedar Creek National Park. It is an easy walk of only a few hundred metres to the falls which tumble (gently rather than spectacularly) down into a series of deep rock pools which are great for swimming. There are a number of good walks through the rainforest. The area is well known for its gemstones and lucky hunters have been known to find common opal, agate and chalcedony, which is a popular ornamental stone.

7 BEENLEIGH

From Cedar Creek Falls the road dips down to the tiny township of Tamborine. At this point take the road north to Beenleigh. Do not take the road west to Beaudesert. The road north makes its way along the valley of the Albert River until it reaches Beenleigh on the Pacific Highway just south of Brisbane.

Beenleigh's one claim to fame, and its one great attraction, is the local Beenleigh Rum Distillery. It stands there right beside the Pacific Highway, tempting drivers to come and inspect it and sample the product.

In 1864 Robert Johnston, the first settler in the area, grew arrowroot (mainly used for pharmaceutical products but also in biscuits) and sugarcane there. The following year two men, John Davey and Frank Gooding, arrived in the region and established a farm which they called Beenleigh after their birthplace in Devon, England.

The district, due to its soil, climate and proximity to Moreton Bay, quickly developed into an important sugar-growing area. The first sugar mill was built by Davey and Gooding in 1867 and by 1885 there were 30 mills in the district. Now there is only one, in Woongoolba.

There was a time when the SS *Walrus*, a floating rum distillery, moved from one mill to the next treating the by-products of sugar manufacture and converting them into rum. Today the town still boasts one of the few rum distilleries in the country. The distillery is justifiably proud of one of its stills which was originally built in 1864 and is now the oldest functioning still in the country and one of three in Queensland. It is possible to visit the Beenleigh Rum Distillery which has an interesting series of displays and guided tours of the works.

Cedar Creek, Joalah National Park.

The view from Rotary Lookout, Tamborine Mountain.

14 HOLIDAY RESORTS AND RURAL TOWNS

■ DRIVING TOUR ■ 302KM ■ 1 DAY ■ EXPLORING THE HISTORY OF SOUTHERN QUEENSLAND

Beyond the Gold Coast the cool retreat of the Tamborine Mountain National Park and the small townships and villages which dot the area stand in sharp contrast to the razzamatazz of the Gold Coast.

1 CANUNGRA

Head south-west out of Nerang along Price St as it becomes the Beaudesert–Nerang Rd (Highway 90). About 4km out of town, branch to the right, following the Canungra–Beaudesert–Warwick signpost. This is still the Beaudesert–Nerang Rd. The road winds up the escarpment. Follow the signs to Canungra, which is 24km from Nerang.

Canungra is a small, thriving township at the southern end of the Tamborine Mountain National Park. The town describes itself as the 'Gateway to the Mountains'. Visitors intending to explore the area should stop at the Canungra Information Centre – tel: (07) 5543 5156 – where they will be able to obtain maps and information on walks and sightseeing. Canungra is a quiet township located on Canungra Creek. Like much of the Tamborine Mountain area, it survives by selling gifts and providing meals for the visitors who make their way up the mountain.

The main attractions of the area are the beautiful views and the number of rainforests with quiet streams and attractive waterfalls. From the ridge it is possible to get excellent views to both the west and east.

2 BEAUDESERT

From Canungra, continue through the Tamborine Mountain National Park towards Beaudesert. The journey is 34km, most of which is down the western side of the Great Dividing Range. At various points there are impressive stands of eucalypts and the views across to Beaudesert are marvellous.

Beaudesert is a town located on the Mount Lindesay Highway and nestled in the valley of the Logan River.

The town was named after the Beau Desert Station which was established in the area in 1842 and which was itself named after Beau Desert Park in Staffordshire. The area had been explored in the late 1820s by both Allan Cunningham and Patrick Logan after whom the nearby river is named.

The large land-holdings which were taken up in the early 1840s remained until the 1860s when they were broken up. This led to a change from sheep grazing to cattle. The greater density of the population led to the establishment of a settlement. Beaudesert came into existence in 1873 and was proclaimed a town in 1876. The railway arrived in 1888. The town has prospered because of its proximity to Brisbane. Today it is a thriving agricultural centre producing dairy products and beef for the nearby state capital. It has a population of about 5000 and is a popular daytrip destination.

3 BEAUDESERT HISTORICAL MUSEUM AND INFORMATION CENTRE

At the centre of town (where the Nerang–Beaudesert Rd meets the Mt Lindesay Highway), turn sharply south into Brisbane St. On the right-hand side, just one block from the main corner in the centre of Beaudesert, is Jubilee Park and on the corner of Brisbane and McKee sts is the Beaudesert Historical Museum.

For people interested in the history of the region, the excellent Beaudesert Historical Museum and Information Centre in Jubilee Park has a very extensive display of transport equipment and an excellently preserved old slab hut. The Historical Pioneer Cottage was built by Patrick Milbanks in 1875. Milbanks had taken up land in the area which he named Kerry. It was presented to the society by his grandson in 1961 and re-erected in the museum area. The museum is open on Saturdays, Sundays and public holidays from 13:00–16:00, on Wednesdays and Fridays from 12:30–16:00, or contact tel: (07) 5541 1284.

The area is characterised by the kinds of tourist development which occur near to a capital city. There is Rices Honey Bee Farm which is open from 8:00–16:00 Mondays to

St Mary's Church, Beaudesert.

Fridays – tel: (07) 5541 1040 – where the process of beekeeping and honey production can be observed. Woollahra Farmworld, 8km north of the town on the Mount Lindesay Highway, is a dairy farm with picnic facilities offering visitors an opportunity to see dairying in action. Contact tel: (07) 5543 1171 for more details.

4 CHURCH OF ALL SAINTS

Travel west from the town on the road heading towards Boonah. This involves continuing along McKee St and heading out of town on Boonah Road. On the right-hand side, and off the main road by about 100m, is the Church of All Saints which is a very impressive wooden building.

The town's greatest historical attraction is the Church of All Saints, a magnificent timber structure designed by Robin Dods and built in 1915 of hardwood and red cedar. Its recent painting in red and cream has made it a superb local landmark. It is claimed that the architect designed it as a variation on a Welsh church with specific modifications for Queensland. Beyond the Church of All Saints on the Boonah Road is the old racecourse with a delightful old grandstand which dates from the 1890s.

5 TEMPLIN HISTORICAL MUSEUM

Leave Beaudesert and drive west for approximately 57km to Boonah. The road at this point winds through undulating countryside which is rich cattle-grazing land. This is the edge of the Darling Downs and the rich soils are also suitable for crops. Drive past Boonah and continue along the main road heading towards the Cunningham Highway for about 3km to reach the Templin Historical Museum.

The excellent Templin Historical Museum contains a very interesting collection of artefacts and memorabilia which chronicles the history of the area.

6 BOONAH

Return to Boonah and take the road which leads into the town centre.

Boonah is known as 'The Heart of the Fassifern'. It is a very pretty little town with a large number of timber houses. Surrounded by hills, it was established in 1882 as a service centre for the surrounding farms. The area produces vegetables for the nearby Brisbane markets (notably carrots and potatoes), as well as cereal crops, beef, pork and timber.

Originally known rather unromantically as the Goolman Division Board, it changed its name in 1937 to Boonah, an anglicised version of the Aboriginal word 'buna' which supposedly meant bloodwood tree.

Boonah is really a quiet community and its inhabitants are not particularly interested in tourism. Nearby is Lake Moogerah which is a popular haunt for boating enthusiasts and waterskiers.

7 MOUNT FRENCH NATIONAL PARK

Take the road south from Boonah for 1km and follow the signs to the Mount French National Park which lies about 10km west of the town.

The Boonah shire area has many interesting national parks where bushwalking and rock climbing are popular – the 'Frog Buttress' climb is one of Australia's most challenging. Mount French National Park is near the town – the climb to the top of Mount French is rewarded by excellent panoramic views over the Fassifern Valley. This valley is part of the 676ha Moogerah Peaks National Park which includes a number of volcanic peaks and rocky cliffs to the west of Boonah. Mount Moon, Mount Edwards and Mount Greville are the more isolated areas of the Moogerah Peaks National Park and are suitable for experienced bushwalkers.

The main street of Boonah, at the heart of the Fassifern region.

QUEENSLAND'S NATIONAL PARKS

Governments in Queensland have had a long history of creating national parks and protecting local flora and fauna. The first act of nature conservation occurred in 1877 when legislation was passed protecting native birds and fining and imprisoning those who broke the law. The first protection given to native mammals was in 1906 when the state started to protect koalas and possums (between November and April) as well as tree kangaroos, wombats, echidnas and pygmy gliders.

There are no fewer than 11 national and environmental parks in the Boonah–Beaudesert region.

1. Mount French has picnic facilities, short walking trails and scenic lookouts.
2. Mount Edwards has a 3–4-hour walk from Lake Moogerah to the summit.
3. Mount Greville has a 4-hour walking track to the summit.
4. Mount Moon has a pleasant walk but access is through private property. Permission to enter has to be gained from the owners of the property.
5. Cunninghams Gap has a wide range of camping facilities and some excellent walking trails.
6. Spicers Gap has a scenic lookout and a pioneers' cemetery.
7. The Head has picnic facilities, a scenic lookout and the Teviot Falls.
8. Mount Barney is ideal for experienced bushwalkers.
9. Tamborine Mountain is a popular tourist destination.
10. Mount Beau Brummel Environmental Park has excellent views and plenty of opportunities for sighting local fauna.
11. Lamington National Park, which is 20 200ha in area, is rich in the diversity of attractions it offers.

8 RATHDOWNEY

Return to Boonah and take the road to the south towards Rathdowney which is located about 49km to the south-east of Boonah.

This is a quiet service centre which is often seen as the starting point for people wishing to drive into the mountains and the national parks on the New South Wales–Queensland border. It has an information office which provides the traveller with details about Mount Barney National Park and Mount Maroon National Park.

9 BOYS TOWN

Travel from Rathdowney to Beaudesert. The journey is 34km. Boys Town is situated 2km before Beaudesert.

This famous home for boys is a totally self-contained village with its own mayor and council. Well worth a visit, it can be seen by arrangement, tel: (07) 5541 1511.

CHAPTER 3
DARLING DOWNS
AND BEYOND

15 HISTORIC IPSWICH

■ DRIVING TOUR ■ 9KM ■ 1 DAY ■ QUEENSLAND'S BEAUTIFUL DOMESTIC ARCHITECTURE

This tour starts at Queen's Park and takes in a number of interesting buildings. The tour ends at the Ipswich Girls' Grammar School, just across the road from where it started.

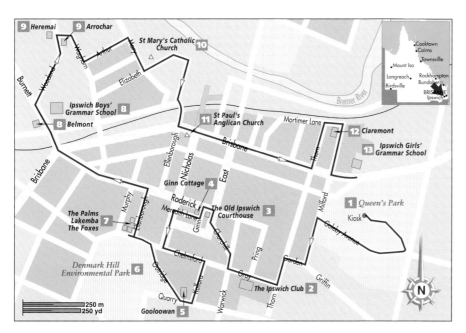

*T*he European exploration of Ipswich was a result of the establishment of the penal colony at Moreton Bay. The Ipswich Municipal Centenary book records the discovery of the Bremer River: 'Two rowboats left the new settlement at Redcliffe on Saturday 16, 1824. In the party were John Oxley, Allan Cunningham, Lieutenant Butler of the 40th Regiment and the boats' crews. They went across Moreton Bay, to make the second survey of the Brisbane River.

'After rowing up the river, they began the return journey on September 25, at 5 p.m. made a camp on the north bank, opposite a tributary, which Oxley named "Bremer's Creek".'

The first European into the Ipswich area was Major Lockyer. He was followed by Captain Logan, the commandant of the Brisbane colony. The next explorer through the region was Allan Cunningham who, in 1828 while writing to Governor Darling, observed that the Bremer River was a navigable stream. 'It is, therefore, highly probable that upon the site of these limestone hills, a town will one day be raised.'

Around this time, convicts from Brisbane were already in the area and a limestone kiln had been built which was producing 300–400 baskets of lime a week. The lime was mixed with mortar to construct Brisbane's stone buildings.

By 1840 a small settlement, probably nothing more than a couple of houses and a general store, had grown up in the area. In 1842, when the area around Brisbane was opened to free settlers, the squatters who were already on the Darling Downs came through Cunninghams and Spicers gaps and quickly took up land. Between 1840 and 1860 industry in the area was dominated by wool production and Ipswich, the furthest navigable spot on the Bremer River, became the point from which wool was shipped to the coast.

Development of the township was rapid. It was proclaimed a municipality in 1860, and the railways to Grandchester and Brisbane were completed in 1864 and 1876 respectively. By 1904 Ipswich, which had started life with the rather unprepossessing name of Limestone, had become a city.

During this time coal was also discovered nearby in the region of Redbank. Mining began in 1843 and a number of coal mines (there were as many as 50 at one time) were established in the area.

1 QUEEN'S PARK

Start your tour of Ipswich at Queen's Park. You can see the city from a number of vantage points near the kiosk. There are also excellent views across the city from the Lion's Lookout at the park's northern end.

Queen's Park has an animal sanctuary and an attractive rotunda with delicate late-Victorian cast-iron lacework. At the southern end of the park is the interesting Walter Burley Griffin Incinerator which has been turned into a theatre. Although Burley Griffin is famous for his design of Canberra he also designed a number of municipal incinerators around Australia.

2 THE IPSWICH CLUB

Head out of Queen's Park along Goleby Ave to the park entrance at Milford St. Turn left into Milford St and follow it until you reach the intersection with Griffith and Garden sts. Turn right into Garden St and continue until you reach the T-junction. Turn left into Thorn St. Take the first right into Gray St. On the left-hand side, opposite Pring St, is the Ipswich Club.

This interesting and impressive building was built in the rich Queen Anne-style which dominated in the early years of the 20th century. It is elaborately ostentatious which was common in the architecture of the time.

3 THE OLD IPSWICH COURTHOUSE

Continue along Gray St to the next intersection. Turn right into Warwick Rd and take the first left into Churchill St. At the T-junction turn right into East St and at the next intersection on the corner of East and Roderick sts is the Old Ipswich Courthouse.

The main courtroom and office of the Old Ipswich Courthouse has an impressive sandstone facade which was completed in 1859. The building was designed by Charles Tiffin, Queensland's first architect, who had been given the position after the state became independent from New South Wales. The building is listed by the National Trust of Queensland and owned by the Queensland Government. Like most public buildings it has had a number of additions. The side wings were probably added in the 1880s and the rear portion in the 1930s.

4 GINN COTTAGE

Turn left off East St into Roderick St. There is a great concentration of historic buildings in this area. Just off Roderick St, on the corner of Ginn St and Meredith Lane, is Ginn Cottage.

William Ginn purchased this piece of land in 1858 and the small Georgian-style cottage was built at around the same time. Ginn Cottage is one of the oldest surviving brick buildings in Ipswich. Although the cottage is quite modest, William Ginn was an important member of Ipswich society being both a merchant and the founding director of the Ipswich and West Moreton Building Society. The cottage is listed by the National Trust of Queensland.

5 GOOLOOWAN

Drive along Meredith Lane and turn left into Nicholas St. At the T-junction turn left and drive along Chelmsford Ave. Take the first right into Kallara Ave. At the T-junction turn right into Quarry St and at the corner of Quarry and Outridge sts is Gooloowan.

Gooloowan is an elegant two-storeyed, cement-washed brick mansion built between 1862 and 1864 for Benjamin Cribb whose family played an important role in the social and economic development of the area. The house has verandahs supported by dual timber columns on both levels with cast-iron balustrades and elegant shuttered French windows. The house is next to Denmark Hill Environmental Park behind large camphor laurels and giant bamboo.

6 DENMARK HILL ENVIRONMENTAL PARK

Travel up Outridge St. On your left is the Denmark Hill Environmental Park.

This picturesque park offers a quiet retreat from the city. It has pleasant walking tracks, an artificial waterfall and, at its northern end, the Water Tower Lookout. There are also some excellent vantage points 100m up the road with scenic views of the city.

7 THE PALMS, LAKEMBA AND THE FOXES

Continue travelling along Outridge St and turn left into Chelmsford Ave. At the top of Denmark Hill between Ellenborough St and Murphy St are three more elegant homes.

The Palms and Lakemba are two large and impressive dwellings. The latter is characterised by beautiful ironwork and was built around the turn of the century. Around the corner, up Ellenborough Street, is The Foxes, a large turn-of-the-century timber house.

8 BELMONT AND IPSWICH BOYS' GRAMMAR SCHOOL

Drive up Ellenborough St and turn left at the T-junction into Roderick St. Drive for 500m until you cross the railway line into what becomes Burnett St. On the left, at 11 Burnett St, is Belmont.

Belmont is an extraordinary two-storeyed sandstone townhouse surrounded by lacework verandahs. It was built in 1865 and, as such, is one of the earliest domestic buildings in Ipswich.

Across the road from Belmont is Ipswich Boys' Grammar School with its distinctive castellated towers and projecting gables. Built in 1863, it is the oldest secondary school in Queensland.

9 HEREMAI AND ARROCHAR

Turn right off Burnett St into Woodend St which is at the eastern end of the schoolgrounds. Follow the road to No 14.

Heremai at 14 Woodend Street is a fine example of a single-storeyed Victorian timber house and is notable for its attractive lacework. Across the road, there is a right-hand turn into Waghorn Street. On the right-hand side of the street is Arrochar which was built in 1893 by the well-known architect, George Brockwell Gill. It is a classic 'Queenslander', a style of house noted for its wide verandahs and elevation so that breezes cool it down from underneath in summer. It is enhanced by a beautiful lattice-work verandah with symmetrical stairways and an ornate central portico.

10 ST MARY'S CATHOLIC CHURCH

Continue down Waghorn St and take the first left into Arthur St. At the T-junction turn right into Mary St and take the first left into Elizabeth St. On your left you will find St Mary's Catholic Church.

St Mary's Catholic Church, built in the 1870s, is one of the most substantial rural churches in Australia. Notable for its two Gothic spires (which can be seen from most vantage points around Ipswich), St Mary's

has impressive stained-glass work, elaborate ceilings and Italianate arches, and makes extensive use of marble. Its keystones feature sculpted mitres and bishops' heads.

11 ST PAUL'S ANGLICAN CHURCH

Continue along Elizabeth St. The road swings to the right into Ellenborough St. Take the first turn on the left into Brisbane St. At the corner of Brisbane and Nicholas sts, opposite the mall, is St Paul's, Ipswich's other major church.

St Paul's Anglican Church was built in 1858 and 1859. Hailed as 'one of the nicest churches in New South Wales' by the clergyman who held the first service there on 12 June 1859, it is the oldest Anglican church in Queensland. Designed in a Victorian Gothic Revival style, it has a finely proportioned interior.

12 CLAREMONT

Continue along Brisbane St across East St and turn left into Thorn St. Turn right into Mortimer Lane and on the corner with Milford St is Claremont.

Near the present site of Claremont, Captain Patrick Logan came ashore from the Bremer River and discovered the Limestone Hills in 1826. Built on sandstone in 1858 for the merchant John Panton, Claremont is a fine example of Colonial Georgian architecture. George Thorn, who had been appointed overseer of stock at the ploughed station at Limestone (Ipswich), purchased Claremont in 1863. The property was purchased by the National Trust of Queensland in 1975.

13 IPSWICH GIRLS' GRAMMAR SCHOOL

Continue along Milford St to the first intersection and turn left into Brisbane St. On the left is Ipswich Girls' Grammar School.

The buildings of Ipswich Girls' Grammar School were designed in 1892 by George Brockwell Gill in the fashionable Classical Revival style. Well worth noting are the cottage near the front gate and the trees lining the drive.

The Ipswich Club.

View of Ipswich from Lions Lookout, Queen's Park.

16 THROUGH CUNNINGHAMS GAP

■ DRIVING TOUR ■ 313KM ■ 1 DAY ■ EXPLORING THE DARLING DOWNS

Queensland is more than just a coastline, it is also a thriving farming region. Towns like Boonah are quiet and attractive while well-established settlements like Warwick are rich in history.

1 BOONAH

Leave Ispwich on Warwick Rd heading south through Churchill. When the road reaches the Cunningham Highway do not take the major route. Instead, continue travelling on through Loamside, Purga, Peak Crossing, and Coulson until you reach Boonah. Covering a distance of about 48km, this is known as the Ipswich–Boonah Road (Route 93).

Boonah is known as 'The Heart of the Fassifern' and is a very pretty little town with lots of timber houses. Surrounded by undulating hills, it was established in 1882 as a service centre for the various farms in the area. The region produces vegetables for the nearby Brisbane markets (most notably carrots and potatoes), cereal crops, beef, pork and timber.

Originally it was known as the Goolman Division Board, but it changed its name in 1937 to Boonah, an anglicised version of the Aboriginal word 'buna' which supposedly means bloodwood tree.

Boonah is rather a quiet community and its inhabitants are not particularly interested in tourism. Nearby lies Lake Moogerah which is a very popular haunt for boating enthusiasts and waterskiers.

2 MOUNT FRENCH NATIONAL PARK

Take the road heading south from Boonah for about 1km and follow the signs to the Mount French National Park which lies 10km west of the town.

The Boonah shire area has a number of interesting national parks where bushwalking is possible. One of these is Mount French National Park. The climb to the top of Mount French is well worth the effort for the excellent panoramic views over the

Fassifern Valley. It is part of the 676ha Moogerah Peaks National Park (situated to the west of Boonah) which includes a number of volcanic peaks and rocky cliffs. Mount Moon, Mount Edwards and Mount Greville are some of the more isolated areas of the park and are suitable for more experienced bushwalkers.

3 TEMPLIN HISTORICAL MUSEUM

Return to Boonah and travel to the west along the road (about 13km) that connects with the Cunningham Highway.

On the road between Boonah and the Cunningham Highway (about 3km out of town) is the excellent Templin Historical Museum which contains an interesting collection of artefacts and memorabilia chronicling the history of the area.

4 CUNNINGHAMS GAP

Approximately 25km to the south of the Boonah turn-off on the Cunningham Highway is Cunninghams Gap, one of the most historically significant vantage points in Queensland.

While exploring the Darling Downs in 1827, Allan Cunningham discovered the gap in the mountain range which he believed would provide access to the Downs from Moreton Bay. He later also explored the area to the

east of the Gap, arriving at Moreton Bay and exploring the upper reaches of the Brisbane River valley.

5 WARWICK

Travel 68km along the Cunningham Highway from the Boonah turn-off to reach Warwick.

Warwick is a thriving town and can lay claim to being the first important settlement in inland Queensland.

The area was first settled by the Leslie brothers (Patrick and George) who established the Canning Downs run in 1840 and built a home in 1846. Inevitably the station became an important centre for the region with a blacksmith, a store and accommodation and eating facilities.

In 1847 the New South Wales government gave Patrick Leslie permission to select a suitable site for a town on his Canning Downs station. At first, it was going to be known as Canningtown, although the local Aborigines knew the area as Gooragooby, but the name Warwick was finally chosen. The site of modern-day Warwick was duly surveyed in 1849 and pieces of land were first sold in 1850. Warwick then grew to become a municipality in 1861 and a city (the second largest city on the Darling Downs) in 1936.

The arrival of the railway in 1871 resulted in a boom in local industry. For a short time Warwick was the end of the line and this led to the establishment of a brewery (1873), a cooperative flour mill (1874), and a brick works (1874). The tasteful use of sandstone and the extensive construction which was undertaken as the town grew and prospered in the 1880s

Boonah is surrounded by a number of National Parks.

The Criterion Hotel, Palmerin Street, Warwick.

The Town Hall, Palmerin Street, Warwick.

and 1890s has left quite a large number of buildings which are noted for their graciousness and splendour.

The best way to discover historic Warwick is to park your car in Palmerin Street and walk up one side and down the other. There are several historic buildings all within close proximity of each other.

The Warwick Post Office (built in 1891) in Palmerin Street is an enormous two-storeyed building with Saracenic arches on the first floor, and a large cupola and Tuscan columns on the ground floor. It was built from locally quarried sandstone.

The Town Hall (dating from 1888) in Palmerin Street was also constructed from local sandstone. It can lay claim to being one of the oldest local authority buildings in Queensland and is distinguished by a large and elegant clock tower. When the building was completed the local newspaper, the *Warwick Argus*, wrote 'The comely edifice has been completed and a monument to the shrewdness and foresight of those aldermen who saw further than the 'morrow now stands where once a humpy reared its unpretentious head.'

Over the years the Town Hall has played host to a variety of unusual and interesting entertainments. In 1900 the Mayor stood on the balcony and called for cheers for Colonel Baden Powell to celebrate the news of the relief of Mafeking. In 1908 a biograph company showed simple movies in the hall. Peter Dawson performed in the hall in 1914, and in 1952 Sister Kenny was the celebrated guest at the Anzac Day celebrations. Today the Town Hall contains the city's Tourist Information Centre.

Other buildings of importance are located in Palmerin Street, including St Mary's Church (1864), a lovely sandstone Gothic Revival building distinguished by its lancet windows and large rose window on the eastern side, and the Criterion Hotel (1917) which today still retains much of its early charm. This elegant hotel (its latticework and bar are particularly distinctive) was also built in 1917.

Nearby, all located in Fitzroy Street, are the old Courthouse (built in 1885), the Police Station (1890) and the Warwick East State School (1862) which is one of the oldest schools in the state and one of the few school buildings in Australia which dates back to the 1860s.

Among the city's other impressive and interesting buildings are St Mark's Church in Albion Street, which was completed in 1868 although the belfry is more recent, and Pringle Cottage (dating from 1869) at 81 Dragon Street which was built by John McCulloch, a Scottish builder, in the style of the Scottish cottages of the time. It was a school for many years and has recently become part of the Warwick and District Historical Society Museum. The Pringle Cottage complex also includes an old general store and a shepherd's hut.

Also of interest is the National Hotel (built in 1890) in Grafton Street. Of particular note is the hotel's superb verandah with its cast-iron columns and balustrades. The Warwick Masonic Hall (completed in 1886) situated in Guy Street is a remarkably ostentatious hall with a Classic facade and Doric columns.

Australia's most famous sheep shearer, John Robert Howe, better known as Jackie Howe, was born at Canning Downs on 26 July 1861. His memory is honoured by a statue which is located in the main street of Blackall, and in 1983 Warwick established the Jackie Howe Memorial at the Jackie Howe Rest Area on the corner of Glengallan Road and the Cunningham Highway. This memorial is notable for the large pair of shears mounted at the top.

In recent times Warwick has promoted itself as Queensland's 'Rose and Rodeo City' because of the fame of the Warwick Rodeo which is held each October and coincides with the Warwick Rose Festival. Warwick is also the headquarters of the Australian Rough Riders Association and it proudly boasts that George Leslie held the very first rodeo on Canning Downs Station back in the 1860s. This is actually a somewhat dubious claim as feats of horsemanship were quite common throughout the country during that time.

Return to Ipswich along the Cunningham Highway. The journey is about 164km and can easily be done in under two hours.

BILLY HUGHES VISITS WARWICK

Fame came to the town of Warwick in 1917 when prime minister Billy ('the Little Digger') Hughes paid a visit to the town in order to press his case for conscription.

The townsfolk of Warwick, together with the majority of Australians, were very much against conscription and there was one brave person in the crowd who demonstrated this by hurling a well-aimed egg at the unfortunate prime minister. Billy Hughes demanded that the egg thrower be arrested on the spot, but the local policeman protested that, as no Queensland law had in fact been broken, he could not arrest the offender.

It is widely claimed that this incident and the intractibility of the protesting policeman were the factors that led directly to the establishment of the Commonwealth Police Force in Australia.

17 THE RAILWAY TOWNS

■ DRIVING TOUR ■ 119KM ■ 1 DAY ■ A WORLD OF TIMBER AND STEAM

This tour starts in Ipswich and takes in Rosewood, Grandchester, Laidley and Gatton, which has a most interesting history, including an unsolved multiple murder.

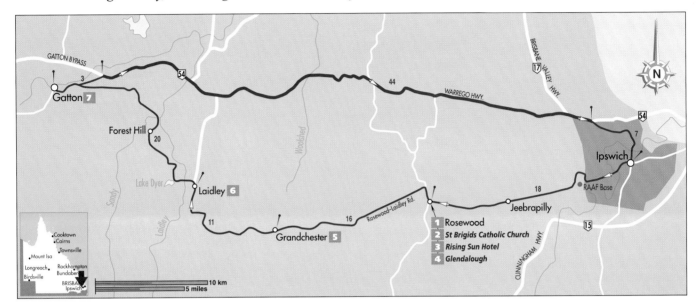

1 ROSEWOOD

Leave the centre of Ipswich on Warwick Rd which becomes the Cunningham Highway at the Showground. Turn right at the RAAF Base turn-off, 11km out of Ipswich. Travel 2km and turn left at the crossroads. Continue through Jeebrapilly to Rosewood. The journey from Ipswich to Rosewood is 18km.

Rosewood, like so many of the small towns that lie between Brisbane and Toowoomba, is easy to pass by, and yet a brief stay yields interesting treasures.

The town came into existence when the railway from Ipswich to Grandchester was

Das Neumann Haus, Laidley.

St Brigids Catholic Church, Rosewood.

built during the 1860s. Rosewood became a stopover point until the area surrounding the town yielded coal (in 1881 the Walloon–Rosewood coalfield started operation) and agriculture developed the rich soils for dairying and mixed farming.

2 ST BRIGIDS CATHOLIC CHURCH

Turn left from the main road and drive a couple of kilometres through the tiny township. On the southern side of the town is St Brigids Catholic Church.

The town's greatest claim to fame is the remarkable St Brigids Catholic Church in Matthews Street. It claims to be the largest wooden Catholic church in Australia and is truly magnificent. The woodwork inside, the feeling of openness and the sense of care and craftsmanship which has gone into the building evoke the kind of religious commitment which is such a characteristic of the great churches of Europe. This is an edifice constructed out of faith.

It was designed by Father Andrew Horan and opened on 13 February 1910. It is claimed that it was made entirely of timber, with even the foundations being timber stumps set on timber bed logs. The church is divided into three parts – the nave and two side aisles – each of which is characterised by a separate cross and gabled window. Inside are some unusual frescoes – one has the symbols of grain (bread) and grapes (wine) with the inscription *O memoriala mortis domini* (In memory of the death of our Lord) while another depicts angels and was probably painted as recently as the 1940s.

Other features of particular interest are the pressed-metal ceiling, the altar which although made of wood has been painted to

look like marble, and the statues of the three saints – St Brigid, St Agnes and the now discredited St Philomena.

3 RISING SUN HOTEL

Return to the main street and continue further south to the Rising Sun Hotel which is located on the left just past the railway line.

The Rising Sun Hotel was built in 1908 and still retains its unusual corner roof turret and its delightful verandah and awnings.

4 GLENDALOUGH

Drive back up the main street until you reach the roundabout. On the corner you will find a beautiful old timber house.

At the other end of the town (adjacent to the main roundabout on the corner of Langfield Road and John Street) is 'Glendalough', a large timber house built in 1910, which, like so many of the houses in nearby Ipswich, is a fine example of the opulence which was possible at that time when timber and craftsmanship were combined with large amounts of money.

5 GRANDCHESTER

Follow the Rosewood–Laidley Rd for 16km west of Rosewood until you reach Grandchester.

Grandchester (named after the beautiful village outside Cambridge in England) is a tiny settlement whose two main claims to fame are the Grandchester Railway Station, which was constructed when the railway from Ipswich terminated at Grandchester, and the Grandchester Steam Timber Mill.

The area was first explored by Allan Cunningham who arrived there in May 1829. Cunningham's party camped beside what is now known as the Railway Lagoon while searching for the Brisbane River.

Originally known as Bigges Camp, after the pioneering pastoralist Frederick Bigges, it was little more than a watering hole for transients until the arrival of the railway from Ipswich in 1865. This short section of railway line was the first railway built in Queensland and Governor Bowen, feeling that the terminus deserved something better than Bigges Camp, renamed it Grandchester.

The Grandchester Railway Station probably dates from around 1865 although, as a single-storeyed timber construction, it has been modified significantly over the years.

But for all the interest that the local history has – and indeed the railway station is listed by the National Trust – it is the Grandchester Sawmill which is the town's treasure. The sawmill began production in 1945 and even today it uses a steam engine which was manufactured in 1911. In an age of environmental awareness the Grandchester Sawmill is a reminder of the extraordinary economies which can be had from the use of steam. The owner actually fires the steam engine with the sawdust which is made by the mill. The sawdust heats the water, which drives the engine, which cuts the timber, producing sawdust which heats the water, and so on.

6 LAIDLEY

Continue westward along the Rosewood–Laidley Rd for 11km to reach Laidley.

Laidley is a sleepy township calling itself the 'Country Garden of Queensland' because the rich soils surrounding it support mixed farming, vegetable growing for the Brisbane markets, dairying, and cotton fields.

The first European to explore the Laidley area was Allan Cunningham who, travelling through the area in 1829, named it after the New South Wales deputy commissary general James Laidley.

The General Store, Laidley Pioneer Village.

Inside the Grandchester Steam Timber Mill.

The area was settled in the 1840s by J P Robinson who called his property Laidley Plains Station. The town wanders through the countryside and apart from a statue of a Clydesdale in the main street (symbol of the contribution made to the town by the animal), Das Neumann Haus and an interesting pioneer village museum, it is without distinction.

The Clydesdale statue gives notice that once a year the Queensland branch of the Commonwealth Clydesdale Society uses the town as the venue for its Show and Field Day. Animals come considerable distances to compete in the show.

Das Neumann Haus, located just off the main street on the corner of William and Patrick streets, is one of those fascinating idiosyncratic buildings which can make an ordinary town seem quite special. It was built by Herman Neumann, a local carpenter and cabinet-maker, and for many years was used as the family residence as well as a furniture showroom. It was handed over to the local council in 1983.

Laidley has an excellent pioneer village with a superbly preserved slab hut as well as an old gaol, general store, butcher's shop and a number of other interesting buildings.

The pioneer village is located where the old road to Toowoomba used to go. It is fascinating to think that after 1865 it was the first stopping place for passengers on the train from Ipswich to Grandchester who were heading further west to Toowoomba, the Darling Downs and beyond.

The Laidley Historical Society Museum is open on Sundays from 14:00–16:00 or by appointment and is located to the south of the town on the site of an old paddock which used to be a resting paddock for the Cobb & Co horses.

7 GATTON

Leave Laidley and travel 20km north-west past Lake Dyer and Forest Hill to Gatton.

Gatton was one of the earliest settlements in Queensland. The region was explored as early as 1825 when Major Edmund Lockyer (after whom the Lockyer Creek was named) passed through the area. He had been instructed to explore the Brisbane River and, in a small boat, managed to reach the present site of Ipswich (where he found coal) and discover the Stanley River.

The area was settled in the 1840s after the land around Moreton Bay was opened up to free settlers. By 13 April 1855 the village of Gatton (it was probably named after Gatton, Roxburghshire, Scotland) was gazetted and by 1858 it had become an important stopover point on the road from Brisbane to the Darling Downs; it was also a changeover point for the horses on the Royal Mail. By 1875 the railway line from Ipswich had reached the area and the town expanded rapidly as a service centre for the surrounding farms.

Today Gatton lies at the heart of a rich farming area where the fertile black soils provide huge crops of vegetables such as

THE GATTON MYSTERY

One of the most intriguing chapters in Gatton's history is the unsolved multiple murder known either as 'The Gatton Tragedy' or 'The Murphy Murders'.

On 26 December 1898 the sisters Norah and Ellen Murphy and their brother Michael were murdered under strange circumstances. The Murphy family, who had lived in the Gatton area for over 20 years, farmed outside the town. On the night of 26 December it was decided that Michael would take his sisters to a dance at the Gatton Divisional Hall. They left their parents' farm by cart at about eight that night and arrived in Gatton at nine. The dance had been cancelled due to a lack of young women. The trio decided to return home and on the way they were waylaid by the murderer. When their bodies were found the next morning Michael and his sister Ellen lay back to back with their hands tied behind them while Norah was on a neatly spread rug with her hands also tied behind her back. They had all been beaten to death and the carthorse had been shot.

The subsequent investigation was a litany of stupid bungling by virtually everyone involved. Within hours the paddock where the Murphys had been killed had up to 40 people in it – all destroying what evidence there was. The police took a day to arrive from Brisbane. The first doctor failed to find a bullet lodged in the head of Michael Murphy (it was only found later when his body was exhumed and a second post-mortem carried out) and the prime suspect, an itinerant labourer named Thomas Day, simply walked out of the town two weeks later and was never heard of again.

The graves of Michael, Norah and Ellen Murphy can be seen in the Gatton cemetery.

potatoes and onions for the Brisbane markets. The area is also well known for its beef and dairy industries.

An insight into the history of the town and the Gatton area can be gained by visiting the Gatton and District Historical Society Museum located beside Lake Apex. The lake, beside the highway on the Toowoomba side of town, is a bird sanctuary and popular picnic spot. The museum, open every Sunday from 13:30–16:00 or by appointment, has a fascinating collection of local buildings as well as interesting memorabilia from the area. Contact tel: (074) 62 1580 or (074) 62 2884 for more information.

Drive 3km east from Gatton, heading towards the Warrego Highway. Join the highway and continue east for 44km. Take the exit for Ipswich. The centre of the town is located 7km from the turn-off.

18 FROM THE HIGHLANDS TO TEXAS

■ DRIVING TOUR ■ 381KM ■ 1 DAY ■ WINE, HISTORY AND CATTLE

In south-eastern Queensland, the New England Highlands push as far north as Stanthorpe and it is common for these regions to receive snow. Further west the land gives way to cattle country.

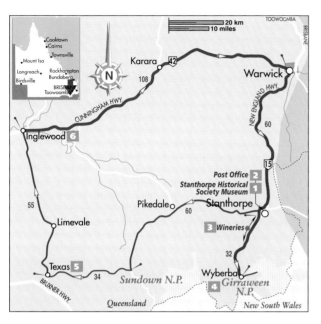

Stanthorpe is a pretty town set in the middle of a farming area where activities range from vine and fruit growing to sheep and cattle grazing. Located on the New England Highway 223km from Brisbane, Stanthorpe is unusually cool for Queensland. In winter, its night-time temperatures often fall below zero – the average minimum temperature for July is 0.3°C. The town once recorded -14.6°C – the coldest temperature ever recorded in Queensland.

The first European to explore the area was Allan Cunningham who passed through the area in 1827. Stanthorpe was first settled 30 years later when a coach station was established. It remained a lonely outpost until the discovery of tin on the Quart Pot Creek in 1871 brought an influx of miners to the area. The name Stannum (Latin for tin) was adopted at this time. The coach station became a regular stopover point for Cobb & Co and the town grew quickly.

The railway arrived in the town in 1881 and in the 1890s there was an influx of German settlers into the area. After World War I soldier settlements were established to the north of the town and during and after World War II a considerable number of Italian POWs and migrants arrived.

1 STANTHORPE AND DISTRICT HISTORICAL SOCIETY MUSEUM

Entering Stanthorpe from the north, the Stanthorpe Museum is on the right-hand side of the road.

The Stanthorpe and District Historical Society Museum is a well-developed rural museum which includes a shearer's hut (1842), the North Marylands School Residence (1891), the Stanthorpe Shire Council Chambers, a small gaol, some interesting railway artefacts (commemorating the Amiens branch line for the soldier settlement area), and a vast collection of local memorabilia. All of the buildings have been beautifully preserved. The setting, next to the Top of the Town Caravan Park at the top of Main Street, is delightful.

Opening times for the museum are restricted to 14:00–16:00 on Sundays and public holidays, but it will open at other times. There is a list of telephone numbers of liaison officers outside the building.

2 POST OFFICE

Continue into the centre of the town. The main street, High Street, deviates to the left at Railway Street and on the corner is the town's impressive Post Office.

Stanthorpe's other major building of historical interest is the Post Office in the centre of town. Built by the government architect in 1901, it has a commanding position on the main street and its front is decorated by the British coat of arms. It is a good example of Edwardian Classical design with arched windows and an ornamental ceiling.

The chief attractions of Stanthorpe, however, tend to be the natural features rather than the historical ones. Stanthorpe lies at the heart of what has become known as 'the Granite Area', a region which extends for 50km north of the New South Wales border – the town is totally surrounded by large granite outcrops. The two most important parks in the area are the Girraween National Park, which has a 35-minute 'Granite Arch Discovery Walk', and Sundown National Park, where campers can enjoy waterfalls and quiet swimming holes.

The historic Post Office, Stanthorpe.

3 THE WINERIES SOUTH OF STANTHORPE

One of the main attractions in the area to the south of Stanthorpe is the wineries. Take the New England Highway south. On either side of the road, signs indicate the location of a variety of wineries.

Elsinore Wines is located at the tiny settlement of Glen Aplin. It is open only on Saturdays, Sundays and public holidays from 8:30–17:00 and specialises in exclusive boutique wines. Contact (076) 83 4234.

Kominos Wines is located near Severnlea on the New England Highway. With vineyards growing chardonnay, semillon, chenin blanc, shiraz and cabernet sauvignon grapes, the winery produces a wide range of reds and whites. Tours are by appointment. Contact tel: (076) 83 4311.

Rumbalara Vineyards is renowned for its fortified wines and ciders. It provides picnic facilities and is open seven days a week. Contact tel: (076) 84 1206.

Stone Ridge Vineyards and Winery is located off the New England Highway at Glen Aplin. Specialising in varietal table wines, especially shiraz and chardonnay, the winery is open from 10:00–17:00 and can be contacted on tel: (076) 83 4211.

Bungawarra Wines at Ballendean offers award-winning reds, whites and fortified wines including a vintage port and liqueur muscat. Open from 10:00–16:00 daily with picnic and barbeque facilities, this winery can be contacted on tel: (076) 84 1128.

Winewood Wineries is one of the newest wineries in the area, having only started production in 1985. It specialises in red and

The Eye of the Needle, Mount Norman, Girraween National Park.

white table wines. Open seven days a week from 9:00–17:00, the winery can be contacted on tel: (076) 84 1187.

Sundown Valley Vineyards boasts the largest wine vats in the Stanthorpe area. From these vats have come award-winning reds and whites as well as a sparkling wine. It is open seven days a week from 9:00–17:00 and can be contacted on tel: (076) 84 1226.

Robinson's Family Vineyards was established in 1969. The predominant grapes are chardonnay and cabernet sauvignon. The winery is open for tastings and sales seven days a week from 9:00–17:00. Contact tel: (076) 84 1216.

4 GIRRAWEEN NATIONAL PARK

This national park is located 32km south of Stanthorpe and is reached by taking the turn-off from the New England Highway at Wyberba.
There are a number of walking tracks in the area ranging from a 25-minute walk along Bald Rock Creek to a six-hour hike to Mount Norman and the Eye of the Needle. Queensland National Parks and Wildlife Service has an informative brochure available which explains the background of the park (it was acquired in 1932 after a long history of sheep grazing), its distinctive fauna including two species of gliding possum, and provides detailed maps of how to get to the famous Balancing Rock, Sphinx Rock, Turtle Rock, the Pyramids and some other impressive granite outcrops. The park ranger can be contacted on (076) 84 5157. Camping facilities are available.

5 TEXAS

Return towards Stanthorpe. Instead of entering the town take the New England Highway by-pass and then take the turn-off to Pikedale. The town is approximately 32km to the west of Stanthorpe. From Pikedale the road turns south for about 29km before turning west once again. Travel 34km along a less-than-perfect road until you reach Texas.

The town of Texas is located 101km from Stanthorpe and 159km from Tenterfield on the Dumaresa River and is actually a very small community serving the surrounding grazing area. Like so many of Queensland's rural settlements, it has spread out and there is a large amount of vacant land within the town's boundaries.

First settled in 1842, the town was named after the nearby 'Texas Station' – the largest landholding in the area. In the 1870s the area became a centre of tobacco growing and in 1876 established its own factory which converted the tobacco leaves into cakes and plugs. But it was still far from being a major town. A report of 1886 states that 'the town [of Texas] only exists on paper' and describes it as a hotel, a store, a few cottages and the factory.

The famous flood of 28 March 1890 wiped out the tobacco factory and what there was of the town. People were forced to climb trees and wait until the flood waters receded. The town moved 2km north to higher ground, but the association with tobacco continued for nearly a century until it started to decline in the late 1950s. Today, there is little evidence of tobacco growing.

The town has a nice sense of humour about its unusual name: in the main street there is a Dallas Gift Shop.

The Texas Historical Museum, located in the old police house (not the police station) which was built in 1890 after the floods, is the town's most interesting feature. It is open on Saturdays from 10:00–15:00. However, a call to the numbers listed on the gate – (016) 53 1169 or 53 1410 – will get the museum opened promptly during the week.

In recent years the museum (which is organised so that local pieces of memorabilia have been placed in the appropriate rooms) has expanded beyond the police house and now includes a shop that was moved from Smithfield, the old gaol (with special steel reinforcement between the

timbers to ensure that even the most desperate inmate could not escape), a special room for a telephone display and some interesting old farming equipment.

Down the street from the museum is a disused building displaying a Cobb & Co sign. This was used by their South Queensland Transport company until quite recently.

6 INGLEWOOD

Leave Texas heading north to Limevale. Travel about 55km to reach Inglewood.
Once an important tobacco-growing town, Inglewood's past is evocatively recalled with a thoroughfare named 'Tobacco Road'. However, it is now a service centre for a mixed agriculture area.

The town was originally known as Brown's Inn (after the local hotel). After it was surveyed in 1862, the name changed to Inglewood. There is some confusion over the origin of the name; some sources claim the town was named after a forest in England while others claim that 'ingol' is an Aboriginal word for cypress pine.

The area around the town prospered while Inglewood itself remained small. It was only in 1907, with the arrival of the railway, that the town's continued existence was ensured. The railway authorities wanted to call the siding 'Parriegana' but the locals objected and actually pulled down the sign insisting that the name remain Inglewood.

The major attraction in the area is the Coolmunda Dam which lies 20km east of the town. A popular place for fishing, boating and waterskiing, it provides the Macintyre Brook, which runs through the town, with a permanent supply of water.
Leave Inglewood on the Cunningham Highway and continue east to Warwick which lies 108km away. From Warwick take the New England Highway south for 60km to Stanthorpe. This stage of the journey will take around 2 hours.

Stanthorpe Historical Society Museum.

Texas Historical Museum.

19 HISTORIC TOOWOOMBA

■ DRIVING TOUR ■ 26KM ■ ½ DAY ■ EXPLORING GRACIOUS HOMES AND PUBLIC BUILDINGS

Toowoomba is a substantial city with a number of interesting historic buildings. It was a popular retreat for Brisbane's powerful and wealthy residents throughout the 19th century.

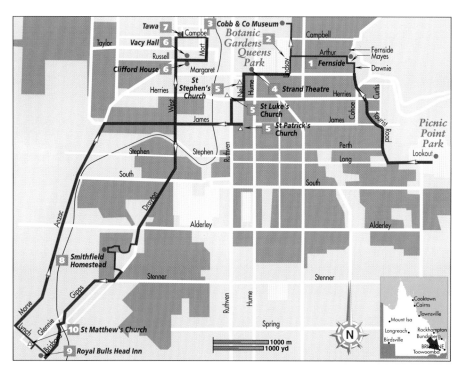

T*he area around Toowoomba was first explored by Allan Cunningham who discovered and named the Darling Downs after the New South Wales Governor, Sir Ralph Darling. Toowoomba as a township grew up in the 1840s as a convenient stopping point on the route from Moreton Bay (Brisbane) to the pastoral holdings in the west. Toowoomba has a surprisingly elegant and gracious city centre with many handsome old buildings and wide streets.*

A first stop for anyone coming from Brisbane should be Picnic Point Lookout and the Camera Obscura – signposted from the Warrego Highway on the eastern side of town. The Lookout, on the edge of the escarpment, offers superb views over the Lockyer Valley and the bare Tabletop Mountain dominates the landscape. The Camera Obscura (open from 10:00–14:00) is a marvellous device which allows visitors a 360° view of the city and surrounding countryside.

1 FERNSIDE

Leave Picnic Point, heading west along Tourist Rd, and follow it for 500m. The road which then continues to the west is actually Long St; Tourist Rd bends to the right in a northerly direction and, after 700m, appears to finish in James St. Turn left, ignoring the immediate right into Curtis St, but take the next right a few metres further on: this is still Tourist Rd. When it joins with Cohoe St at the 4-way intersection, keep heading in the same basic direction. When you reach an intersection with Margaret St to the left, continue straight on as Tourist Rd becomes Dawnie St. At its end you have no option but to turn into Mayes St. Take the first turn right into Fernside St. Halfway along this short street you will find Fernside.

Fernside is a large brick residence built in the early 1870s on a 9.7ha piece of land which included a coach house and stables. In the early 1880s it was used as a summer retreat by Sir Arthur Kennedy, the governor of Queensland (1877–1883).

2 BOTANIC GARDENS

About halfway up Fernside St, turn left into Arthur St. Follow Arthur St all the way to the end and, at the T-junction with Lindsay St, turn right. On your left are the Botanic Gardens.

The beautiful Botanic Gardens are central to the city's annual Carnival of Flowers festivities. Over the years Toowoomba has been known variously as the 'Regional Capital of the Darling Downs' (an accurate description) and 'The Garden City' (a fair description given the number of parks and public gardens and the proliferation of tree-lined streets).

3 COBB & CO MUSEUM

Past the intersection with Campbell St you will find the Cobb & Co Museum at 27 Lindsay St. It is part of the Queensland Museum.

Toowoomba's most notable tourist attraction is the Cobb & Co Museum, tel: (076) 39 1971. It is open from 10:00–16:00 on Mondays to Fridays and from 13:00–16:00 on weekends and public holidays. It is more comprehensive than its name suggests, tracing the history of horse-drawn transportation in Australia from the old timber wagons and bullock drays to Cobb & Co coaches and a landau used by the Duke of Edinburgh when he visited in 1876.

4 STRAND THEATRE

Head back, going south along Lindsay St for 700m to the intersection with Margaret St. Turn right and drive down the hill with Queens Park on your right. At the bottom of the street is the intersection with Hume St. Across the road and to your right is the Strand Theatre.

The Strand Theatre has a very distinctive semi-circular window and an unusual central balcony. Across the road is the Courthouse which was built in the 1870s in the Classic Revival style. It is a suitable accompaniment to the Post Office at 136 Margaret Street which was designed in an Italianate style by the government architect in 1878. Over the years it has been greatly altered but the clock tower and the two-storeyed loggia are original features of this imposing building.

5 CHURCHES IN THE CITY CENTRE

Toowoomba has a number of distinctive churches in the central business district. To view St Stephen's Church, keep on the left-hand side of Margaret St and take the next left turn into Neil St. It is on your right just past Jessie St.

To get to St Luke's and St Patrick's, continue along Neil St to the intersection with Herries St, turn right and the next street on the left is Ruthven – St Luke's is on the corner. Then head along Ruthven St to the intersection with James St and turn left – St Patrick's is 100m along on the right-hand side.

St Stephen's Church was built in 1884 and is now nothing more than a shadow of its former glory. There is also the Gothic magnificence of St Luke's (1891), while the Gothic style of St Patrick's Roman Catholic Church (1889) dominates James Street at the top of the town centre.

6 VACY HALL AND CLIFFORD HOUSE

To get to Vacy Hall head back along James St, cross Ruthven St and continue to the next major intersection turning right into West St. Head north across Herries and Margaret sts and take the next turn right into Russell St. On your left at number 135 is Vacy Hall.

Blacksmith, Cobb & Co Museum, Toowoomba.

Vacy Hall is now an historic guest house. Built in the 1880s, the house is characterised by beautiful bay windows, a magnificent surrounding garden and extensive areas of patterned parquetry floors.

Clifford House at 120 Russell Street, across the road from Vacy Hall, is recognised by many as Toowoomba's finest old home. Now functioning as a restaurant, it was built in 1860 as a residential club for squatters. It is a superb example of the way stone and timber can be integrated: the sandstone gives the building a solid feel while the upstairs timber verandah appears almost delicate by contrast.

7 TAWA

Continue down Russell St, take the first left into Mort St, cross Taylor St and turn left into Campbell St. Cross Price and Gowrie and take the next right into Boulton St. On your left is Tawa.

Tawa is the oldest remaining cottage in Toowoomba. It is quite a small cottage built from homemade bricks with simple pit-sawn timber floors and a shingle roof; it was completed in the 1850s on a site originally owned by the famous pastoralist Thomas Mort.

8 SMITHFIELD HOMESTEAD

Go back down Boulton St, turn right into Campbell St and take an immediate left into West St. Follow West for 1.5km across Margaret, Herries and James sts and just past Stephen St take the right fork down Drayton Rd. Continue through the roundabout at Alderney St and take the next right into Corriedale Crescent. Take an immediate left into Wessex St which curves to the right becoming Brangus St. Take the first right into Cheviot St and then the first left into Panda St which bends around to Smithfield Homestead.

This historic home is now surrounded by suburbia and has been converted into an exclusive restaurant and reception centre which is used for weddings and other formal occasions. It was designed by the architects J Marks and Sons, probably for the grazier and landowner James Taylor, and is a superb rural residence having been built in stone with wide verandahs and elegant paired timber columns.

The building's most famous occupant was a successful German industrialist, Oscar Flemmich, who kept thoroughbred horses and employed a large number of grooms and servants. It is said that when he left the area he shot all his horses and dogs rather than let them go to another owner.

9 ROYAL BULLS HEAD INN

Continue along Panda St, turn left into Chilla St, take the first turn left into Brangus, the first right down Smithfield St, the first left along Friend St and turn right into Drayton Rd. Turn right into Stenner St, then take the second left and follow Gipps St until you enter the township of Drayton. Cross the railway line and continue for 300m, pass the police station and on your right is the Royal Bulls Head Inn.

Drayton can lay claim to being the first town established beyond the Great Dividing Range in Queensland. It was settled in 1842 and by 1847 the Royal Bulls Head Inn had been built. It was a popular haunt for the local squatters and their workers. The first proprietor was William Horton, a convict from Worcestershire in England who, so rumour has it, was actually descended from the local aristocracy.

The Royal Bulls Head Inn was the venue for the first Church of England service on the Darling Downs, held in one of the rooms in 1848 by Rev Benjamin Glennie.

FROM SWAMP TO CITY

In 1852 the squatter, Thomas Alford, settled to the north of Drayton and called his property Toowoomba. Slowly a settlement grew up in this area. Its original, and rather unromantic, name was 'The Swamp'. This was changed in 1858. Toowoomba was officially declared a municipality in 1860, became a town in 1887 and was declared a city in 1904. In the 1860s the town expanded rapidly, soon outstripping the smaller Drayton.

The building was extended in 1859 and for some time it was known as the best building on the Darling Downs. It was certainly good enough for the Governor of Queensland to stay the night there.

Today this remarkable building is owned by the National Trust. It is open between 10:00 and 16:00 from Thursday to Monday. The original 1847 kitchen, the rooms of the hotel, and the interior have all been lovingly restored and preserved by the Trust.

Drayton managed to have a separate life from Toowoomba until the 1860s when it was overwhelmed by the increasing importance of the nearby township.

10 ST MATTHEW'S CHURCH

Return towards Toowoomba, travelling up Brisbane St to Lynch St where you turn left. Take the first turn left down Glennie St, on the right is St Matthew's Church.

Drayton also boasts the interesting St Matthew's Church which was built in 1887 and has the knocker from the Royal Bulls Head Inn on its door.

Continue on Lynch St and turn right at the T-junction into Morse St, which becomes Anzac Ave. Follow this road for about 3.5km and turn right at James St (Warrego Highway). Follow this road for another 2km and turn left into Ruthven St. Follow the signs back to the centre of Toowoomba.

East Creek Park, one of Toowoomba's many public gardens.

War memorial to Toowoomba's servicewomen.

20 HISTORY ON THE DARLING DOWNS

■ DRIVING TOUR ■ 166KM ■ 1 DAY ■ EXPERIENCING RURAL QUEENSLAND

The highlight of this tour would have to be a visit to the well-known Jondaryan Woolshed Tourist Complex, where the Australian Heritage Festival is held each year at the end of August.

1 OAKEY

Leave the centre of Toowoomba heading west on Bridge St, which becomes Gowrie Rd and later the Warrego Highway. Travel 29km to Oakey.

Oakey is a small country town situated 402m above sea level. It was named, rather unimaginatively, after the river oaks on the nearby creek.

Like so much of the Darling Downs, Oakey was first settled in the early 1840s when pastoralists moved into the region and claimed large areas of land for grazing. It was not until 1867, and the arrival of the railway line, that any kind of a township was created. In 1871, one rather daring entrepreneur opened a short-lived meat-works near the town. The plan was to tin and export kangaroo and wallaby under the dubious marketing name 'Australian Game'. The enterprise was unsuccessful and closed down in 1876.

2 AVIATION MUSEUMS

Stop at the Tourist Information Centre, located on the Warrego Highway on the southern side of town.

The town has two aviation museums. The small one in the Tourist Information Centre next to the Jondaryan Shire Office contains memorabilia from World War II.

3 STATUE OF BERNBOROUGH

Nearby, on the Warrego Highway adjacent to the Shire Office, is the statue of Bernborough.

Oakey's moment of glory came with the birth of the brilliant horse Bernborough at Rosalie Plains in 1939. For the first four years of his life Bernborough was restricted to racing in the local area (because of a ban the Queensland Turf Club had placed on his owners) and he became something of a legend on the tracks around Toowoomba. But then in 1945 he was sold to the well-known Sydney restauranteur, Azzalin Romano, who bought him for 2600 guineas.

Over the next 18 months, trained by Harry Plant and ridden by a young Athol Mulley, Bernborough became a legend. Carrying horrendous weights (he won the Doomben Cup carrying 10 stone 11 pounds and the Doomben 10 000 carrying 10 stone 5 pounds) he won 15 consecutive races in three states between 22 December 1945 and 19 October 1946. His memory is honoured by the life-size bronze horse cast (the first in Australia) which stands outside the Jondaryan Shire Office. His trainer Harry Plant believed that Bernborough was the greatest horse ever to race in Australia.

4 OAKEY AIR BASE

Continue along the Warrego Highway which becomes Bridge St. After the railway station cross the railway line and take the turn off the Warrego Highway to Acland, then turn right across the railway line. The Air Base is signposted at the northern end of Oakey.

At the Oakey air base is the Museum of Australian Army Flying. It recalls the special role flying has in the Army as opposed to the Air Force. Recognised as a superb collection, the museum has quite a lot of material from World War I.

Oakey is now the home of the $13 million Australian Army Aviation Centre and it seemed appropriate that a museum should be established to record the history of Army flying as well as the history of flight and the early history of the RAAF. The museum's

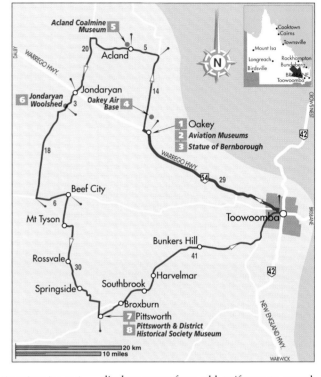

displays range from old uniforms to actual aircraft. There is a replica of a Box Kite as well as every aircraft flown by the army. These include the Sioux helicopter, the Link Trainer, an old Spitfire and a replica of Sir Charles Kingsford-Smith's Southern Cross. The museum is open from 8:00–16:00 on Wednesdays to Fridays and also from 11:00–17:00 on weekends.

5 ACLAND COALMINE MUSEUM

Continue northwards towards Acland. About 14km north of Oakey the road turns left, and 5km further west is the Acland Coalmine Museum.

Acland has one of the most interesting coalmining museums in the country. Privately run, the museum is sited on the old Acland coalfield which was still operating as recently as 1984 and is regarded as the smallest coalmine in Australia. Each visitor is given a tour of the mine during which all the equipment and the entire process of coalmining are explained.

6 JONDARYAN WOOLSHED

Travel west for 10km, then south for 10km and you will reach the small township of Jondaryan which sits astride the Warrego Highway. Cross the Highway and, following the signs, head 3km south of Jondaryan township to the Jondaryan Woolshed Complex.

Jondaryan is a superb example of a tiny, insignificant settlement exploiting its one famous and important historical building in

The rich volcanic soils of the Darling Downs make fertile farming land.

The Jondaryan Woolshed Tourist Complex.

Sheep shearing at the historic woolshed.

order to create an entire tourism industry out of it. The town itself consists of nothing more than a hotel, a few shops, and a few houses. It would be fair to suggest that the town is there merely to direct traffic towards the Jondaryan Woolshed Tourist Complex.

The Jondaryan Woolshed is a major tourist attraction which is well organised and interesting. The complex consists of a large number of buildings but the centre-piece is the Woolshed itself which has been listed by the National Trust.

Jondaryan was first settled by Charles Coxon in 1842. It was named, so the accepted wisdom goes, after the Aboriginal word 'Jondooyan', the name given to a waterhole in the Oakey Creek. The property changed hands a number of times in the 1840s and 1850s until in 1856 it was purchased by Robert and Edwin Tooth (famous for their beer as well as for their involvement in the establishment of the Bank of New South Wales and the Colonial Sugar Refining Company).

The highlight of each year at Jondaryan is the nine-day Australian Heritage Festival which is held at the end of August. During this period people come from all over Australia to display traditional bush crafts and all the machinery in this remarkable museum complex becomes operational.

The Jondaryan Woolshed Historical Museum is a remarkable example of local enthusiasm and enterprise. In 1972, after a ball was held in the woolshed on the anniversary of the first ball 111 years before, it was decided to use the Woolshed as the focal point of a park which would become a 'living memorial to the historic pastoral industry and the pioneers of rural Australia'. In 1976 the society received a grant of $10 000 from the Federal Government to restore the deteriorating woolshed.

Slowly the complex began to expand. The original Jondaryan blacksmith's shop (dating from 1850) was moved onto the land in 1977. That same year the old Woodview

School (1886) arrived and in August the first Australian Heritage Festival was held.

The following year the sulky shed and an old shepherd-boundary rider's hut were acquired and in the same year the Youth Hostels Association established a hostel in the old shearers' quarters.

In 1979 the complex was expanded by a blacksmith-made windmill and the Evanslea wheat-handling shed. Then, in 1980, the old police lockup from Peranga was added. 1984 saw the arrival of the Lagoon Creek homestead (now a restaurant for visitors) and more recently the beautiful old Bank of New South Wales building has been turned into a reception and souvenir shop near the car park. The Jondaryan Woolshed is open daily from 8:30–17:00.

7 PITTSWORTH

Travel 18km south of the Jondaryan Woolshed and turn left at the T-junction. Travel 6km east until you reach the crossroads at Beef City. Turn south and continue a further 6km to Mt Tyson. Take the road through Rossvale and Springside to Pittsworth. The distance from Mt Tyson to Pittsworth is 24km.

Pittsworth portrays itself as a town with many interesting buildings and places of historical importance. Unfortunately this image is not matched by the quiet reality of an attractive town with tree-lined streets and a couple of interesting buildings in the main street. The ANZ Bank (1905), the gracious St Stephen's Catholic Church (1908) in Hume Street and the substantial Pittsworth Folk Museum where the old town Post Office (1886) is the most prominent building are the most noteworthy.

The town was originally known as Beauaraba but the name was changed to Pittsworth in 1915 after a prominent local family who settled the area in 1854 when they took up land at Goombungee.

Dating from 1876, the town grew up around a hotel which attracted itinerant rural workers and local landholders. The settlement of the area was greatly helped by

the arrival of the railway in 1887 and, with the transition to smaller holdings and the move from sheep to dairy farming, the town opened its own Co-operative Dairy Company in 1896. By 1914, Pittsworth had a number of dairy factories which were producing approximately 80 per cent of all the cheese being manufactured on the Darling Downs. In 1924, on the invitation of the Australian Committee of the Empire exhibition, the town made a single block of 'Pittsworth Mild' cheese weighing 1.5 tonnes which was duly shipped off to the World Dairy Show in London.

8 PITTSWORTH & DISTRICT HISTORICAL SOCIETY MUSEUM

As you leave the town you will see signposts to the museum which is well worth visiting. It is located on the northern outskirts of town and is signposted at the first street off the bypass.

Like so many of the folk museums on the Darling Downs, the Pittsworth Museum is a combination of fine old buildings – old schools, the Post Office, an 1895 cottage – and fascinating memorabilia. The museum makes much of items such as a chantilly lace wrap which once belonged to Florence Nightingale, a love letter written by Governor Bligh's mother, and memorabilia connected with Arthur Postle who, in 1906, was proclaimed 'the fastest man in the world' when he won the World Championship Cup for the 220-yard dash. It is a very interesting and well-presented local folk museum which includes an outdoor display of carts and farm equipment. Last but not least, there is also a display of the complete cheese-making process by the Pittsworth Cheese Factory.

Today Pittsworth is an attractive, small service centre for the surrounding farms which grow cereal crops, cotton, linseed and sunflowers, and breed beef cattle.

From Pittsworth, travel to Toowoomba. The journey covers 41km and passes through the tiny settlements of Broxburn, Southbrook, Harvelmar and Bunkers Hill.

21 COTTON AND CATTLE COUNTRY

■ DRIVING TOUR ■ 410KM ■ 2 DAYS ■ QUEENSLAND'S RICH AGRICULTURAL HEARTLAND

Dalby is a thriving centre in the heart of the Darling Downs, which have a number of large and prosperous service centres that reflect the wealth of the region.

Historically, the rich volcanic soils around Dalby have produced high yielding grain crops and excellent grasses for the raising of beef cattle, sheep and pigs. Today, Dalby is also the centre of a thriving cotton industry which spreads from St George in the south-west across the Goondiwindi and north to Dalby. The town also services the wheat, maize, millet, stock feed and butter producers in the surrounding districts. Dalby is a typical large country town with pleasant picnic spots beside the river, a lovely park in the centre of town, wide streets (particularly Cunningham, the main street) and plenty of attractions although, in fairness, most of these are located outside town.

The town's main historical attraction is The Crossing which is located on the Myall Creek. It was here that Henry Dennis set up a camp in 1841 which eventually became the township of Dalby. Driving from the east on the Warrego Highway you turn left just before the creek and the Criterion Hotel. Today, it is nothing more than a plaque commemorating the first settlement of the area.

Just over the road from The Crossing in Gray Park there is a gravestone to the town's first resident, Samuel Stewart, who ran the pub. He died in February 1851 and was buried beside the river. Further along the road is the beautiful old home Randwick – a fine example of a 'Queenslander' with the elaborate timber architecture which makes these buildings so distinctive and attractive.

After the arrival of Henry Dennis (who was really taking the land on behalf of his wealthy employer Charles Coxen), Dalby was declared a township in 1854 and became a municipality in 1863. It is said that the town was named after Dalby on the Isle of Man although in recent times one disgruntled local alderman, tired of taking on the burden of the local citizenry, decided the name should be an acronym for 'Do a little bit yourself!'

The power of the local landholders, particularly Thomas Bell at Jimbour, ensured that the vast sheep and cattle runs which characterised the area were not broken up. Thus the railway line arrived in Dalby in 1868 and the town became an important railhead. But it wasn't until after World War II that the land was opened up to settlement by soldiers who were given land grants.

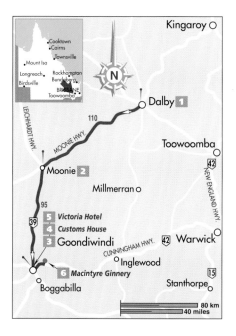

The Crossing, site of first camp in Dalby.

1 DALBY

Among this town's attractions is the Thomas Jack Park, on the main route through Dalby from Brisbane to Longreach. Large and attractive, with good stands of native trees and bushes, it is an ideal stopping place for travellers passing through the town.

Nearby in Cunningham Street is St Joseph's Roman Catholic Church which was consecrated in 1921. It is notable for its use of different coloured bricks. This unusual brick mosaic has given the building an almost Byzantine feel.

At the western end of town is the Pioneer Park Museum which has a number of interesting buildings including a well-preserved blacksmith's shop.

Running though the town is Myall Creek, which offers the chance to hook a silver perch or a Murray cod. On the banks of the creek is a tribute to the cactoblastis moth which was introduced by government scientists in 1925 to combat the prickly pear cactus plague, deadly to stock and crops.

2 MOONIE

Drive north-west out of the centre of Dalby on Drayton St. At the junction of Nicholson St and the beginning of the Warrego Highway at the western edge of the town, turn south-west into Nicholson St. The road turns west at Loudoun St which becomes the Moonie Highway. About 110km from Dalby the road passes through the tiny township of Moonie.

To call Moonie a township is to give it a status which would probably surprise most of the residents. Located close to the Weir and Moonie rivers (noted for their quality fishing) it is not really much more than a service station, a few houses, a motel and a caravan park.

The area was first settled in the 1840s but it only came to prominence in December 1961 when it became Australia's first commercial oilfield. In reality it is only a small oilfield accounting for less than one per cent of Australia's oil and gas reserves but the excitement which was associated with its success led to the establishment, in 1969, of a pipeline which joined the fields to

refineries in Brisbane. The area around Moonie is known as the Surat–Bowen Basin.

It is possible for visitors to inspect the oilfields (they are not immediately obvious from either the Leichhardt or Moonie highways) and tours can be arranged from the motel or caravan park.

3 GOONDIWINDI

At Moonie turn south onto the Leichhardt Highway and continue for about 95km until you reach the outskirts of Goondiwindi.

Located 805km from Sydney and 362km from Brisbane (or so the prominent and interesting road sign on the corner of the main street declares), Goondiwindi is a typical rambling Queensland settlement which spreads for kilometres around the old Customs House on the banks of the Macintyre River.

Pronounced 'gun' rather than 'goon', Goondiwindi is important because of its position at the junction of the Cunningham,

Dalby is an important railhead for the Darling Downs.

Newell, Bruxner, Barwon and Leichhardt highways on the border between New South Wales and Queensland. The town's fame has grown throughout Australia because of a horse named Gunsynd which was the subject of a 1973 hit song titled 'The Goondiwindi Grey'.

The town has made much of this famous horse and beside the river in Apex Park is a plaque commemorating the glories of Gunsynd, owned by the publican and three regular patrons of the Goondiwindi Hotel. In the late 1960s and early 1970s the horse had 29 wins including the 1971 Epsom Handicap and the 1972 Cox Plate. It came third in the 1972 Melbourne Cup.

The area around Goondiwindi was first explored in 1827 by Allan Cunningham. He named the Macintyre River after Captain Peter Macintyre who had provided horses and drays for the expedition.

Settlers arrived in the 1830s and one of the properties was named 'Gundawinda' which, some authorities claim, is the local Aboriginal word for 'a resting place for the birds'. Others claim the name comes from the Aboriginal words 'goona winnah' meaning 'dropping of ducks or shags'.

Goondiwindi grew up in the 1840s as a riverside camp for the teamsters bringing supplies from the north of New South Wales to the outlying properties in western Queensland. Its status was greatly increased when Queensland became a separate colony in 1859 and the Macintyre River became the border. The establishment of a Customs House in Goondiwindi ensured the settlement's continuing importance.

CUSTOMS HOUSE

Drive south down the Cunningham Highway. Just past Bowen St, on the right-hand side of the road before the Macintyre River, is the old Customs House.

The Customs House was probably first built in 1859 but over the years it has gone through a number of alterations. Between 1872 and 1894 it operated as a centre for staff employed to police and control illegal trading between Queensland and New South Wales. Customs duties were collected at a desk in the open air until Federation in 1901 when this was no longer necessary.

The old Customs House became a private home. In the 1970s it was converted into the Goondiwindi Museum and contains many interesting local artefacts.

VICTORIA HOTEL

Turn around at the museum and return along the Cunningham Highway. Turn left at the Post Office. This is the intersection with the Barwon Highway. One block to the west is the Victoria Hotel.

Apart from the Customs House (and the charming old cottage beside it) the other superb building in Goondiwindi is the Victoria Hotel, the oldest pub in town. Located on a site which was apparently a popular place for the local Kamilaroi Aborigines to launch attacks against the invading Europeans, the Victoria Hotel (1898) is a beautifully preserved and highly original Queensland country pub with wide verandahs and an unusual tower which makes it look rather like a wedding cake. Gunsynd is remembered here as well with a good collection of equine memorabilia.

MACINTYRE GINNERY

Turn east on Marshall St and continue across the Cunningham Highway. Continue about 2km out of town. On the northern side of the road is the Macintyre Ginnery.

Another feature of the town, and something well worth a visit, is the Macintyre Ginnery where the local cotton is processed 24 hours a day. In the cotton-picking season the streets of the town are filled with the roar of huge trucks as they make their way from the cotton fields to the ginnery. The Macintyre Ginnery actually encourages visits and is open from 8:00–17:00 between April and late August or September.

The processes inside the gin are simple yet fascinating. After it is picked mechanically the cotton is compacted into 12-tonne blocks by a 'module-maker' and taken to the ginnery. Following yellow guiding lines the visitor can see the raw cotton balls being fed into the machine and can follow the cotton as it is cleaned and prepared until, by the end, it is ready to be semi-automatically baled and shipped away for carding, drawing and roving. A booklet called *The Australian Cotton Story* is available from the office at the Ginnery.

Due the fertility of the surrounding farmlands, Goondiwindi also boasts the largest wheat-receiving depot in Queensland. It is located on the outskirts of town and can be reached by following Russell Street (the Barwon Highway) out of town.

Return to Dalby via the Leichhardt and Moonie highways. It is possible to travel east to Inglewood and then north to Dalby via Milmerran but the roads are not of the same quality as the major highways.

Massive silos at Dalby store much of the region's grain.

22 ALONG THE WARREGO HIGHWAY

■ DRIVING TOUR ■ 533KM ■ 2 DAYS ■ A WORLD OF HISTORY AND ADVENTURE

This tour enables the traveller to experience the flatness of western Queensland. Towns visited along the way include Boonarga, Chinchilla, Miles, Roma and Mitchell.

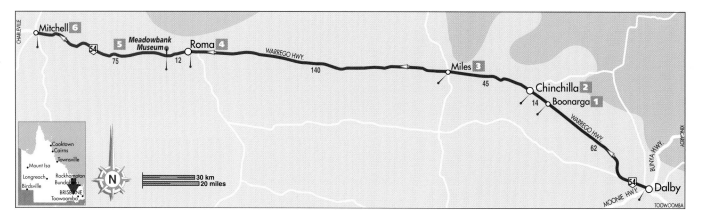

1 BOONARGA

Drive north-west out of the centre of Dalby on Drayton St. Take the Warrego Highway at the western edge of the town and continue for 62km to Boonarga.

It is hard to visualise today but by the 1920s 24 250 000ha of Australia were covered with prickly pear. The cactus had been introduced into Australia in 1839 and by 1862 it had reached the Chinchilla area. Farmers tried to fight it by cutting and burning but their labours met with little success. In 1925 the Commonwealth Prickly Pear Board, realising the scale of the problem, introduced the cactoblastis moth and larva from South America. Initially 3000 eggs arrived from Argentina and from a population of 527 females a total of 100 605 eggs were hatched. Half of these eggs were sent to the Chinchilla Prickly Pear Experimental Station and half were kept in Brisbane. The moth was spectacularly productive: at the height of the operation, Chinchilla was sending out as many as 14 million cactoblastis eggs a day.

The Boonarga Cactoblastis Hall was built by the local farmers and dedicated to the redoubtable insect which had managed to eat its way through the jungles of prickly pear. At the time it was seen as the saviour of rural Australia and thus it is entirely understandable that a hall should have been dedicated to its memory.

Artefacts at the Chinchilla Folk Museum.

2 CHINCHILLA

Continue on the Warrego Highway for 14km to the small township of Chinchilla. Although it claims to be the town that saved Australia from the prickly pear, it is Boonarga which celebrates the fact.

Chinchilla is a thriving rural settlement which boasts one of the finest transportation museums in Australia. The area around the town was first explored by Allan Cunningham in 1827 but it wasn't until the 1840s that Europeans began to take up land. By 1844, when Ludwig Leichhardt began his epic journey from Queensland to the Northern Territory, the furthest outpost of white settlement was Jimbour which lay some kilometres to the east of the present site of Chinchilla.

Chinchilla Station was established in 1848 as an extension of Wongongera Station which had been leased in 1846. It was probably named after a corruption of the local Aboriginal word for the cypress pine which Ludwig Leichhardt had recorded as 'jinchilla'.

During both the 1890s and the early part of the 20th century, the Queensland Government developed the area around Chinchilla with programs of closer settlement. While the first program failed, the second one in 1906 was far more effective and the next decade saw the population of the area increase dramatically. The new settlers became successful dairy farmers and this drove the economy of the area for the next 50 years. It was during this time that Chinchilla wrote itself into the history books as the town at the heart of the eradication of the dreaded prickly pear.

The highlight of any visit to Chinchilla must be a visit to the Chinchilla Folk Museum in Villiers Street (it is to the south of the town). This specialises in transportation and has one of the country's true rarities – a photocopy of the first ticket ever issued by Qantas (to a Mr A Kennedy) for

the first flight from Longreach to Cloncurry. The original ticket is in the local ANZ Bank. Apart from this the museum has a huge display of working steam engines, a rare three-cylinder engine which can move effortlessly into a reverse cycle, and extensive displays of dairy equipment, clothing and the usual materials of a folk museum. It is also home to the old Wongongera Slab Cottage, which dates from the 1880s.

The museum also prides itself on its steam-driven sawmill which is fired up on special occasions.

The town's other major attraction is the presence of petrified wood in the area. There are some good examples at the museum but the best example is in the town's main street next to the library in Fuller Park.

3 MILES

Drive west from Chinchilla for 45km along the Warrego Highway to reach the township of Miles.

Miles is situated on Dogwood Creek which was named by the explorer Ludwig Leichhardt when he passed through the area in 1844 on his journey from Jimbour to Port Essington in the Northern Territory.

The town developed in 1878 when the railway from Brisbane ran into trouble crossing the Dogwood Creek. The delay meant that railway workers settled in the area, shops, stores and pubs were established, and, for a short time, it became the railhead for supplies to the west. At the time the town was known as Dogwood Crossing but this was later changed to the less romantic Miles in honour of William Miles, the owner of Dulacca Station, who was a local Member of Parliament and the Queensland Colonial Secretary.

There is little doubt that the town's major attraction is the excellent Miles Historical Village – a first-class re-creation of a pioneer village in rural Queensland. The highlight of the village is Pioneer Street, an accurate reflection of a Queensland country town's main street at the turn of the century. Pioneer Street includes a post office, general store, bakery and pub. There is also the old Australian Bank of Commerce, the *Murilla Express* building, an old cafe, and Andersen's Smithy where the famous Condamine cow bell was first made. This bell was tied around the necks of cattle and used to locate them whenever they strayed in the bush. It was so successful that, according to Dame Mary Gilmore, it actually made the cattle deaf. This is a superb museum and is a suitable companion piece to the equally excellent one at Chinchilla. They were developed concurrently and are designed to complement each other and offer the visitor a comprehensive picture of the early history of the area.

4 ROMA

Continue west from Miles for another 140km to the major centre of Roma.

Roma is an attractive town of nearly 7000 people. Lying at the heart of a rich sheep- and cattle-grazing area, it boasts the largest store cattle market in Australia.

Lying to the west of the Darling Downs, the Roma district was first explored by Europeans when, in 1846, Sir Thomas Mitchell, the New South Wales surveyor-general, passed through the area looking for a route from Sydney to the north coast of the continent.

In 1848 Allan Macpherson reached the region and laid claim to about 400 000 acres (162 000ha) of land which he called Mount Abundance Station. Here Macpherson built a simple wooden hut.

On 4 April 1848 he was visited by Ludwig Leichhardt who was attempting to cross Australia from east to west. Leichhardt wrote his last letter in Macpherson's hut.

The first sign of a township occurred in 1861 when a couple of rough public houses were built near to the Mount Abundance homestead. The owner at the time, Stephen Spencer, objected to this change in land use but agreed with a Government surveyor that a town could be laid out at a place known as Reid's Crossing. The town was gazetted in 1862 and it had three hotels before any homes were built. The new town, or rather the trio of pubs, was named Roma after Lady Roma Bowen, the wife of the Queensland governor at the time. Before her marriage she had been known as Countess Diamantina Georgina Roma. The locals resisted the change and continued to call the settlement either The Bungil or Reid's Crossing.

Roma has the distinction of being the first town gazetted in the new colony of Queensland. It grew quite quickly once the area had been surveyed and by 1863 it had its own court of petty sessions, police station, doctor, chemist, and postmaster. It was proclaimed a municipality in 1867.

The railway reached the town in 1880 and the census a year later revealed that the town had a population of 1838.

The present Courthouse which was built in 1907 stands beyond the Empire Hotel (to the west) and is an impressive country town building. The original Courthouse was located to the west of the present building.

Wyndham Street, which runs at right angles to the main street, has two very impressive rows of bottle trees which were planted shortly after World War I. There is supposedly a tree for each soldier from the district who was killed in the war.

5 MEADOWBANK MUSEUM

Drive out of Roma on the road to Charleville for 12km. On the northern side of the road there is a sign to the Meadowbank Museum. The visitor has to drive on good dirt roads and open a couple of gates to gain access to this excellent museum.

The highlight of any visit to Roma is a visit to Meadowbank Museum, which has one of the finest and most unusual collections of memorabilia in the country. Of particular interest is the deadly 'man trap' used to trap Aborigines who were stealing cattle. It is a huge and ugly variation of a rabbit trap devised to break the leg and is almost impossible to open once triggered. There is a wonderful collection of old horse-drawn vehicles and old motor cars (including a model T Ford) and a hayloft which dates from 1859. This is only a hint of the riches the museum offers. There are bird and animal enclosures, a picnic and play area, and for people who enjoy exploring a vast collection of local artefacts, there is enough to keep even a cursory visitor busy for half a day.

6 MITCHELL

Continue on from the museum for a further 75km to the township of Mitchell.

Mitchell is a tiny town on the very edge of the Darling Downs and Maranoa region. The town was named after the great explorer Sir Thomas Mitchell who travelled through the area in 1845 and 1846 searching for a route from New South Wales to Port Essington and who was eager to find a great river which ran north through the area.

Steam engine at Chinchilla Folk Museum.

Mitchell left Sydney in December 1845 and by June 1846 he had established depots on the Maranoa, Warrego and Belyando rivers. He travelled through the area for nearly 12 months and upon his return to Sydney on 29 December 1846 he announced that the land which lay to the west of the Darling Downs was suitable for grazing. Thus Mitchell did much to encourage the settlement of the region.

Today Mitchell is a small settlement with few attractions. There is a pleasant park with picnic facilities in the centre of town and at 48 Edinburgh Street (about 300m off the Warrego Highway) there is a private Museum which specialises in working farm and transport equipment. The museum has Cobb & Co coaches and an excellent display of blacksmith's tools.

From Mitchell the Warrego Highway continues for 178km to Charleville (see Tour 71).

Bottle trees are found in the extensive grounds of Roma Courthouse.

CHAPTER 4
THE SUNSHINE COAST

23 THE TOWN THAT SAVED QUEENSLAND

■ DRIVING TOUR ■ 125KM ■ 1 DAY ■ GYMPIE'S GOLDMINING GREATNESS

This tour starts at Noosa, passes through several villages and ends at Gympie, known affectionately as 'the town that saved Queensland' because gold was fortuitously discovered here.

1 TEWANTIN

Depart from Noosa via Hastings St, turning left into Noosa Dve, and at the roundabout at the main shopping centre, turn west into Noosa Dve again. Continue heading west, following the signs to Tewantin. As you drive through Tewantin, turn right off Poinciana Ave (the main street) into Moorindil St. Gympie St is two blocks to the north and Myles St is three blocks to the east of Moorindil St on Gympie St.

Although Tewantin is the older settlement, the twin tourist destinations of Noosa Heads and Tewantin have merged and it is only the newness and shopping of Noosa that distinguish the one from the other.

Tewantin is basically a shopping centre and a residential area and its two major attractions are commercial enterprises – the Big Shell Museum and Hattery in Gympie Street, and the House of Bottles which is situated at 19 Myles Street.

2 COOROY

Return to Poinciana Ave, turn west and continue along the Cooroy–Noosa Rd for 21km to Cooroy.

Cooroy is a tiny township which appears to spend most of its time watching the seemingly endless stream of traffic roar past and servicing the surrounding timber and dairy workers. The only real attraction, and one that can't be missed from the Bruce Highway, is the rather unusual Passengers Restaurant located in a railway dining car next to the Butter Factory.

3 POMONA

Turn east off the Bruce Highway at Cooroy and travel 10km to the small township of Pomona.

Statue commemorating Gympie's gold pioneers.

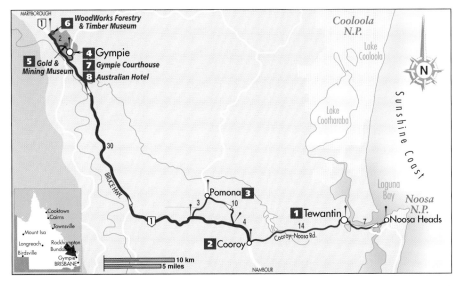

Pomona is a delightful village with dramatic Mount Cooroora looming over it. Each year in July, mountain runners from all over the world come to the town to participate in the 'King of the Mountain Race'. These fitness fanatics actually run up the 439m volcanic plug. More sensible people can relax in the town's delightful old-style Pomona Hotel or see a movie in the Majestic Theatre (across the railway line) which claims to be Queensland's longest running cinema. At one point it had Rudolf Valentino's *Son of the Sheikh* running for over 156 weeks.

4 GYMPIE

Return to the Bruce Highway, then follow the highway north for 30km to reach Gympie.

Gympie is a complex and rather unwieldy town which stretches for kilometre after kilometre over hill and dale to the point where, if you don't take the correct turning off the Bruce Highway, the town centre can be quite hard to locate.

Gympie proclaims proudly that it was 'the town that saved Queensland', a claim that is actually based on fact rather than wishful thinking. In 1867 Queensland, less than a decade old, was facing possible bankruptcy (there was widespread unemployment and two banks had closed in Brisbane) when James Nash discovered gold near the present site of Gympie. Overnight the wealth from the goldfield (it was to go on to produce over 99 million grams of gold) led to Queensland's first gold rush and pulled the state back from potential disaster.

The story of Nash's discovery is pure good fortune. Nash was so down on his luck at the time that he literally had nothing more than a dog, a pick and a panning dish. When his pick broke he walked to Maryborough where, with an ounce of gold which he had panned, he bought rations and some more equipment. He returned to the Gympie area, went up a dry creek bed and within a week had 75 ounces of gold which he sold in Brisbane for £200. He registered his find and the rush was on.

Briefly called Nashville after him, the town officially became known as Gympie in 1868 – named after a stinging tree which the local Aborigines reputedly call 'gimpi gimpi'. At this time all that existed was a mining shanty town with endless tents and numerous small stores and liquor outlets.

The growth of Gympie was remarkable. Within months there were 25 000 people on the goldfields. Within a year a gold battery had been built. Gympie was proclaimed a municipality in 1880, became a town a decade later and was a city by 1905. The railway arrived in 1881 and in 1888 Gympie became one of the few towns in Australia to have its own stock exchange. The gold-mining continued until 1925 when the city became the most important regional centre for the area, servicing the rich variety of agricultural activities that spread from the coast into the hinterland.

Today, Gympie is the centre of the Mary River Valley agricultural district where beef cattle and pigs are raised, tropical fruit and vegetables are grown and an active dairy industry operates.

The town has two really superb tourist attractions which should not be missed. The Gold and Mining Museum, complete with the house of Andrew Fisher, Australia's first Labor Minister for Trade and Customs, is set in attractive parklands which are ideal for picnics. There is also the WoodWorks Forestry and Timber Museum which has to rate as one of the best and most fascinating working museums in Australia. Both these attractions are located on the Bruce Highway and both are clearly signposted.

5 GOLD AND MINING MUSEUM

Continue on the Bruce Highway bypass. The Gympie & District Historical and Mining Museum is located on the east of the road, adjacent to Lake Alford. About 150m before the entrance there is a large statue depicting the discovery of gold in the town. Turn right into the parking lot near the end of the long elevated tramway, or gantry.

Spread over several hectares and located beside attractive lakes and lawns, the Gold and Mining Museum is an outstanding folk museum with a very interesting range of buildings. One of the highlights of the museum is the Retort House of the Scottish Gympie Gold Mines which, remarkably, is the only mining building still standing in Gympie. It is listed by the National Trust. Here gold was extracted from quartz by amalgamating it with mercury.

In the museum grounds is a 100-year-old, four-roomed, simple timber cottage with verandahs running down two sides; this was once Andrew Fisher's house. Fisher went on to become Australia's first Labor prime minister. He was prime minister three times in the years leading up to World War I and is credited with the famous declaration of Australia defending the British Empire to her 'last man and last shilling'.

Also included in the complex are buildings ranging from old school houses to a blacksmith's shop; the displays include an old camera and movie room and a trophy room celebrating Gympie's sporting achievements. There is also an agricultural and dairy exhibit. The museum is open daily from 9:00–17:00 and detailed brochures on all the buildings in the complex are provided with each entry ticket.

Near the entrance to the park beside the Bruce Highway is a large statue commemorating the gold miners who 'saved Queensland'. There is also a granite memorial to James Nash outside the Town Hall.

6 WOODWORKS FORESTRY AND TIMBER MUSEUM

Return to the Bruce Highway and continue north. Located about 2km beyond the northern end of the town is the Queensland Department of Forestry's WoodWorks Forestry and Timber Museum.

The WoodWorks Forestry and Timber Museum proudly declares that it has old tools and equipment including bullock wagons used in the early timber industry, a 1925 Republic truck used to winch logs, timber sample displays of 101 species, a number of videos on aspects of the timber industry, and a cross-section of a 619-year-old kauri pine which was logged in north Queensland in 1939.

Outside, there are displays of pit sawing and cross-cut sawing at which visitors are also welcome to try their hand, as well as demonstrations of the old tools by experienced timber cutters and explanations of the transport equipment and techniques. There is also a timber cutter's bark hut, a shelter shed with shingle roof, a blacksmith's shop and a steam-driven sawmill. The sawmill is only operated about eight times a year and for dates it is wise to contact the museum on tel: (074) 82 2244. The working demonstrations of pit sawing and cross-cut sawing and other timber cutting activities are held on Wednesdays at 10:00 and 13:00 and Sundays at 14:00.

7 GYMPIE COURTHOUSE

Return to Gympie on the Bruce Highway and turn left at Channon St (sometimes known as the Gympie Connection Rd). Pass Barter, Reef and Duke sts and carry on until you reach King St. The Courthouse is located on the corner.

There are several attractive and historic buildings in the town. The most important is the Gympie Courthouse on the corner of Channon and King streets, which was designed by the Queensland Government Architect and built between 1900 and 1902 at a cost of £6000. An imposing brick building with an impressive corner tower, it is a significant landmark in Gympie.

8 AUSTRALIAN HOTEL

Turn back down Channon St and then turn left into Mary St, heading south. Continue along Mary St for approximately 600m until you reach the five-way crossing at Caledonian Hill. On the corner is the famous Australian Hotel.

The Australian Hotel, one of the many historic buildings in Gympie, has remained largely unchanged since it was built in 1883 and it still retains many of the original fixtures. Another interesting feature of the town is on display across the road from the

A replica of the old goldmine head, Gympie.

Interior of Andrew Fisher's home, Gympie.

Australian Hotel at Murphy's Convenience Store. On the front of the building there is a tethering ring which was once used by customers when they arrived at the general store by horse.

Continue on down Caledonian Hill which crosses Mary Terrace and becomes Apollonian Vale and Red Hill Rd before joining Brisbane Rd, which is sometimes known as Tin Can Bay Rd. Turn right into Brisbane Rd. About 2km further to the south the road joins the Bruce Highway. Return from Gympie to Noosa via the Bruce Highway and the Cooroy–Noosa Rd. The journey is 61km on good sealed road.

Andrew Fisher's home in the grounds of Gympie & District Historical & Mining Museum.

24 NOOSA AND THE BLACKALL RANGE

■ DRIVING TOUR ■ 209KM ■ 1 DAY ■ NATIONAL PARKS AND TEA HOUSES

The Blackall Range, with its peaceful villages and green pastures, has lovely views across to the ocean. A daytrip from Noosa into the mountains is an escape from the hustle and bustle of the coast.

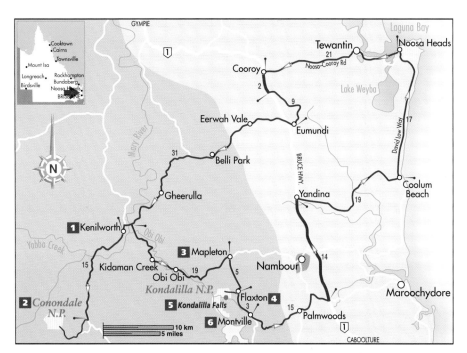

1 KENILWORTH

Travel from Noosa on the Noosa–Cooroy Rd. At Cooroy, take the Bruce Highway and head south for 2km to Cooroy West. Turn left and follow the road for 9km to Eumundi. Turn right at Eumundi (crossing the Bruce Highway), travelling towards Eerwah Vale. Continue along this road through Belli Park and Gheerulla to Kenilworth. The road rises from the flat coastal country into the Blackall Range and at various points there are excellent views overlooking the coast.

Kenilworth is a tiny settlement which is notable more as a bushwalkers' retreat than a township. The area contains a number of streams and waterfalls and the local fauna includes skinks, sugar gliders and an interesting variety of birds.

The Kenilworth Historic Homestead offers adventure holidays with horse riding, bushwalking, swimming and canoeing, and fossicking for gemstones. Visitors are also attracted to the Kenilworth Country Foods Cheese Factory which has both tours and tastings, and the interesting Movie Museum.

Additional information on the Kenilworth area can be obtained at the Montville Tourist Information Centre. Contact tel: (07) 5442 9409.

2 CONONDALE NATIONAL PARKS

Travel south out of Kenilworth for 15km and turn right to reach the Conondale National Parks.

The substantial Conondale National Parks (there are two of them) cover 2126ha of rainforest and wet schlerophyll which includes bunya pines and flooded gums. Both parks are managed as wilderness areas and it is necessary to gain a forestry access permit before entering. Contact tel: (074) 82 4189. This is an ideal location for bushwalkers eager to explore both wet eucalypt and subtropical rainforest.

3 MAPLETON

Return to Kenilworth and drive back towards Cooroy for 1km, then turn right onto a partially sealed road. Travel about 19km, through Kidaman Creek and Obi Obi, to reach Mapleton.

Mapleton is perched on the top of the mountain range behind Nambour. Like Maleny (*see* Tour 28), it is remarkably unpretentious and relatively unaffected by the sudden burst of development which has made Montville and Flaxton such bizarre settlements in recent times.

Mapleton's chief attraction is the lily ponds, officially opened in 1988. These lie behind the main shopping centre and provide an ideal picnic environment for visitors.

Equally impressive are the Mapleton Falls in the Mapleton National Park. The park is quite small (25.9ha) but the lookout from

N oosa Heads is an island of sophistication in a huge area where the beaches have become the focal point for tourism. However, it was originally a sleepy little village known only to a few fishermen and beachcombers.

The first European to come to Noosa was the convict 'Wandi' (David Bracefell) who managed to escape from Moreton Bay with almost monotonous regularity (between 1828 and 1839 he escaped four times). Each time he escaped he fled north and lived with the Noosa Aborigines. Finally free, he accompanied Henry Russell Petrie's exploration of the coast in 1842.

There seems to have been no great urgency to develop Noosa or Tewantin in the 19th century. Around 1865 timber cutters moved into the area and a sawmill was built at Tewantin. The possibility of using the area as a port resulted in the Noosa estuary being surveyed in 1869 and the following year Tewantin was opened as a port, shipping timber out and bringing gold prospectors in to the Gympie goldfields.

It wasn't until after World War I that the area began to develop as a tourist resort. A surf lifesaving club was formed in 1927, the Noosa National Park was established in 1930 and tourist development started in earnest in the late 1940s.

The road which winds along the banks of the Noosa River from Tewantin provides a number of picnic spots. There is a ferry across the river at Tewantin and a gravel road leads to Teewah Beach which is famed for its coloured sands. The cliffs, which are up to 200m high, are made up of as many as 72 different coloured sands which have been produced by combinations of iron oxide and leached vegetable dyes. It is likely that the sands have been forming since the last ice age, although the Aborigines have a story which explains the formation of the sands in terms of the killing of a rainbow by a huge boomerang.

In recent times, the area has been the subject of considerable controversy. Conservationists have had to battle plans to mine sand (in 1970 two sandmining companies put forward plans to mine the sands in the Cooloola National Park) while there is also a feeling that the village atmosphere is being destroyed by unsympathetic high-rise and canal development.

A view of Noosa Heads from Laguna Lookout.

the falls (which tumble down the cliff face for 120m rather than as a sheer drop) offers excellent views over the dense rainforest of the valley. The National Park has a number of interesting rainforest walks. Mapleton Falls are located a few kilometres from the village centre – turn south near the Mapleton Hotel Motel and follow the signs.

4 FLAXTON

Head south out of Mapleton and travel approximately 5km to reach Flaxton.

Flaxton is probably the prettiest of all the Blackall Range settlements. It manages to achieve a balance between the old and the new, lacking the crassness of Montville or the ordinariness of Maleny. It has a golf course, a great deal of mountain accommodation and some rather beautiful arts and crafts shops. The town offers access to the Kondalilla National Park, which consists of 128ha of lush tropical rainforest on the edge of the range. This is a particularly lovely area for bushwalking. The Flaxton escarpment is also a popular weekend hang-gliding destination.

5 KONDALILLA FALLS

Continue south from Flaxton. Take the turn-off to the Kondalilla National Park which lies to the west of the main road.

The Kondalilla Falls are part of the small (327ha) Kondalilla National Park. The area protects remnants of wet eucalypt and sub-tropical rainforest. The Kondalilla Falls tumble from a height of 80m over the escarpment to form a series of beautiful pools which are popular swimming spots.

6 MONTVILLE

Return to the main road and travel further to the tiny settlement of Montville, 3km south of Flaxton.

Montville has a genuinely interesting village green. It also has such overt tourist attractions as a Swiss Chalet which houses a chemist and an Irish worker's cottage which houses a real estate agent.

This tiny settlement works hard to get the visitor to stop. Buildings announce proudly that they were 'Established 1984' or, like the Montville Mountain Inn, 'Established 1989'.

Continue along the same road to Palmwoods. Drive 3km past Palmwoods and turn right. Drive 2km to the Bruce Highway. Turn left onto the Bruce Highway and travel north through Nambour to Yandina. At Yandina turn right and follow the Yandina–Coolum Rd back to Coolum Beach. Once at the beach turn left and then return to Noosa along the David Low Way.

The coloured sand cliffs at Teewah Beach, Cooloola National Park.

Connemarra Cottage, Montville.

Montville Mountain Inn.

25 THE BEACHES OF THE SUNSHINE COAST

■ DRIVING TOUR ■ 121KM ■ 1 DAY ■ SUN, SURF AND SUGARCANE

Noosa Heads is the most popular destination on the Sunshine Coast. It is the centre for a number of excellent daytrips that explore the region's major attractions and popular beaches.

1 NOOSA HEADS

Hastings Street is Noosa's main street. It is unlike any other main street in an Australian beachside town. While it has a large number of eateries (few are fast-food outlets) and gift shops, it has managed to retain a village atmosphere and has attracted specialist clothing shops and boutique delicatessens which give it an inner-city feel. Many aspects of Noosa and Tewantin are charming; there is a sense of style which is missing from much of the Queensland coast.

2 NOOSA NATIONAL PARK

To reach the Noosa National Park follow Park Rd north beyond the Noosa township. There is a car park and picnic area. Beyond this are a number of excellent walking trails to the headland which provide views over Noosa, Little Cove and the estuary.

The Noosa National Park, located on the headland beyond Little Cove, is a small coastal park of 382ha where several species of birds and small mammals find refuge in the native flora. The bushwalks and picnic spots are a quiet retreat from the tourism of the surrounding area.

3 SUNSHINE BEACH

Return to Noosa Heads shopping centre via Park Rd. Turn into Noosa Dve at the roundabout. At the second roundabout turn left into Sunshine Beach Rd. Continue straight ahead at the third roundabout into David Low Way, which briefly becomes Edward St before continuing as David Low Way.

The shopping centre, Noosa Heads.

Noosa National Park car park.

While Noosa may dominate the Sunshine Coast, it is only one of a number of impressive beaches. To the south is a series of excellent surf beaches including Sunshine, Marcus, Peregian and Coolum. Although each has its own charm, it is common for Australians to select a beach by how crowded it is at any particular time and also whether the surf looks inviting.

4 COOLUM

Continue along David Low Way past Marcus Beach and Peregian Beach to get to Coolum.

Coolum was first settled in 1871, but today it is a typical beach-resort town with lots of high-rise buildings. The popularity of the area is due to the unspoilt cliff faces of Mount Coolum and the beautiful long beaches which are a magnet for surfers all year round. There is a surf patrol which operates through the summer months. Fishing around the rocky headlands and bays is also a popular pastime throughout the year for locals and visitors. Near to the beach is a panoramic view of the surrounding district and the ocean from Lows Lookout.

5 YANDINA

At Coolum Beach turn left into Beach Rd just before the Coolum Esplanade. Beach Rd becomes the Yandina–Coolum Rd. Continue along this road for 19km to reach Yandina. To visit Gingertown (see opposite), turn right at the sign just before entering Yandina and continue for 200m into what seems like an industrial estate. On the left is the large entrance to Gingertown. Return to the main Coolum–Yandina Rd and continue into Yandina township.

Yandina is an attractive little town – one of the first surveyed in the region – with a delightful and unspoilt old pub. However someone decided it needed a focal point and so the 'Big Cow' appeared beside the road just to the south of the town. The Big Cow, which you can actually walk into, has had a chequered history and is currently being used as an antique shop. The rest of the town is a service centre for the surrounding rural industries.

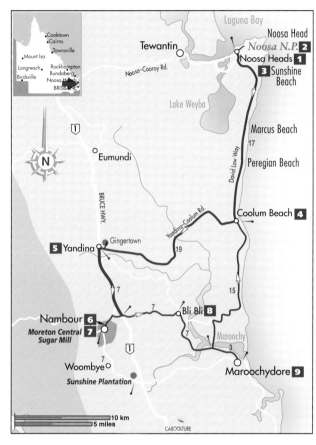

6 NAMBOUR

Drive south down the Bruce Highway for 7km and take the Nambour Connection Rd from Yandina to Nambour. This road becomes Coronation Ave, which becomes Station St upon entering Nambour. The directions to Nambour off the Highway may seem confusing but visitors shouldn't have any problems if they follow the road signs.

Nambour was probably named after the local Aboriginal word for a red flowering tea-tree. It is a town of supermarkets rather than historic buildings and serves both the travellers on the Bruce Highway and the surrounding agricultural population. The sugar railway line crosses the Bruce Highway and runs down the middle of the main street; at crushing time it is commonplace to see a cane train winding its way through town.

The district was settled by Europeans in the 1860s but it wasn't until the arrival of the railway in 1890 that the local agriculture was focused on sugar production.

Nambour is the most southerly of Queensland's major sugar towns and, interestingly, sugar was still cut by hand in the area as recently as the 1970s. However, this was only because of the hilly terrain which was not suitable for cane-cutting machines.

Noosa's main beach, situated on Laguna Bay.

GINGERTOWN

Gingertown is situated just outside Yandina. The whole town is primarily a factory which produces the bulk of the world's ginger for confectionery purposes. It is fascinating to stand on the observation platform at the factory and watch the entire production process. The owners have created a total tourist experience where, after you have bought ginger in every possible shape, size and packaging, you can go on a river cruise, see a video on the Australian ginger industry, check out a doll's museum or board the Ginger Bus for a tour of a ginger farm.

7 MORETON CENTRAL SUGAR MILL

The Moreton Central Sugar Mill is located off the main street of Nambour. Turn right off Curie St into Bury St. The Mill is located at the end of the street.

In 1896 the Moreton Central Sugar Mill began crushing. Tours of the sugar mill can be arranged during harvest and crushing time (July to December) by contacting tel: (07) 5441 1411.

In recent times the agricultural base of the area has expanded to include a variety of tropical crops – macadamia nuts, citrus fruits, bananas and pineapples are the ones which have tended to dominate.

8 BLI BLI

Travel north out of Nambour on Nambour Connection Rd. Turn right just past the Showground onto the Nambour–Bli Bli Rd. Drive 7km to Bli Bli.

Bli Bli's one and only claim to fame is a huge medieval castle (which looks as if it came straight out of a child's picture book) located at the centre of the tiny township. The castle entertains tourists with a huge doll's museum and lots of activities based around 'things medieval'.

9 MAROOCHYDORE

At the Bli Bli roundabout, head to the south along David Low Way which follows the Maroochy River into Maroochydore.

Maroochydore is a classic Queensland holiday destination: high-rise blocks of flats are interspersed with lower developments from the 1950s stretching virtually uninterrupted down the coast all the way to Caloundra. It is the heart of the Sunshine Coast with kilometres of golden beaches, pleasant beach parks, small shopping centres geared to the tourists, and a little industrial development in the hinterland.

The first European 'holiday-maker' to arrive in the Maroochydore area was the Irishman John Graham who was taking a break from his convict duties at Moreton Bay. Graham was sentenced to seven years transportation for stealing six and a quarter pounds of hemp. He arrived in Sydney in April 1825 and in October 1826 was sentenced to another seven years for petty theft; the following January he was shipped to Moreton Bay. In July, labouring under the delusion that he could row to China, Graham escaped. He tried to avoid the Aborigines on the coast as they had a fierce reputation, however he eventually walked into a camp near the present site of Maroochydore and was immediately accepted as the ghost of one woman's dead husband. The woman died within a year but Graham continued to live with the Aborigines for the next six years. In 1833 he returned to Moreton Bay and gave himself up. Three years later he featured prominently in the rescue of Eliza Fraser from Fraser Island. He was given his ticket of leave the following year and nothing is known of his later life.

Timber cutters were in the area by the early 1850s and a depot handling timber was established on the river by 1856. The explorer Andrew Petrie passed through the region in 1862 and gave the Maroochy River its name. Maroochydore was probably named after the local Aboriginal word 'marutchi' meaning 'black swan' or 'marutchi dora' meaning 'water where the black swan lives'.

The township of Maroochydore was established in 1900 but it wasn't until the 1960s that the area really became a major tourist destination.

Today there is little of historical interest unless you want to experience the incongruity of passing from a lazy Australian beach culture into a medieval castle with dungeons and armour. The improbable fairytale castle sits perched on a hill near the ocean between Noosa and Maroochydore. It is open from 9:00–17:00 and further details can be had by contacting tel: (07) 5448 5373.

To return to Noosa Heads, leave Maroochydore on the David Low Way which eventually winds its way back to Noosa Heads.

Visitors can enjoy beautiful coastal walks through Noosa National Park.

26 UP THE ESCARPMENT

■ DRIVING TOUR ■ 37KM ■ 1 DAY ■ PIONEER COTTAGES AND BIG PINEAPPLES

The Sunshine Coast's beaches are often quite uncrowded and its mixture of tourist attractions include the Sunshine Plantation (the 'Big Pineapple') and SuperBee, as well as quiet villages such as Buderim.

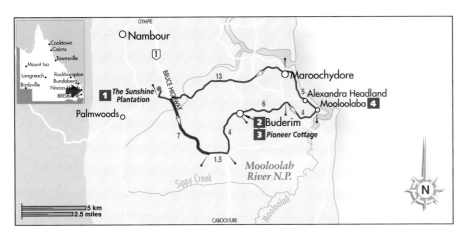

▮1 THE SUNSHINE PLANTATION

Depart from the Maroochydore shopping centre on Ocean St and turn right at the traffic lights into Maroochydore Rd. Continue along Maroochydore to the Bruce Highway. Cross the highway and continue until you reach the Sunshine Plantation.

The area's main attraction is Sunshine Plantation which is a typical Queensland theme park. It is a place where visitors can spend money on tropical fruits and gifts while clambering up the Big Pineapple (16m high), take the train through the Tropical Plantation, hop aboard the Nutmobile for a journey through 'Nutcountry', or visit the Animal Nursery.

The park has a licensed restaurant, a special macadamia display, and a huge greenhouse, all of which are specifically designed to entertain the visitor. The gift shops are full of pineapple drinks, dried pineapples and macadamia nuts packaged in every way you can think of.

▮2 BUDERIM

Travel south along the Bruce Highway for 7km and turn left towards Mooloolaba. Travel 1.5km to Crosby Hill Rd, then turn left and proceed 4km to Buderim.

Buderim has become a kind of Sugar Coast hill retreat. It is a cool and luxuriant town characterised by gardens in which tropical flowering trees such as hibiscus, bougainvillea, poincianas, and frangipani flourish. People who work in very urbanised centres on the coast and those who want to escape from hot, overcrowded and overdeveloped areas often decide to retreat to tree-lined, leafy Buderim.

The first Europeans to explore Buderim and the surrounding mountain range were timber cutters. Richard Jones moved through the area in 1854 looking for suitable timber for Pettigrew's Mill and he was followed by others eager to extract the cedar, beech and pine trees from the mountain forests. In 1862 Tom Petrie followed Jones

up the mountain and became the first European to cut and extract the local timber.

From these earliest times the mountain was known to Europeans as Buderim. The early timber cutters had heard the local Aborigines using the term (it was sometimes spelt 'Badderam' and 'Budderum') which, it is now widely accepted, was the word for the hairpin honeysuckle that grew in great profusion on the mountain.

The mountain or plateau (it is over 7km long, 4km at its widest point, and between 152m and 182m above sea level) was first surveyed in 1869. During the following year several people purchased land which they duly cleared. They built houses and planted crops of sugarcane, citrus fruits, bananas and coffee.

▮3 PIONEER COTTAGE

Entering Buderim from the south on Burnett St, turn right at the first set of traffic lights into Ballinger Rd and left again into Ballinger Crescent. Pioneer Cottage is on the right.

In 1876 a sugar mill was built in Buderim to process the local produce. In that same year the beautiful Pioneer Cottage, which is now the home of the Buderim Historical Society, was built by John Burnett out of pit-sawn cedar and beech.

It is a sad comment on the changes which have occurred on the Sunshine Coast in recent times that Pioneer Cottage at Buderim is one of the few historical buildings left on the mountain. This beautifully preserved old house, surrounded by tall palm trees in pleasant subtropical gardens and filled with remarkably interesting displays, is open to the public from 10:00–16:00. Pioneer Cottage contains a wealth of material about the surrounding area, including an excellent booklet titled *The History of Buderim Mountain* which was produced by students of Buderim State School in 1979. There is also a booklet on the history of Pioneer Cottage and the project which revitalised this important building.

The Pioneer Cottage, Buderim, occupied by the Burnett family for 74 years.

Interior of the Pioneer Cottage.

The Big Pineapple, a well-known landmark just off the Bruce Highway, Nambour.

SUPERBEE

SuperBee is situated on the western side of the Bruce Highway at Tanawha. This unusually shaped venue celebrates the produce of the bee. Entry to SuperBee is free, and visitors are offered free tasting of more than 24 varieties of Australian honey, a wide range of beeswax products and, every hour, a 30-minute Bee Show demonstrating how honey is taken from the hive. The attractions for children include the House That Jack Built, Snow White and the Seven Dwarfs and the cottage of the Three Bears. It is also an ideal place to have a picnic. The gardens, a cool retreat from the heat and bustle of the coast, offer pleasant shady walks.

It was around the time of the establishment of the mill and Pioneer Cottage that the local farmers began using Kanaka labour on their sugar plantations. The Kanakas planted, cultivated and harvested the cane and were kept in conditions of virtual slavery although one prominent citizen in the area, Joseph Dixon, who was a Quaker, built a slab and shingle shed near the sugarcane mill. This shed was used as a school and Sunday school by the Kanaka children. By 1875 there were 19 children living in the area, enough to justify the establishment of a provisional school.

In 1883–1884 the first crop of Buderim bananas was added to the produce from the area. Grown by James Lindsay, they were taken down to the coast and shipped to the markets in Brisbane. Like the sugar before them, the bananas presented the small community with a major transportation headache. There were years when the whole crop rotted on the wharves while waiting for boats to carry the bunches to the markets.

Buderim has always been confronted with a certain mountainous isolation. In the early days the local produce had to be carted to the coast by bullock dray. When the railway reached Landsborough, the Buderim farmers moved their produce to the railhead. In 1914, after much lobbying, a tramway was built between Buderim and Palmwoods. From 1914–1935 the Buderim Tramway connected with the railway but it was soon to become redundant because of improvements in roads and road transportation.

In the late 1880s coffee was grown in the area. Production peaked in 1907 when 40 360 lb of coffee were produced on the mountain. However, the crop which really boosted the economy of the region was ginger. The first ginger was grown here as early as 1916, but it wasn't until 1941 that the Buderim Ginger Growers Co-operative Association was formed. It experienced hard times after the war but by the 1970s Buderim was one of the country's major producers of ginger.

Today, Buderim is a delightful mountainside commuter town which seems to be a world away from the bustle of the coast. There are a number of art galleries, antique shops and nature reserves in the area to provide visitors (especially those from the coast) with a sharp and pleasant contrast to the coastal attractions.

4 MOOLOOLABA

Leave Buderim and travel east on King St which becomes the Buderim–Mooloolaba Rd. Follow this road until you reach Mooloolaba.

Mooloolaba is the largest of all the tourist developments on the Sunshine Coast. There are several canals behind the town centre where developers have dredged out the swampy lowlands and converted them into waterfront residential areas. These canals run off the Mooloolah River. Not surprisingly, this development has attracted a huge number of people. During the past decade, the residential development around Maroochydore and Mooloolaba has rivalled the suburban sprawl on the Gold Coast.

In spite of development, the origins of the township are still in evidence. There is a large trawler fleet operating out of the town, the local yacht club is successful and the marina attracts boats from the surrounding area as well as being a welcome port of call for people cruising up and down the coast.

Drive north from Mooloolaba along the Mooloolaba Esplanade. It eventually becomes Alexandra Parade which runs along the beachfront into the township of Maroochydore (see Tour 25).

The Wharf, Mooloolaba, at the mouth of the Mooloolah River.

27 A NECKLACE OF GOLDEN BEACHES

■ DRIVING TOUR ■ 42KM ■ 1 DAY ■ HOLIDAYS FULL OF FISHING AND FUN

The Sunshine Coast was the second major coastal area of Queensland to become highly developed – large numbers of high-rise apartments and beaches, close to shopping centres, cater for the tourists.

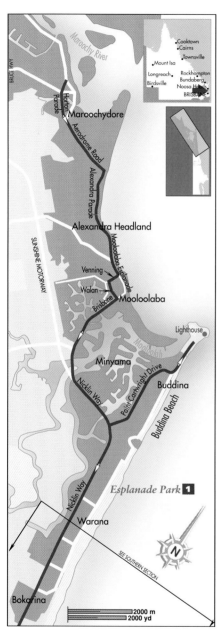

1 ESPLANADE PARK

Depart from the Maroochydore shopping centre on Ocean St and turn left at the lights into Horton Parade, which becomes Aerodrome Rd. Once you reach the beach, turn right into Alexandra Parade, which becomes the Mooloolaba Esplanade. Turn right at the traffic lights on the Esplanade into Venning St. Turn left into Walan St and then right at the traffic lights into Brisbane Rd. Follow Brisbane Rd across the Mooloolah River to join Nicklin Way. Continue along Nicklin Way and turn east into Point Cartwright Dve which leads out to the lighthouse and to Buddina Beach.

Esplanade Park runs for the length of Buddina Beach which, to the south, becomes Warana, Bokarina and Wurtulla beaches. Many of these beaches are unpatrolled and it is sensible to assess the surf conditions before going for a swim.

2 DICKY BEACH

The distance between the beach and Nicklin Way is short and nearly all the roads heading west will take the visitor back to the main Mooloolaba–Caloundra Road. After crossing the Currimundi Lake, turn left into Buderim St and proceed towards Dicky Beach. When you reach the beach, keep an eye out for the Caravan Park, located between the road and the beach.

Near the Caravan Park at Dicky Beach (in fact, it's right in front of the toilet block) is the propellor from the SS *Dicky* which ran aground at Dicky Beach on 1 February 1893. Several attempts to relaunch the SS *Dicky* proved to be unsuccessful, so it was used for local dances until someone knocked over a kerosene lamp and it was burnt down to the waterline.

3 CALOUNDRA

Continue south from Dicky Beach, turning east into Beerburrum St and then south into Elizabeth St. Continue travelling south until you reach the main Caloundra Shopping Centre.

In recent times Caloundra has changed considerably. Once a truly classic Queensland retirement town – units with ocean views, elderly people making their way carefully along the beachfront, men tossing their fishing lines into the Pumicestone Channel – it has now become a mixture of young commuters, holiday-makers and retired people all enjoying the attractions.

On any morning, in the narrow strait between Caloundra and the northern tip of Bribie Island, people can be seen fishing for their breakfast (or possibly for their lunch or dinner). Caloundra is that kind of place. It is no wonder most sources claim that the Aboriginal word 'callanda' means either 'beautiful' or 'beautiful place'.

The city of Caloundra, with its 13km of delightful beaches – Currimundi, Dicky,

*T*he great attraction of this area is the beautiful 12km-long surf beach which stretches from Mooloolaba to Caloundra. It is so long, and has so many access points, that it is always possible to find a quiet place away from the small crowds which gather around the patrolled areas. The beach immediately to the east of Mooloolaba is often crowded, but south to Buddina there is a row of peaceful beaches stretching beyond Point Cartwright. From Point Cartwright, just to the south of central Mooloolaba, the beaches are Buddina, Warana, Bokarina, Wurtulla, Currimundi, Dicky, Moffatt, Shelly, Kings, Bulcock and Golden.

The area's most recent attraction is Underwater World, a comprehensive introduction to the magic of the reefs and rock platforms found around Mooloolaba. Included in the complex is an Oceanarium, Ocean Discovery Centre, speciality shops, restaurants and an amusement centre.

Moffatt, Shelly, Kings, Bulcock and Golden – its greenery, its near-perfect climate, and its easy lifestyle, is the most southerly resort on the Sunshine Coast. The quiet, protected waters of Pumicestone Channel are a mecca for watersports enthusiasts, including windsurfers, sailors, anglers and swimmers.

The first European to sight the Caloundra area was Captain James Cook who noted and named the Glasshouse Mountains in May 1770. Seeing a similarity between the unusual shapes of these volcanic plugs and the glass furnaces in his native Yorkshire, he named them the 'Glass Houses'.

The next explorer in the area was Matthew Flinders who, in 1799, entered the narrow passage which lies between modern-day Caloundra and Bribie Island. Because of the pumicestone on the shoreline he named it the Pumicestone River, and it subsequently became known as Pumicestone Channel. Flinders also came ashore here and climbed Mount Beerburrum on 26 July 1799.

The first European settler in the area didn't arrive until 1862. The rush to grab land after 1842 had concentrated on the Darling Downs and the fertile lands north of the Brisbane River valley.

It was during the 1880s that Caloundra began to gain its reputation as a seaside resort. The first hotel was built in 1885 on Shelly Beach and by 1905 Wilson's Guesthouse offered holidays on 'Dicky's Beach'. A bakery was built in 1909 and the first general store appeared in 1910.

While the fertile inland soils were used to grow maize, oats, sugar and tobacco and the local dairy industry prospered, tourism was all that Caloundra could really offer. Today the city has a number of interesting reminders of its past.

4 H.M. BARQUE *ENDEAVOUR*

Continue south to Bulcock St which runs west until it becomes Bowman Rd. Near the corner of Bowman Rd and Landsborough Parade is the replica of the H.M. Barque Endeavour.

The two-thirds-size replica of Cook's H.M. Barque *Endeavour* is located at 3 Landsborough Parade (on the way to Golden Beach). This excellent reproduction is made to a scale which allows visitors to experience what it must have been like to sail in the ship. It is open daily from 9:00–16:45.

5 CALOUNDRA LIGHTHOUSE

Continue along Landsborough Parade. The road runs alongside Pumicestone Channel and provides excellent views of the northern extremity of Bribie Island. On the western side is an interesting old lighthouse.

On Golden Beach is Caloundra's third lighthouse – it replaces the previous two which were taken down. Located next to the Caloundra Power Boat Club this lighthouse, which was built at the top of Canberra Terrace in 1898, was moved to its present site in 1970. It is currently owned by the National Trust and a modern control tower now directs ships in the area.

6 QUEENSLAND AIR MUSEUM

Return towards Caloundra and turn west onto the Bowman–Caloundra Rd. The Caloundra Airport is on the southern side of the road. Turn south into Pathfinder Dve to reach the Air Museum.

The Queensland Air Museum, located at the Caloundra Aerodrome, is a major attraction. Queensland is central to the history of aviation in Australia and the exhibition is an interesting depiction of the state's involvement in the industry. It is the country's only community-owned air museum and has a number of interesting historic aircraft and memorabilia on display.

The lighthouse, Caloundra.

7 CALOUNDRA ROAD ENVIRONMENTAL PARK

A few kilometres further along Caloundra Rd is the Caloundra Road Environmental Park.

To the west of Caloundra, adjacent to the highway, is the long, narrow 10ha swamp known as Caloundra Road Environmental Park. Apart from the superb displays of Christmas Bells (for which it is very well known) and its natural scenic appeal, it also has substantial stands of banksia, boronia and melaleuca.

Drive about 11km westward to the Bruce Highway. Travel north on the highway for 16km as far as Maroochydore Rd. Turn right into Maroochydore Rd and drive 11km to reach Maroochydore town.

Underwater World, Mooloolaba.

Underwater World, a children's paradise.

A replica of HM Barque Endeavour, *Golden Beach, Caloundra.*

28 HILLSIDE FESTIVAL COUNTRY

■ DRIVING TOUR ■ 140KM ■ 1 DAY ■ TIMBER TOWNS AND QUIET VILLAGES

The hilly hinterland behind Caloundra and the Sunshine Coast is a delightful mixture of small villages (many geared to the tourist industry), rural farmlands and alternative-lifestyle artists and craftspeople.

1 LANDSBOROUGH

Leave Caloundra by way of Caloundra Rd, heading west. Travel 11km to the Bruce Highway. Cross the Highway and continue 9km along the Glasshouse Mountains Rd to Landsborough.

Located 76km north of Brisbane, at the southern end of the Blackall Ranges and to the north of the Glasshouse Mountains, Landsborough is one of those towns rich in local history but, by accident of geography, not reaping the economic benefits of tourism which have become the staple of the Sugar Coast's economy since the 1960s.

The area was first settled in 1871 by Isaac Burgess. At the time the tiny settlement was known as Mellum Creek. Almost immediately it became a stopping point for Cobb & Co on the route from Brisbane to Gympie. Business was so good that by 1877 Burgess had acquired 572 acres and built a two-storeyed hotel, a store and a butcher's shop to service the passing trade as well as the local residents.

The area developed rapidly – not only because of Burgess' activities but also as a result of the arrival of the timber cutters. Large stands of red cedar, beech, hoop and bunya pine on the Blackall Ranges were cut and then hauled to the Mellum

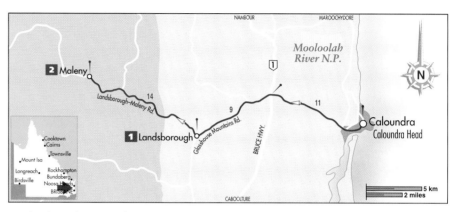

Creek where they were floated downstream to the waiting steamers. The railway arrived at Landsborough in 1890. The settlement continued to grow although it was always overshadowed by the larger settlements that surrounded it.

The highlight of any visit to Landsborough is the Shire of Landsborough Historical Museum which has to be one of the finest and most comprehensive folk museums in Australia. Located just 300m to the west of the railway line, its displays are interesting and detailed, giving the visitor an insight into how the town once was. It

occupies two buildings in the centre of the tiny township. The exhibits include pioneer timber tools, machinery, old bottles, photographs, antiques, furniture, and a pioneer bedroom and kitchen.

2 MALENY

Leave Landsborough on the Landsborough–Maleny Rd. The road rises from the flat plains of the Sunshine Coast into the gently undulating hills until, after about 14km, it reaches Maleny.

Maleny is a charming, unspoilt little township on the southern edge of the Blackall Range. It is an area of timber cutting (the

Uniting Church, Landsborough.

Landsborough Shire's Historical Museum.

WILLIAM LANDSBOROUGH

Landsborough was named after the explorer William Landsborough (1825–1886) whose great claim to fame was that he was chosen by both the Victorian and Queensland governments to lead a search for Robert O'Hara Burke and William Wills, the first Europeans to cross the continent from south to north, who had disappeared on their return journey south. Landsborough arrived in the Gulf of Carpentaria in November 1861 and, although he didn't find Burke and Wills (their bodies had already been recovered), he did become the first explorer to traverse the continent from north to south. He was criticised for working for pastoral interests and it is true that his expedition did result in a land grab throughout the Gulf country. After an extraordinary life he retired to Caloundra in 1882 where he bought a property which he named Loch Lamerough. He died four years later. He was, by any measure, a remarkable and controversial man. The town of Landsborough is a suitable acknowledgment of the part he played in opening up large areas of Queensland.

Western Queensland, Carpentaria and the Gulf Rivers area were first explored by Burke and Wills but, with a bizarre sense of disregard for common sense and the rules of exploration, they made no contribution to the understanding of the area. The *Australian Dictionary of Biography* entry on Robert O'Hara Burke makes the observation that:

> ... it took four months to do the 1500 miles. They walked from 5 am to 5 pm with only a single day of rest in the whole period ... It was magnificent, but it was not exploration. Burke kept no journal; there was no time for scientific observation, and nothing useful was discovered ... Indirectly, discovery was promoted because, although Burke's journey was worthless as exploration, solid gains in geographical knowledge were made by explorers Howitt, McKinlay and Landsborough who led parties in search of him.

The expeditions of William Landsborough, Frederick Walker and John McKinlay scoured the area for the ill-fated Burke and Wills and in the process discovered both the pastoral and mining potential of the region. William Landsborough referred, somewhat inaccurately, to the area as the 'Plains of Promise'. In fact they were marginal lands with not a great deal of promise.

town has named many of its streets after types of timber, including Maple, Myrtle, Cedar and even Macadamia Drive), dairy farming (predominantly with Friesians), and growing macadamia nuts.

In contrast to the other towns in the area (notably Montville and Flaxton), Maleny has remained relatively untouched by tourism.

As far as can be determined, the first European to come into the Maleny area was Ludwig Leichhardt, who seemed to be describing the Blackall Range when he wrote a letter in 1844 in which he said: 'There is a little valley, an open plain, in the midst of these brushes which cover perhaps an extent of 50 miles long and 10 miles broad. This plain they call Booroon and it seems to be the rendezvous for fights between the hostile tribes who come from near and far to enjoy the harvest of the Bunya'.

Timber cutters moved into the region and, by the early 1870s, there were also teamsters, a blacksmith and a timber mill in the area. A settlement was beginning to form. The first selection of land at the present site of Maleny was made by Isaac Burgess on 13 November 1878. Slowly the land was cleared, and dairy and beef cattle were brought into the area to feed on the rich grasses that were produced by the annual rainfall of 2056mm on the red volcanic soils of the range. No one knows exactly where the town's name came from, but it is likely that it is a misspelt version of a tiny Scottish hamlet named Malleny.

There can be little doubt that the Blackall Range is one of the most interesting and dramatic mountain terrains in Queensland. Rising sharply behind Nambour and then

A cafe in Montville.

Local handicrafts in Montville.

winding its way across the range to Maleny and Landsborough to the south, the road runs along the ridges, allowing visitors the rare opportunity of viewing the rolling mountains and valleys to the west and the coastal plain and Pacific Ocean to the east.

There are a number of towns in the region, as well as a series of small national parks (all protecting areas of rainforest), literally dozens of holiday locations (mainly guesthouses and leisure resorts), and hundreds of speciality shops selling crafts, antiques and gifts.

The Landsborough Museum contains a number of very interesting books from which visitors can find out more about the history of the surrounding region. These include *Recollection of the Early Days in Maleny* and *By Obi Obi Waters: Maleny 1878–1978*, both of which contain interesting early photographs of the area.

Leave Maleny on the Maleny–Landsborough Rd heading towards Landsborough. Once you reach Landsborough, return to Caloundra along the Glasshouse Mountains Rd, across the Bruce Highway and then along Caloundra Rd.

Mapleton, at the northern edge of the Blackall Range.

29 THE GLASSHOUSE MOUNTAINS

■ DRIVING TOUR ■ 80KM ■ 1 DAY ■ FIELDS OF PINEAPPLES AND VOLCANIC PLUGS

The Glasshouse Mountains, a series of volcanic plugs which rise glowing out of the surrounding area, are one of the wonders of Queensland. There are no easy roads to the base of any of the mountains.

1 GLASSHOUSE MOUNTAINS

Leave Caloundra via Caloundra Rd, heading west. Travel 11km to the Bruce Highway. Cross the highway and continue for 9km along the Glasshouse Mountains Rd to Landsborough. Travel a further 6km to Beerwah. There is a small township called Glasshouse Mountains which is just off the main road. The road to the main lookout point is clearly signposted and passes through extensive fields of pineapples. A number of pleasant drives run through the area. Climbing the mountains is difficult and is not encouraged for the inexperienced. The main lookout point (which can be reached by car) offers an excellent vantage point from which all the mountains can be seen in the larger context of the plains and the Pacific Ocean to the east.

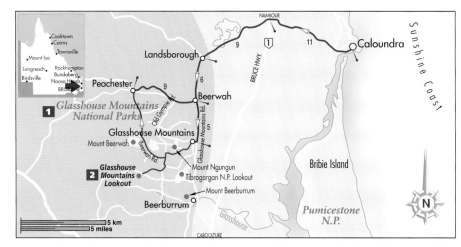

The first European to see the Glasshouse Mountains was Captain James Cook. On 17 May 1770 he wrote in his journal:

… however, if any future navigator should be disposed to determine … whether there is a river in this place, which the wind would not permit us to do, the situation may always be found by three hills, which lie to the north-ward of it, in the latitude of twenty-six degrees fifty-three minutes. These hills lie but a little way inland, and not far from each other: they are remarkable for the singular form of their elevation, which very much resembles a glass house, and for this reason I called them the Glass Houses: the northernmost of the three is the highest and largest; there are several other peaked hills inland to the northward of these, but these are not nearly so remarkable …

The next European to visit the area was Matthew Flinders, who spent 16 days sailing around Moreton Bay in July–August 1799. During his explorations he came ashore and climbed Mount Beerburrum from which he surveyed the whole of Moreton Bay. The excellent booklet *Matthew Flinders in Moreton Bay 1799*, published by the Redcliffe Historical Society, records Flinders' visit to the Glasshouse Mountains:

… Flinders took the boat up a small creek that pointed towards the peaks.

The volcanic soil adjacent to the Glasshouse Mountains is ideal for farming.

Beerwah, the highest of the 13 volcanic Glasshouse Mountains.

About half past nine he left the boat accompanied by two seamen and a native. The country … was swampy, covered with mangroves, they waded through rocky swamps. In observing the flat-topped peak (Tibrogargan) it was considerably nearer than the highest Glass-house (Beerwah) that he had first meant to visit, but seeing one of the round mount (Beerburrum) with sloping sides was nearer, he altered course for it and after walking about nine miles from the boat he reached the top.

The view … was very extensive, to the south were several distinct columns of smoke visible. The mount was a pile of loose stones of many sizes, which had made the ascent quite difficult.

Today the Glasshouse Mountains have become one of the premier tourist attractions on the Sugar Coast. Not only are they important to the European history of southern Queensland but they also play a major part in the Aboriginal culture of the area.

The Glasshouse Mountains are a series of volcanic plugs (the surrounding material has been slowly eroded away) of rhyolite and trachyte which are estimated to be between 24 and 25 million years old. There are actually 13 volcanic plugs in the area but only 10 dominate the landscape.

The only plug (mountain) which can be climbed relatively easily by bushwalkers is Ngungun. There is a strong incentive for entering the various national parks and walking in the area. The wildlife, which ranges from koalas and wallabies to echidnas and lizards, is bountiful and the bush is a dramatic change from the high-rise development of the nearby coastline.

2 GLASSHOUSE MOUNTAINS LOOKOUT

The route through the Glasshouse Mountains is singularly complex. The roads are poorly signposted and there are few good maps available. Continue along the Glasshouse Mountains Rd from Beerwah for about 5km to reach the tiny township of Glasshouse Mountains. Then head west from Glasshouse Mountains township and follow the signposted roads to the Tibrogargan National Park Lookout. There are a number of turns. You know you are heading in the right direction when you pass a tea-house on the crest of a hill. The Glasshouse Mountains Lookout is a couple of kilometres further on.

The view from the lookout is well worth the effort of finding it. All of the major volcanic plugs can be seen. They are placed in the larger context of the whole area – the lookout is high enough for visitors to be able to see the sea. There are descriptive placards and signs to help visitors identify each of the mountains. More information can be obtained from the Beerburrum District Office, tel: (074) 96 0166.

Return towards the Glasshouse Mountains township but, instead of turning east, continue north on the road to Peachester. This route offers particularly close views of Mount Beerwah. From Peachester, turn east and drive for 9km to the village of Beerwah. To return to Caloundra, drive along the Glasshouse Mountains Rd to the Bruce Highway. Cross the highway and proceed along Caloundra Rd to Caloundra town.

A kookaburra at the Reptile & Fauna Park.

Kangaroo, Reptile & Fauna Park, Beerwah.

To the casual visitor modern Bargara is nothing more than a pleasant holiday town offering excellent fishing, swimming and surfing, but to the more observant visitor, in the area around Mon Repos and Bargara there is quite a lot of evidence of the work of the South Pacific Kanakas who came to Australia in the late 19th century as virtual slaves. Being right at the centre of Queensland's sugar industry, Bundaberg's use of indentured labour was important. The excellent *The History of Bundaberg and Districts* (available at the Bundaberg & Districts Historical Museum) records:

In 1879, a schooner sailed up the Burnett River with the first group of South Sea Islanders (Kanakas) recruited as indentured labourers for the sugarcane industry. They were engaged for three years at a small yearly wage, and plantation owners and farmers had to provide living accommodation and food.

For the next 30 years Melanesian and Polynesian Islanders provided virtually the complete field labour for cane plantations and farms. At one stage, 3000 lived in the district. This labour trade stopped in 1901 when the Commonwealth Government of Australia was established. Some Islanders chose to stay in the Bundaberg district.

In 1882, 80 Ceylonese labourers were brought to Bundaberg under a work contract. This venture was not popular and was not repeated, although some remained in the district.

The stone walls which were built by the Kanakas can be seen today on the southern side of Bargara Road near the edge of town; there are also long walls on the road between Bargara and Mon Repos.

7 THE BASIN

Drive through the small shopping centre until you reach the beachfront. Turn south and continue along the coast road – the Scenic Drive – for about 1km. Upon reaching the car park the rock pool is located immediately to the south.

Bargara is a pleasant seaside holiday resort town which is geared to the tourist trade. The road which runs along the coast – The Esplanade, Miller Street and Woongarra Scenic Drive – is now a near-continuous strip of holiday homes, flats, apartments and motels, all built rather precariously between the beach and the hinterland.

Of particular interest is The Basin (at the very southern end of The Esplanade), a sheltered swimming area which was built out of local volcanic rock by Kanaka labourers.

8 THE HUMMOCK

From the Basin, return to the small shopping centre in Bargara. Head west along Bargara Rd for about 5km and turn left into Rehbein Rd. The Hummock is 500m further down the road.

The Hummock is a low-lying remnant of a volcanic cylinder cone which, although it is only 96m above sea level, offers the visitor excellent views over the whole area. The ocean can be seen to the east while to the west the sugar fields encircle the city, with the smoke stacks of the Bundaberg Rum Distillery on the horizon.

It was Matthew Flinders who named this physical feature 'Sloping Hummock' but it has, over the years, become known simply as 'The Hummock'.

A stone wall built by the Kanakas.

A rock pool built by the Kanakas.

Take Rehbein Rd back to Bargara Rd. Turn left and follow Bargara for about 6km to the west until it forks into Princes and Whittred sts. Veer to the left into Princes St and continue for about 750m to Scotland St. Turn right into Scotland St and take the first turning to the left into Bourbong St East. Turn right into Barolin St about 1km after crossing the Kennedy Bridge. Turn left at Quay St where you will find Burnett Bridge one block further on the right.

A view of the cane fields from The Hummock, Bundaberg.

32 MYSTERY CRATERS AND CAPTAIN COOK

■ DRIVING TOUR ■ 421KM ■ 2 DAYS ■ EXPLORING THE AREA NORTH OF BUNDABERG

The area to the north of Bundaberg is flat sugar country. It was here, millions of years ago, that mystery craters were formed by unknown forces, and it was here that Captain Cook came ashore.

1 SEVENTEEN SEVENTY

From the centre of Bundaberg, cross the Burnett River at Burnett Bridge and turn left at the memorial park into Perry St. Take the next right turn into Queen St and, after turning left at the roundabout into Gavin St, turn right at Hinkler Ave. Turn left onto the Gin Gin Rd at Bundaberg North School. Follow the Gin Gin Rd past the Hinkler House Museum and the Botanic Gardens. Continue across the railway line and turn right into the Bundaberg–Lowmead Rd. Proceed through Booloongie, Takoko Littabella, Watalgan and Rosedale. At Berajondo, turn right onto a partially sealed road and continue past the turn-off to Miriam Vale until you reach Agnes Waters. Continue north from Agnes Waters for 6km to reach Seventeen Seventy.

Seventeen Seventy (sometimes called 'the town of 1770') has one of the most unusual names of any town in Australia. It was so called because it was here that James Cook made his second landing on Australian soil (his first had been at Botany Bay). Or, if you are a patriotic Queenslander, it was here that the first European set foot on Queensland soil on 24 May 1770. This historic occasion is commemorated by the Captain Cook Memorial at nearby Round Hill Head. Cook was impressed by the oysters and the mangroves and palms that lined the beaches, and noted the large numbers of birds in the area. In particular, he remarked that the ducks resembled the English Bustard.

Today the town is a small seaside resort which is noted for its pleasant beaches and good fishing. From November to January, turtles come ashore here to lay their eggs.

2 MIRIAM VALE

Return south through Agnes Waters to the turn-off to Miriam Vale. Turn right and drive 26km to Miriam Vale.

The major town in the area (if it can be called a major town) is Miriam Vale, which is situated on the Bruce Highway 63km west of Seventeen Seventy. It is a small settlement servicing the surrounding dairy industry and providing the basic services, including food and petrol, for travellers between Gladstone and Bundaberg.

3 GIN GIN

Head south along the Bruce Highway for 99km to reach Gin Gin. Take advantage of the service station at Colosseum Creek (16km out of Miriam Vale) as there is no petrol between there and Gin Gin.

Gin Gin is the perfect example of a town that has survived solely because of its location on the main north road from Brisbane.

The Gin Gin area was originally settled by Europeans in 1847 when Gregory Blaxland and William Forster moved into the area. The site where the modern town now stands was once part of the huge Gin Gin Station which was owned by Sir Thomas McIlwraith (three times Premier of Queensland between 1879 and 1893).

The town's one brush with notoriety occurred on 30 March 1866 when one of Queensland's few bushrangers, James Alpin McPherson, known as the 'Wild Scotsman', was captured on Monduran Station about 13km north of the town.

The Mystery Craters on the Gin Gin Road near Bundaberg.

The Mystery Craters, South Kolan.

Bundaberg's sugarcane fields viewed from The Hummock.

Although McPherson is reputed to have rampaged through the Wide Bay area for nearly four years prior to his arrest, he did manage to rob without violence. He was sentenced to 20 years in gaol, served 15, and subsequently became a law-abiding citizen.

Today, Gin Gin is basically one large street (with plenty of trees, flowers and picnic benches in the median strip) surrounded on either side by several takeaway shops, hotels, and service stations which rely on the passing trade.

4 GIN GIN MUSEUM

The Gin Gin Museum is located on Mulgrave St, just off the highway at the south-eastern end of the town. The one place of interest in the town is the impressive Gin Gin Museum, which consists of a delightful old slab barn called 'Euston Barn' and a building which houses local memorabilia and is called, rather impressively, 'The Residence'. This was actually the police sergeant's residence and, at various times, had to serve as the local lock-up and casualty centre. It has been moved from its original location to become the centrepiece of the Museum. The Museum is open on Wednesdays and Sundays between 14:00 and 16:00.

5 BOOLBOONDA TUNNEL

Head out of Gin Gin on the road to Mount Perry. Travel 37km and take the left turn to Boolboonda. The route to the tunnel from Gin Gin is clearly signposted.

One of the most interesting sights in the area is the Boolboonda Tunnel near Mount Perry. Running for 192m in rock that is unlined and unsupported, it has the distinction of being the longest unsupported tunnel in the southern hemisphere. It was constructed between 1883 and 1884 as part of the railway line from North Bundaberg to Mount Perry with the objective of opening up the mineral and agricultural resources of the area. If for no other reason, the trip is well worth making because of the delightful bush track which is like travelling 70 years back in time.

The track passes through stands of hoop pine and rainforest and offers excellent views of the surrounding countryside. Once through the tunnel, the road winds down the side of a hill. Pass through three gates to rejoin the Mount Perry road. Turn right and return to Gin Gin.

6 MYSTERY CRATERS

Leave Gin Gin, heading east on the Gin Gin Rd towards Bundaberg for approximately 25km to South Kolan. The entrance to the Mystery Craters is clearly signposted. It is located just off the road on the southern side. The Mystery Craters are one of the most interesting attractions in the Bundaberg area, partly because they are so substantial and partly because there is just nothing like them anywhere else in the whole of Australia. The Bundaberg District Tourism and Development Board has written of the craters, which have featured in the 'Unsolved Mysteries of the World' TV series, that 'the secrets of the 35 craters formed in a massive slab of sandstone have baffled teams of international geologists. Discovered beneath a layer of silt and sand by a local farmer in 1971, 27 holes were exposed, while another 8 remain in their prediscovered state. An interesting feature is the extremely even distribution of red ochre through the coloured sandstone as if it was once churned in a giant cauldron.

'Some experts think the craters are part of a large meteorite, while Australian geologists say the area is the roof of a subterranean lake that was caused by oil pressure underground, or that it was once the edge of the ocean and is the result of sea action (the nearest beach is 24km away) … It is probably impossible to deduce the exact manner of their formation. One thing is certain: they are at least 25 million years old.'

The craters (on average they are only few metres across but some are several metres deep) can be viewed at close quarters and there is also an observation platform which allows people to get an overview of the whole area. They are open from 8:00–17:00 seven days a week.

Return to Bundaberg on the Gin Gin Rd. At the school, turn right onto Hinkler Ave. Travel past Hinkler Park and turn left into Gavin St. Turn right at the roundabout into Queen St and cross the Burnett Bridge back into the centre of town.

33 SUGAR MILLS AND HISTORIC VILLAGES

■ DRIVING TOUR ■ 148KM ■ 1 DAY ■ THE CHARM OF CHILDERS AND THE SUGAR AREA

Childers must be one of the most charming towns in Queensland. Visitors have the rare opportunity to see such sights as a 19th-century pharmacy and a turn-of-the-century butchery.

1 ISIS CENTRAL MILL

From the Burnett Bridge in the centre of Bundaberg, turn right at the roundabout into Quay St. Turn left into Maryborough St then right into Bourbong St. Continue along Bourbong St and veer to the left where the Isis Highway continues at Takalvan St. Continue along the Isis Highway for 44km to the turn-off to the Isis Central Sugar Mill. The Mill is located to the right, about 1km off the highway.

It is possible to visit the Isis Central Mill between July and November from Monday to Friday at 14:00. This is the only sugar mill in the area which is open to the public. It crushes around 900 000 tonnes of cane each year. Contact the Tourist Information Office or call the mill at tel: (071) 26 6166 for more details.

2 CHILDERS

Return to the Isis Highway and continue for about 9km into Childers. The Isis Highway joins the Bruce Highway as it enters Childers.

Childers is a town that was created and sustained by the sugarcane that flourished in the area until there was a drought lasting eight years. The local council, determined to capitalise on the tourist traffic which drove through town without stopping, then embarked on a campaign which has resulted in the title 'Historic Childers – The National Trust Town'. It now offers those people speeding through, an ideal place to stop and explore a little of the Sugar Coast's interesting past. Given the age of the unusual Brazilian leopard trees that line the main street, it is surprising that people ever drove through the town without so much as a pause of curiosity.

The Childers area was first explored by Europeans in the 1850s. The name of the town comes either from the village of Childre in Oxfordshire (there are other Oxfordshire names in the area including Abingdon, Didcot and the Isis River) or from the Right Honorable Hugh Childers, Auditor General of Victoria.

The area grew slowly as teamsters stopped in town and the surrounding land was taken up by pastoralists eager to raise cattle on the fertile soil. Crops including avocados and vegetables are now grown in the area. In 1902 the town was virtually wiped out by a raging fire which demolished nearly all the buildings on one side of the main street. Those that survived the fire are now the most interesting and important buildings in the whole town.

The real centrepiece of Childers' charm is the Childers Pharmaceutical Museum as well as the Olde Butcher Shoppe, both of which are specialist museums where the history of particular trades can be explored.

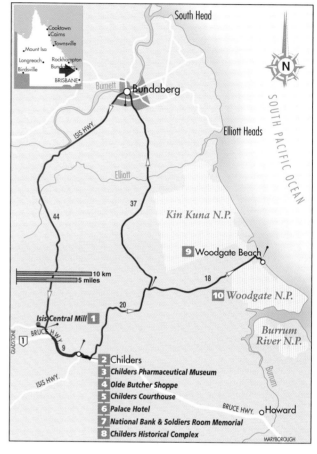

The Federal Hotel boasts original swinging doors and iron lace. It was built in 1907 for around £1250 and was the favoured watering hole of the cane cutters, bullockies and timber getters.

3 CHILDERS PHARMACEUTICAL MUSEUM

As it enters Childers the Bruce Highway becomes Churchill St. Turn left into North St after you have passed the swimming pool to reach the Olde Butcher Shoppe, which is next door but one to the Federal Hotel. Return to Churchill St to the Pharmaceutical Museum, which is located opposite the Post Office. The following historical attractions are all within walking distance of each other.

The Pharmaceutical Museum in the main street (it is also the Tourist Information Office) was originally built in 1894 and retains much of the charm of the late 19th century. The shop fittings are made from cedar, there are old leather-bound prescription books, mortars and pestles that are works of art, and a very early cash register dating back to 1906. The shop is now owned by the local council and it is the centrepiece of the town's regeneration as a

The historic town of Childers, rebuilt after a disastrous fire in 1902.

tourist destination. There are brochures available which list all the interesting historic buildings in town.

4 OLDE BUTCHER SHOPPE

Around the corner from the Federal Hotel (1907) is the Olde Butcher Shoppe which, it is claimed, was the first tiled butcher's shop outside Brisbane when it opened in 1896. The owner is a true enthusiast who happily takes visitors around, explaining early butchering techniques and the history of the building which, by luck, managed to escape the disastrous fire of 1902.

5 CHILDERS COURTHOUSE

Walk east along Churchill St to the Courthouse on the corner of Churchill and Crescent sts. Cross Churchill St to the old Palace Hotel (72 Churchill St).

The Childers Courthouse (1897) is a fine and well-preserved example of the kind of country courthouse built throughout Queensland at the turn of the century. It was originally designed to cater for a town with a population of over 4000.

6 PALACE HOTEL

Undoubtedly the most ostentatious building in the main street is the old Palace Hotel which has recently been converted into Salt's Antiques and Collectables. It has changed its function a number of times although it still looks like a very gracious old country pub.

7 NATIONAL BANK AND SOLDIERS ROOM MEMORIAL

Cross the road again and continue walking east along Churchill St past the National Bank and the RSL to the Soldiers Room Memorial on the corner of Churchill and Lord sts.

The National Bank was built in 1895 and has been preserved in its original state. It was originally a branch of the now defunct Bank of North Queensland.

At the southern end of the main street is the Soldiers Room Memorial, a touching memorial to the soldiers from the area who were killed in all the wars this century. Each soldier is honoured with a bronze plaque and, where possible, a photograph. The images of the young men who were killed are tragic and powerful. The building itself was built in 1926 and is designed in the shape of a Maltese Cross.

8 CHILDERS HISTORICAL COMPLEX

Cross Churchill St and walk past the Roman Catholic Church to Taylor St.

Across the road in Taylor Street is the newly established Childers Historical Complex. It contains a very impressive sugarcane locomotive which was imported from England in 1916, a cottage from Isis Central Mill which was once rented out to mill workers for the modest sum of two shillings a week, and also the old Isis Central Mill School. Both these buildings contain interesting collections of local artefacts and memorabilia. There are also plans to incorporate information on the Aboriginal history of the area into the complex.

Sugarcane burning is a common sight at harvest time.

9 WOODGATE BEACH

Leave Childers via Churchill St, which becomes the Bruce Highway. About 2km out of the town, turn off the highway at Goodwood St, heading towards Bundaberg. Drive about 18km to reach the turn-off to Woodgate Beach. Turn right and continue along this road for another 18km to reach the beach.

Some 38km east of the town of Childers is the seaside resort of Woodgate with its flat, 18km-long beach which is ideal for fishing and sailing. It is a typical retirement village and also a popular holiday resort for people wanting to 'get away from it all'.

10 WOODGATE NATIONAL PARK

The Woodgate National Park extends south along the coast from the town of Woodgate to the Burrum River. It has five walking tracks ranging from the 200m boardwalk near the town to the 6.2km Banksia Track (which has spectacular wildflower displays in the spring) and the 5.8km Melaleuca Track. A comprehensive brochure and map are available from the National Parks and Wildlife office. For more information contact tel: (071) 26 8810.

Woodgate National Park is important because, apart from being home to a wide range of wildflowers and marsupials and over 200 species of bird, it is also an excellent example of wallum banksia heath which is unusual in Queensland. It also features sand dunes, mangroves, wetlands and eucalypt forests. The park offers good picnic facilities and a camping ground (only accessible by 4WD vehicle).

Return 18km to the Woodgate Beach turn-off. Turn right and travel 37km north back to Bundaberg.

The Isis sugar mill near Childers.

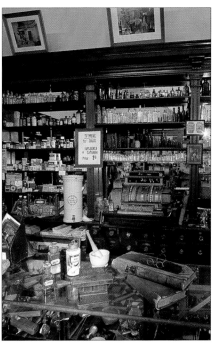

Inside the Childers Pharmaceutical Museum.

34 EXPLORING AROUND HERVEY BAY

■ DRIVING TOUR ■ 100KM ■ 1 DAY ■ MEMORIALS, SHARKS AND SLEEPY SEASIDE VILLAGES

Hervey Bay is a strange mixture of motels, caravan sites and fast-food outlets – the result of highly developed tourism – and sleepy retreats with quiet beaches and pleasant foreshore walks.

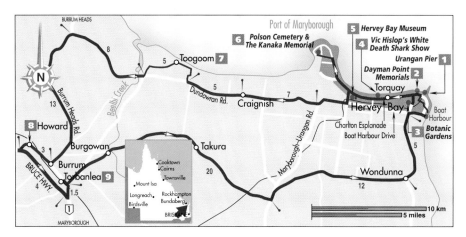

*H*ervey Bay is a loosely connected series of villages – Urangan, Torquay, Scarness, Pialba and Point Vernon – which stretches along the bay in a string of small shopping centres and a seemingly endless run of holiday units, motels, caravan parks and flats. Hervey Bay's great attraction lies in the range of activities it offers: fishing, walking, waterskiing, scuba diving, and exploring nearby Fraser Island. Whale watching has also become synonymous with Hervey Bay. Families of humpback whales migrating south from August to mid-October each year stop and play in the sheltered waters of the bay for a while. A number of operators run whale-watching cruises to view the whales at close range. Beyond these activities are the usual tourist attractions of a wildlife park, a bird sanctuary and an aquarium. There is also an interesting and substantial historical museum and a memorial to the Kanakas who worked the sugar fields in the area.

Its villages once quiet and sleepy, Hervey Bay is in the process of exploding into a major holiday destination. It is now a city encompassing the small villages which all blend together. This is compounded by the fact that much of the beach foreshore is taken up with caravan parks (it actually boasts that it is the 'Caravan Capital of Australia'), creating a very one-dimensional feel about the place – shops on one side of the Charlton Esplanade, then caravan parks, then a narrow, hard-sand beach.

The first European to reach the Hervey Bay area was Captain James Cook, who sailed past Fraser Island and named many of the prominent features. Cook did not sail into Hervey Bay; in fact he was some 6km offshore as he sailed north. This did not stop him naming the bay after the 'English Casanova', Augustus John Hervey, a sailor of some note who had acquired a reputation as a womaniser.

Matthew Flinders passed through the area twice and was the first European to step ashore at Hervey Bay. In 1799, Flinders sailed up the eastern coast of Fraser Island, entering the bay and going ashore at the present site of Dayman Park. It is one of the ironies of history that Flinders, who returned to the area in 1802 on his historic circumnavigation of Australia, did not locate the Fraser Island Straits on either of his voyages.

Hervey Bay was originally part of a cattle station, the Toogoom Run, which was settled in 1854. The first permanent white settler at Hervey Bay was Boyle Martin who, with his wife and child, arrived in 1863. He worked as a timber cutter and it is suggested that he was the first person to grow sugarcane in the area.

The attractions of Hervey Bay were obvious. The fishing was good, the place was quiet, the weather was excellent, and the area around the bay was flat and accessible. All these factors quickly led Maryborough businessmen to take up large waterfront blocks of land for weekend retreats.

1 URANGAN PIER

This journey starts from Urangan Boat Harbour and moves west and north around Hervey Bay. Travel north along Buccaneer St and turn left into Edwin St. At the end of Edwin St, turn right into Pulgul St. Pass Dayman St and take the next left turn into Kent St. After a short distance, there is a four-way intersection where King St branches off to the right of Kent St. Veer to the right into King St and continue past Pilot St. Take the next right turn into Pier St, heading towards the water. Urangan Pier is at the end of the street.

In 1896 Hervey Bay was connected to Maryborough by railway. In 1917 the Urangan Pier was completed and Urangan became an important port for the export of sugar. Stretching 1.4km out into the sea, the pier, a Hervey Bay landmark, is popular with fishermen and people who want a leisurely walk.

2 DAYMAN POINT MEMORIALS

From Urangan Pier, walk west along Point Dayman Park until you reach the memorials to Matthew Flinders and the Z-Force.

During World War II, Fraser Island and Hervey Bay were used as training grounds for the famous Z-Force commando unit. At Dayman Point, near the Matthew Flinders memorial, is a memorial 'dedicated to the men of Z-Force who sank 38 000 tons of Japanese shipping in Singapore Harbour in September 1943'.

Using an old Japanese fish carrier named *Kofuku Naru*, which had been renamed the *Krait*, Z-Force managed to get into Singapore Harbour where, in a daring raid known as Operation Jaywick, they attached limpet mines to several Japanese vessels. In one night they blew up the Japanese ships before returning to Australia.

The Matthew Flinders Memorial is located in Dayman Park which lies between the Urangan Pier and Hervey Bay Marina, overlooking Fraser Island strait. A bronze plaque on the monument reads: 'Erected to the memory of Capt Matthew Flinders R. N. who landed hereabout from HMS *Norfolk* on 6th August, 1799 and Lt Joseph Dayman R.N. who passed here in the schooner *Asp*, after making the first passage of the Fraser Island Straits in 1847.' Dayman found the straits by clinging to the shores of the bay as he sailed down the coast after a surveying expedition in the Port Curtis area.

3 BOTANIC GARDENS

From Urangan Pier, travel west along the Charlton Esplanade and turn into Elizabeth St, the first street on the left. Proceed south for about 1km. The Botanic Gardens are on the right after the intersection of Dayman and Elizabeth sts.

The Botanic Gardens are a delightful retreat from the overt tourism of The Esplanade. They offer the visitor quiet walkways through pleasant tropical displays.

4 VIC HISLOP'S WHITE DEATH SHARK SHOW

Leave the Botanic Gardens and turn left into Elizabeth St, heading north towards the beach. At the end of Elizabeth St, turn left onto the Charlton Esplanade and continue for about 2km, passing through Torquay to the White Death Shark Show.

Vic Hislop's White Death Shark Show has become one of the well-known attractions of Hervey Bay. The huge shark's mouth at the doorway, the large shark announcing the attraction and most people's inevitable fascination with sharks have ensured its continuing existence.

5 HERVEY BAY MUSEUM

From the White Death Shark Show, continue west along the Charlton Esplanade for about 2km. The museum is in Zephyr St on the left.

The Hervey Bay Museum (which is clearly signposted off the Charlton Esplanade) is an interesting and detailed collection of buildings and memorabilia related to the area. The museum is easily located as it has an enormous fish, the 'Fighting Whiting', donated by the local newspaper, placed prominently outside to attract tourists.

6 POLSON CEMETERY AND THE KANAKA MEMORIAL

From the museum, head north along Zephyr St to the Charlton Esplanade and continue until you reach Corser St. Head west along Corser; the cemetery is on the right, just past Barker St.

There is a memorial to the Kanakas at Point Vernon, the westernmost suburb in Hervey Bay. The memorial, located at the back of the Polson Cemetery, is a reminder that these virtual slaves were brought to Australia as conscripted labour from 1863–1906. There were an estimated 12 000 (out of a population of over 50 000) Kanakas living in the Maryborough–Hervey Bay area.

7 TOOGOOM

From the memorial, return east along Corser St to the Charlton Esplanade. Turn right and follow the Charlton Esplanade south for 3km back to Main St. Turn right into Main St and continue south to the intersection with Boat Harbour Dve. Turn right into Boat Harbour Dve and follow it west until it meets the Maryborough–Urangan Rd after 2km. Turn left into Maryborough–Urangan Rd, head south-west and take the second right turn into Dundowran Rd. Continue west for 7km, passing through Craignish. About 5km beyond Craignish the road turns north, and upon reaching the coast it turns west. Follow the road for another 2km to Toogoom.

Toogoom, on the mouth of the Beelbie Creek, has become a popular retirement haunt for people whose idea of bliss is a bit of fishing (both in the creek and on the bay), some boating, sailboarding or canoeing, birdwatching (around 90 species of bird inhabit the area) and lots of lazing in the sea. It is a quiet and sleepy little village.

8 HOWARD

From Toogoom, head south for 3km and take the road heading west to Burrum Heads. Continue west, crossing Beelbi Creek, and then veer north-west. After 8km, turn west into Burrum Heads Rd and follow it for 13km south to Burrum. From Burrum, travel north-west for just under 3km on Burrum Heads Rd to Howard.

Howard is a small service centre for an area in which sugar plantations, citrus orchards and dairy farming flourish in conjuction with coalmining.

There was a time when coalmining made Howard an important centre – miners had moved into the area as early as 1864 when a seam of coal was discovered on the banks of the Burrum River – but a combination of factors has caused it to revert to a sleepy rural settlement. The decision to bypass the town ensured that it did not develop a tourist industry and the growing importance of the port facilities at Gladstone and the coalmines to the north and south of Blackwater reduced its importance as a mining centre.

The town's major 'tourist attraction' is the charming colonial home Brooklyn (across the railway line from the centre of town) which was once the home of Dame Annabel Rankin. She was a successful State and Federal parliamentarian who, after representing the electorate of Burrum in the Queensland State Parliament for many years, became a Liberal Senator for Queensland from 1946–1971.

9 TORBANLEA

From Howard, follow the directions to the Bruce Highway, about 1km south of town. Once on the highway, travel south-east for 4km where the Torbanlea Railway Station is off the highway to the north.

The peaceful village of Torbanlea, just south of Howard, is another old mining centre. The main attraction here is the Torbanlea

Vic Hislop's Shark Show, Hervey Bay.

Mining Museum, a delightful folk museum which chronicles the 100-year history of mining in the area, which once supported 94 coalmines. The museum, built on the site of a railway siding that once served the mining township, combines old equipment (including a very old fire engine) with a row of fascinating shops including a pawnbroker, a general store, a barber's shop, a bottle shop, the original Burrum Railway Station building, a miner's cottage and an authentic slab hut. There is even a Model T Ford bus and a recreated old mining tunnel.

To return to the Urangan Boat Harbour, leave Torbanlea, heading north-east along the road to Burgowan. Travel for 20km, passing through Burgowan and Takura. When the road reaches a T-junction, turn left and head north for a short way until you reach the turn-off to Wondunna. Veer right and continue for 12km, passing through Wondunna. The road swings to the north. Follow Booral Rd north, passing the aerodrome on the left. At the intersection near the cricket grounds, continue straight into Elizabeth St, following it north to the roundabout intersection with Boat Harbour Dve. Turn right into Boat Harbour Dve, proceed east to the Charlton Esplanade and turn left. Travel north along the Charlton Esplanade and take the third right turn into Miller St. The boat harbour is at the end of the street.

The Pier, Urangan, built to service the sugar trade.

35 EXPLORING 'THE GREAT SANDY ISLAND'

■ DRIVING TOUR ■ 117KM ■ 1 DAY ■ SAND DUNES, FRESHWATER LAKES AND TRANQUILLITY

Fraser Island is one of the true wonders of Australia. It has extraordinary freshwater sand-dune lakes, beautiful quiet streams, cliffs with remarkable coloured bands of sand, and rugged headlands.

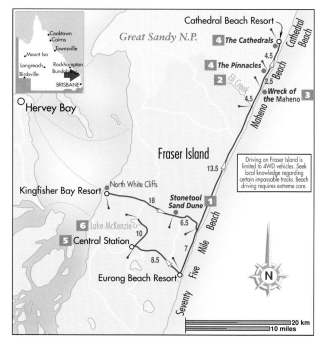

Located just off the coast from Hervey Bay, Fraser Island is 123km long and varies from 7km to 22km in width. It covers an area of 184 000km² and has sand dunes that rise to a height of 240m. It is estimated that the sands which make up Fraser Island extend to over 600m below sea level.

The first European to sight Fraser Island was Captain James Cook who passed along the coast of the island between 18 and 20 May 1770 and named Indian Head after seeing a number of Aborigines assembled there.

In 1799 and 1802 Matthew Flinders sailed past the island. He mapped it both times but on neither occasion did he confirm that it was separated from the mainland. He suspected that it was an island but was unable to sail around it.

The most famous early contact with the island was that of Eliza Fraser (after whom the island is named) and her shipwrecked companions from the brig Stirling Castle. On 13 May 1836, while travelling from Sydney to Singapore, the Stirling Castle struck the Great Barrier Reef about 320km south of Torres Strait. Captain James Fraser, his pregnant wife Eliza and 18 passengers and crew launched the ship's longboat and set course for Moreton Bay. During the next six weeks, Eliza gave birth, but the baby survived for only a few hours. Captain Fraser had been trying to avoid the coast for fear of the Aborigines, but was forced to land for water on the Great Sandy Island (Fraser Island) on 26 June. The local Aborigines stripped the survivors and separated Eliza from her husband. For the next two months the Frasers (until the death of the Captain) and the other survivors were put to work and forced to live in arduous conditions.

Eventually a search party from Moreton Bay led by Lieutenant Charles Otter was sent out to search for the survivors. John Graham, a remarkable convict who had once lived with the Aborigines, found Eliza and escorted her back to Moreton Bay. She subsequently sailed to Sydney where she was feted as a heroine. The people of Sydney, impressed by her bravery, raised a considerable amount of money for her by public subscription.

Before Eliza departed for England, she married Captain Alexander John Greene of the Mediterranean Packet. After such a dramatic life, Eliza slipped into quiet obscurity. She and Captain Greene later returned to the Antipodes. Eliza was accidentally run over and killed in Melbourne in 1858.

This story has captured the Australian imagination. It has been made into a TV program and a film. Sidney Nolan did two series of paintings based on the story.

In 1870, as a result of a series of shipwrecks, a lighthouse was built at Sandy Cape. This was the first permanent European settlement on Fraser island.

Beaches of Fraser Island near Sandy Cape.

Boardwalk at Central Station.

The wreck of the Maheno.

Swimming in refreshing Eli Creek.

The tour described below is the standard one-day trip offered by Kingfisher Bay Resort. Visitors are taken by 4WD bus, and morning tea, lunch and afternoon tea stops are included. You can also undertake the trip in your own 4WD. There is some argument about damage being done to the island. It is up to you to decide whether you believe one 4WD bus carrying 20 people does more damage than up to 10 4WD vehicles doing the same journey. The roads on the island are quite impassable for conventional vehicles.

1 STONETOOL SAND DUNE

Departing from Kingfisher Bay Resort, you travel for approximately 18km to the viewing point overlooking Stonetool Sand Dune.

This huge dune is currently moving across the island, burying everything in its path. The movement, driven by the prevailing winds, is very slow. The size of the dune is remarkable – it is not possible to walk across it. Although the island has been used by Europeans for over 100 years, there is now a genuine environmental concern that recognises the delicate ecology of the region.

2 ELI CREEK

Travel down from the Stonetool Sand Dune lookout until you reach the island's eastern beach. Drive north along the beach until you reach Eli Creek. It is approximately 20km from the Stonetool Sand Dune.

Eli Creek is the largest freshwater stream on the eastern coast of the island and is an area of exceptional and pristine beauty. There are a number of wooden walkways and a short, circular route runs up one side of the creek and down the other. It is possible to swim in the lower reaches of the creek, which is very cool and refreshing on a hot day.

3 THE WRECK OF THE *MAHENO*

Travel north for approximately 4.5km along the eastern beach until you reach the wreck of the Maheno *which is located at the water's edge.*

After some 30 years of service in Australian waters the *Maheno*, a former World War I hospital ship and trans-Tasman luxury liner, was being towed to Japan as scrap when it hit cyclonic conditions off the coast and was washed ashore on 9 July 1935. It was used for target practice during World War II. The past 60 years of waves and weathering have reduced this once huge vessel to nothing more than a small rusting hulk.

4 THE PINNACLES AND THE CATHEDRALS

Continue north for 2.5km until you reach The Pinnacles. About 4.5km further on are The Cathedrals.

These majestic coloured-sand cliffs and formations have been eroded and sculpted by the wind and rain blowing in off the Pacific Ocean. The colours – red, brown, yellow and orange – are spectacular. The size of the cliff faces is a reminder of how large the sand dunes on the island are.

5 CENTRAL STATION

Return the 31.5km to Eurong. The 8.5km track inland to Central Station is well signposted. The Kingfisher Bay Resort tour stops here for lunch and the restaurant is open to visitors.

Central Station was once the centre of the forestry industry on the island and the home of over 100 people. The Woongoolbver Creek which carries clear water through the island's rainforest at Central Station is one of the most beautiful retreats on the whole island. It seems as though this area inspired the Australian Nobel Prizewinner Patrick White, whose description of the island in the novel *A Fringe of Leaves* includes the lines:

Now it hushed the strangers it was initiating. At some stages of the journey the trees were so densely massed, the columns so moss-upholstered or lichen-encrusted, the vines suspended from them so intricately rigged, the light barely slithered down, and then a dark, watery green, though in rare gaps where

the sassafras had been thinned out, and once where a giant blackbutt had crashed, the intruders might have been reminded of actual light if this had not flittered, again like moss, but dry, crumbled, white to golden.

6 LAKE McKENZIE

Follow the trails from Central Station to Lake McKenzie. This is a distance of some 10km.

There are a number of freshwater lakes on the island, including Lake Bowarrady (120m above sea level), Lake McKenzie, Lake Birrabeen, Lake Boomanjin (reputedly the largest perched lake in the world), Ocean Lake, Hidden Lake, and Coomboo Lake. Each is notable for the clarity of the water, the purity of the white sands on the surrounding beaches and the peacefulness of the area. They are ideal places for picnics and swimming.

By the mid-1960s, a number of mining leases had been taken out on parts of the island by Queensland Titanium Mines Pty Ltd and Murphyores. The wealth of the island lay in its rich deposits of rutile, ilmenite, zircon and monazite. The battle raged through both the state and federal courts and resulted in the historic Fraser Island Environmental Inquiry which, in October 1976, decided that all sandmining should be banned and that the island should be recorded as part of the National Estate.

Kingfisher Bay Resort.

36 HISTORIC MARYBOROUGH

■ WALKING TOUR ■ 10KM ■ 3 HOURS ■ ARCHITECTURE PRODUCED BY GOLD

The original settlement of Maryborough is now no more than a collection of plaques in a park on the river bank. The city centre, however, has several fine late-19th-century public buildings.

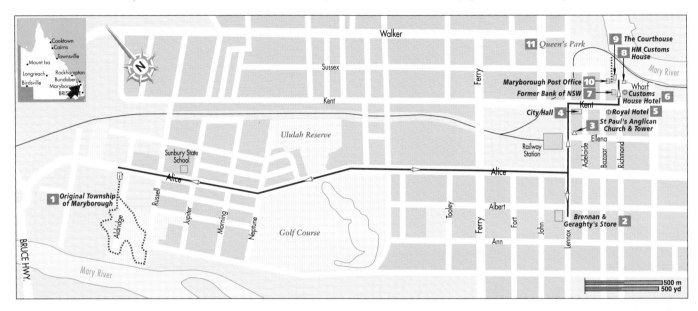

While the coast near Maryborough was charted by Captain James Cook and Matthew Flinders, it was really Andrew Petrie who explored the present city site. In 1842 Petrie sailed up the coast from Moreton Bay in a whaleboat to investigate the economic potential of the harbour which lay behind Fraser Island. Petrie travelled nearly 80km up the Mary River, and although he did not find the bunya trees he was specifically looking for, one of his crew, Henry Stuart Russell, declared after the journey that he had 'seen what looks like a first-rate harbour, and a river in which I yet hope, if I can but find fit country on or near it, goodbye to drays, bullocks, Cunningham's Gap and hells holes – hoorah! for immediate water carriage for wool.'

The hinterland was settled extensively in the 1840s and in July 1847 the Government Surveyor, J C Burnett, surveyed the river and declared that it was 'an eligible position for the establishment of a town as parties will no doubt settle there as soon as there is prospect of trade'. On the result of this survey, Governor Fitzroy named the river Mary, after his wife. Prior to that it had been known as Wide Bay to the Europeans and Booie, Numabulla, Mooraboocoola or Moonaboola to the local Aborigines.

1 ORIGINAL TOWNSHIP OF MARYBOROUGH

Heading to the north-west out of Maryborough, follow Alice St from the southern side of the railway station for just over 2km, passing the golf course on your left and the Sunbury State School on your right. Cross Russell St and continue until you reach the intersection of Alice and Aldridge sts. On the corner is the entrance and information centre of the original Maryborough township.

First settled as a wool port, Maryborough is one of Queensland's oldest cities. In September 1847 George Furber, an enterprising Ipswich businessman, arrived at Wide Bay on the Mary River and built a store, a house for himself, and a jetty. By December that year he had shipped out his first load of 65 bales of wool. The next year Furber found himself in competition with Aldridge and Palmer who had set up on the opposite bank of the river and were offering easier access to the port. Within a year, over 1000 bales of wool were being shipped out and several shops and hotels had sprung up.

The original Maryborough site has been recreated with a series of boards describing the early history of the town. It has a very pleasant heritage walk which winds through the parklands beside the Mary River where the original settlement was established. Although none of the original buildings remain, the walk is dotted with plaques which recount the history of a long-departed house or shop. The only unchanged features are the old Furber graves (most of which have illegible inscriptions) and the gracious Baddow House. The 15 points of interest on the walk include the Teamsters' Paddock, the site of the Bush Inn, the site of Furber's Inn, the wool store, sawpits and sawyers huts.

The walk reaches the river at Baddow House. Though not built until 1883, it dates back to the earliest days of the settlement. Baddow House was built by Edgar Thomas Aldridge, who had followed Furber to the area and established the original Bush Inn (now the Royal Hotel) as well as trading and wool stores on the banks of the river.

Two events in the 1860s ensured that the town would continue to grow and prosper. In 1865 the Maryborough Sugar Company began sugar farming in the area and in 1867 gold was discovered at Gympie, resulting in Maryborough becoming one of the major access points to the goldfields.

2 BRENNAN & GERAGHTY'S STORE

Head back along Alice St until you reach Lennox St on the far side of the railway station, then turn right. At number 64 is Brennan & Geraghty's Store.

This large, single-storeyed timber building dates from 1871, and is a good example of a well-appointed store of the period. Its Victorian brick and stucco facade, six-panel doors and shuttered shop windows all make it an imposing structure. In 1990 it was restored to its original condition.

The excellent *Historical Homes of Wide Bay* records:

The store was similar to a present-day supermarket and many articles apart from groceries were sold.

At the close of business each night wooden shutters were placed on the windows. Produce in the rear section of the store was transported to the front section on a flat topped trolley which ran on wooden rails. A galvanised pipe speaking tube linked the store to the Geraghty home on the northern side of the store.

3 ST PAUL'S ANGLICAN CHURCH AND TOWER

Turn around and head back up Lennox St. One block up from Alice St is Ellena St. On your right is St Paul's Anglican Church.

Located in Lennox Street, St Paul's Anglican Church was the town's third Anglican church when it was completed in 1879. Perhaps of greater interest is the freestanding bell tower, one of the many gifts to the town from one of its first settlers, Edward Aldridge. Dedicated to his wife, the tower was completed in 1887.

4 CITY HALL

Continue up Lennox St and turn right at Kent St. On your right-hand side, occupying most of the block, is the City Hall.

This impressive building was designed in 1908 by Robin Dods in a distinctive American Colonial style. One of the city's true novelties – the Time Gun – is fired daily at 13:00. It has been estimated that the sound of the gun can be heard from as far as 30km away. The gun was a gift to the city from the Premier of Queensland, John Douglas. It had been found on the Torres Strait island of Mobiag and was most probably a gun used by the vessels of the Dutch East India Company during the 17th century. It was presented as a response to the criticism that the town had no clock. The gun was first fired on 21 March 1878.

5 ROYAL HOTEL

Continue down Kent St and across Adelaide St. The next street you cross is Bazaar St. On the far right-hand corner is the Royal Hotel.

The Royal Hotel still has the Royal Crest which gives it the status of a hotel under royal patronage. As the publicity for the hotel proudly declares: 'The Royal Hotel, famous for its hospitality and service since 1856, has been host to Governor Generals, State Governors, Prime Ministers, Premiers, and many distinguished overseas visitors.'

The distinction of royal patronage was bestowed on the Royal Hotel by Governor Bowen when he conducted his very first official function as governor at the hotel. In 1930, Governor Sir Leslie Orme Wilson wrote to King George V questioning the hotel's status, and its royal patronage was confirmed. The hotel's Regal Room still has the Coat of Arms which was presented by Governor Bowen.

6 CUSTOMS HOUSE HOTEL

Continue along Kent St and turn to your left up Richmond St. On your right at the next intersection is the Customs House Hotel.

Built in 1870 at the height of Maryborough's early prosperity, the Customs House Hotel is one of the many highlights on Wharf Street. Its impressive two storeys and fine cast-iron lacework are a reminder of the affluence which characterised Maryborough during the 1860s and 1870s.

7 FORMER BANK OF NEW SOUTH WALES

Directly opposite the Customs House Hotel is the Maryborough Family Heritage Insitute, the former Bank of New South Wales.

The Maryborough Family Heritage Institute building in Wharf Street was the former Bank of New South Wales. Erected in 1878 with iron columns and elaborate cast-iron lacework, it was one of Maryborough's three major banks during the Gympie gold rush. Fortunes were deposited in this bank by successful miners.

8 HM CUSTOMS HOUSE

Just past Wharf St, along Richmond St, the Customs House is on your right.

Maryborough got its first Customs Officer in 1859. Customs House was completed in 1901. It features a coat of arms and is a fine example of the elaborate brickwork which was commonplace during the period. The building has high windows to improve ventilation in summer.

9 COURTHOUSE

At the end of Richmond St, on the corner with Queen's Park, is the Courthouse.

At one corner of Queen's Park stands an impressive group of solid Victorian buildings, the highlight of which is the Maryborough Courthouse and Lands Office, a huge two-storeyed Victorian Classical Revival building which was built between 1875 and 1877 for £7345.

10 MARYBOROUGH POST OFFICE

Wander across the park and down to the corner of Wharf and Bazaar sts to the Maryborough Post Office.

The Post Office was constructed in 1869. It reflects the affluence which came to Maryborough as a result of the Gympie gold rush. It is a typical Victorian Classical Revival building with arcaded verandahs and a clock tower which was added in 1879. A gracious two-storeyed building, it is an important part of the streetscape near Queen's Park which includes the Customs House, Courthouse, bond store, warehouses (many of which are in the process of being restored) and a number of hotels.

11 QUEEN'S PARK

Queen's Park is located on the banks of the Mary River. If you head to the north from the Post Office towards the river, after a short distance you will reach the Band Rotunda.

Established over 100 years ago, Queen's Park can lay claim to being one of the most delightful parks in the whole of Queensland. The huge banyan tree, the elegant Band Rotunda, the City Fernery, waterfall, lily pond and the views over the river all make it an ideal place to relax.

The lace-trimmed Band Rotunda is a very early example of prefabrication. It was actually built in Glasgow and shipped out to be constructed in the park in 1890. Originally it included the 'Fairy Fountain' – an ornate drinking fountain – which has been removed and relocated nearby. The fountain was removed in order that the floor could be raised so that audiences could have better views of the performer.

Near the Band Rotunda are some 13cm-gauge railway tracks. The local Model Engineers and Live Steamers Association bring their trains to these tracks on the last Sunday of each month.

Maryborough Town Hall.

HM Customs House, Maryborough.

Boats on the Mary River, Maryborough.

37 FROM GOLD TO PEANUTS

■ DRIVING TOUR ■ 354KM ■ 1 DAY ■ EMU AND PEANUT FARMING

In the often overlooked areas beyond the coast there are rolling pasturelands, the heartland of Australia's peanut industry and one of the country's most successful Aboriginal communities.

1 KILKIVAN

Head north out of Gympie along the Bruce Highway (Route 1). The WoodWorks Forestry and Timber Museum (see Tour 23) is situated on the highway just a few kilometres from the town. Some 14km from Gympie you will reach a junction where the Bruce Highway heads north to Maryborough and the Wide Bay Highway branches west. Follow the Wide Bay Highway for 38km to Kilkivan.

Kilkivan is a small, pleasant township nestled into the eastern hills of the Great Dividing Range. The area was settled in the 1840s and the town of Kilkivan takes its name from a property which was established around that time. A Scot named MacTaggart selected 1600 acres which he then named Kilkivan. European settlement of the area was slow until a gold reef, the Rise and Shine (the town was briefly named after the reef), was discovered at nearby Mount Neurum in 1868.

In its heyday, the town had a population of around 2000 miners serviced by a number of grog shanties, four hotels and several general stores. Within about four years the alluvial gold in the area had run out. Fortunately the Black Snake reef was discovered in 1874 and the economy of the town was sustained until 1902.

2 MOUNT CLARA COPPER SMELTER

Access to the Mount Clara Copper Smelter is not easy. Travel 1.5km out of town towards Gympie then turn

Carved Emu Eggs at Cherbourg Emu Farm.

Wondai Post Office.

right and travel for 11.5km along Rossmore Rd. The copper smelter is located 3km from the road.

In 1872 copper was also discovered at Mount Clara on the Fat Hen Creek. A smelter was established which today is part of the National Estate.

The National Estate, in its assessment of the old copper mine ruins, states that: 'To process the ore eight reverbatory furnaces were built, the remains of which include a collapsed reverbatory furnace, fragments of railway line used to carry timber to the furnace, and a chimney 16.5m high. The chimney is constructed of locally hewn stone of pleasant colour and texture and bonded with clay mortar. The site is notable for the absence of modern intrusions and as a relic of early mining activity in the area.'

3 KINBOMBI FALLS

Return to the Wide Bay Highway and continue south-west. After about 19km, take the road south-east off the highway to the beautiful Kinbombi Falls. About 4km down the road is a signposted turn-off to the left. Follow this road for 1km.

The Kinbombi Falls are spectacular in wet weather. There is a 200-step walk to the pool at the bottom of the falls and the pleasant picnic facilities include barbeques. Toilets are available.

4 MURGON

Return to the Wide Bay Highway and continue west. About 6km from the turn-off is the small township of Goomeri. From Goomeri head south for 2km along the Burnett Highway (Route 17) then turn off onto the Bunya Highway, heading south-west to Murgon, which is 19km from Goomeri.

The tiny township of Murgon has an historical museum and a sign announcing that it is the home of Australia's champion cheese.

Murgon probably means either 'spring', 'lily-covered pond' or a specific variety of lily in the language of one of the local Aboriginal groups.

The first European settlers were Ferriter and Uhr who arrived in the area in 1843 and took up land which they called Barambah. A house built on Barambah Station in 1905 with superb wide verandahs and an unusual hexagonal corner pavilion has been listed by the National Estate. While not the first house built on the property (this has long

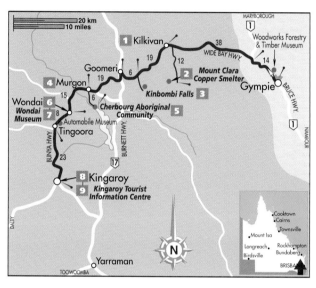

since disappeared), the current Barambah Homestead is a fine example of Queensland timber architecture. Unfortunately it is not open to the public.

The development of the town did not start until the early years of this century. The butter factory was opened in 1913 and a grain shed was built the following year.

Today the town is a quiet rural service centre. Its major attractions include the Queensland Dairy Industry Museum which is open on Saturdays and Sundays from 13:00–16:00. Other times can be arranged by contacting tel: (071) 68 1499. The museum is located on the Gayndah road at the eastern edge of Murgon and exhibits include a three-bail dairy, laboratory displays and also the equipment used for making cheese and butter.

Nearby on the Bunya Highway opposite the Gayndah turn-off is the Goschnick's Machinery Museum which has an excellent display of working vintage tractors.

5 CHERBOURG ABORIGINAL COMMUNITY

Head to the south-west from the Murgon town centre across the railway line and along Lamb St. Just 1km from the railroad track is a signposted turn-off to the south. Follow this road for 6km to the Cherbourg Aboriginal Community.

This Aboriginal community was established in 1904 when the government brought Aborigines from 21 different groups to the area and forced them to live together. It was to Cherbourg that the survivors of the decimated Aborigines from Fraser Island were sent. Somehow over the years these widely differing groups have managed to work together so that now the town, with a population of 1600 and a school which has a student population of nearly 300, is a huge success. It is managed by the Cherbourg Community Council.

Cherbourg (which was supposed to be 'Chirbury' but, due to a series of errors, was changed firstly to 'Cherberg' and later to 'Cherbourg') is a remarkably self-sufficient community with a successful dairy farm, an active town council, and, most interestingly, an experimental emu farm. There are conducted tours which take approximately 30–45 minutes and guides will explain everything you need to know about emus. Add to that the community's active production of boomerangs, spears and Aboriginal art (all of which are for sale) and Cherbourg is an interesting experience.

6 WONDAI

Return to Murgon and rejoin the Bunya Highway. Head west out of town on the highway and follow it for about 15km to Wondai.

Like so much of southern Queensland, Wondai was settled in the 1840s after the government of New South Wales decided to open the land around the Moreton Bay penal colony to free settlers. A number of large stations (first sheep and later cattle) were established in the Wondai region but it wasn't until 1902 that the town was officially gazetted.

The establishment of the town occurred with the arrival of the railway line and, in 1901, the resumption of large tracts of land which were subsequently subdivided, resulting in more intensive land use.

Today it is a typical rural centre, servicing the surrounding properties where peanuts, wheat and cereal crops are grown and dairy and beef cattle are raised.

To the west of Wondai are fields which are popular with gemstone fossickers.

7 WONDAI MUSEUM

Follow the Bunya Highway to the south as it enters Wondai from Murgon. After passing Bicentennial Park, go through the roundabout and take the first right turn into Mackenzie St where you will see the Wondai Museum on the left.

Visitors who are interested in the history of the area should visit the Wondai Museum in Mackenzie Street (open from 10:00–16:00 Mondays to Fridays). It is a typical folk museum and is filled with informative and unusual memorabilia from the area. It includes the reconstructed operating theatre from the old Wondai Hospital which dates back to 1915.

8 KINGAROY

Return to Scott St, turn left and then left again at the roundabout, and then turn south onto the Bunya Highway. About 8km along this route is the little hamlet of Tingoora which has a solitary hotel and an automobile museum boasting over 2000 exhibits. Continue travelling south along the Bunya Highway for another 23km to Kingaroy.

Kingaroy proudly boasts that it is both the 'Peanut Capital of Australia' and the 'Baked Bean Capital of Australia'. The region around Kingaroy also produces maize, oats, barley, and soya beans.

The town was probably named after the Aboriginal word 'kinjerroy' which was a term used to describe a particular type of red ant (although there was a 'King' among the early settlers).

Kingaroy was opened up in the 1840s when Henry Stuart Russell and the Haly brothers moved into the area. Taabinga Station homestead (listed on the National Estate) was built in 1846. Located some 5km south of Kingaroy, it is closed to the public but can be opened for groups. Enquiries should be directed to the Kingaroy Tourist Information Centre.

In 1904 the railway arrived in Kingaroy (ensuring the town's continuing existence), the post office and police station were built, and the first hotel was constructed.

The next stage in the town's development occurred in the 1920s when the first really significant crops of peanuts (using seeds supplied by Chinese market gardeners from the nearby town of Nanango) were harvested and the first silo was built (1928). Today the town seems to be run by peanuts. There are big peanut signs in the street, selling points known as 'The Peanut Van' are located at either end of the town, the silos dominate the town, and even the Tourist Information Office sells peanuts. The huge silos are 29m high and capable of holding 12 000 tonnes.

9 KINGAROY TOURIST INFORMATION CENTRE

Follow the Bunya Highway south into the centre of the town (where it becomes Youngman St). Turn left into Haly St, 750m past the hospital. The information centre is at No 128 Haly St, just past King St.

The Kingaroy Tourist Information Centre is the starting point for the twice-daily (10:30 and 13:30) tours of the Peanut Board facilities. The tour combines a video with a 15-minute tour of the facilities.

In recent times Kingaroy has become a major producer of navy beans (known to everyone as the beans in baked beans) and the Information Centre has details on the local production.

Next to the Information Centre is the town's Bicentennial Heritage Museum which is open daily from 9:30–12:30. It has a good folk museum display which chronicles the agricultural and pastoral history of the area and is worth a visit.

To return to Gympie, retrace the route along the Bunya Highway, the Wide Bay Highway (from Goomeri) and, for the final 14km, the Bruce Highway.

Each year around 50 000 tonnes of peanuts are delivered to the silos at Kingaroy.

Rolling pastures near Kingaroy.

The Peanut Van, Kingaroy.

CHAPTER 6
OUTBACK QUEENSLAND

38 THE WILDS OF OUTBACK QUEENSLAND

■ DRIVING TOUR ■ 931KM ■ 2 DAYS ■ A WORLD OF RED DESERT AND BORE WATER

This flat, inhospitable country on the edge of the desert is the world of the lizard contest, of the church that has an altar made from thunder eggs, and of miners hoping to discover a fortune.

The area around Cunnamulla was first settled in the late 1840s after it had been explored by Sir Thomas Mitchell who passed through the area in 1846 searching for a route to the Gulf of Carpentaria. It was during this time that Mitchell discovered the 'Victoria' River which he believed flowed north into the Gulf. After the party returned to Sydney, Mitchell's second-in-command, Edmund Kennedy, returned to the area to find the mouth of the Victoria. Kennedy passed near Cunnamulla in 1847 on an expedition which determined that Mitchell's 'Victoria' was in fact the Barcoo and that it flowed into Cooper's Creek.

The township of Cunnamulla was created by Cobb & Co who, on 3 September 1879, drove the first coach through from Bourke. Cunnamulla was one of many settlements that grew up in south-west Queensland as a result of the activities of Cobb & Co but it is the only one to have survived.

The survival of Cunnamulla was undoubtedly linked firstly to the reliable water supply provided by the Warrego River and secondly to the arrival of the railway line in 1899. Today it is still an important railhead for the surrounding area as it is the end of the branch line which runs south from Charleville.

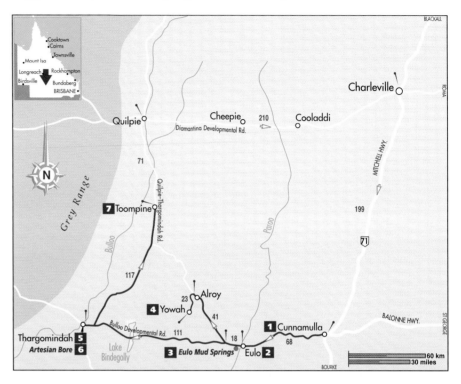

Memorial Fountain, Cunnamulla.

A 'Queenslander', Cunnamulla.

1 CUNNAMULLA

Cunnamulla is the administrative centre for the vast Paroo Shire which covers about 47 617km² of south-west Queensland. With a population of 1600, Cunnamulla is significantly larger than the other three towns – Eulo, Yowah and Wyandra – in the shire.

Cunnamulla has a distinct old world charm. The hotels in the main street have remained unchanged for over half a century, the shops still have a pre-supermarket feel to them, and the tree-lined streets evoke the world of the country town long past.

Around 200 bird species have been recorded in the area.

There is an interesting historical museum in the Shire Hall at 49 Stockyard Street and, if you continue to the southern end of the street, about two blocks beyond the Council Offices, there is a solitary tree on a sand dune where the bank robber Joseph Wells hid after robbing the local bank. Wells' escape was, however, short-lived. The locals, whose money he had stolen, chased him and he was captured.

2 EULO

Leave Cunnamulla heading west on Louise St. Cross the river and drive for approximately 68km to Eulo on the Bulloo Developmental Rd.

Eulo has little more than one pub and one general store and yet it has a charm which makes it something more than just another outback Queensland town.

As you enter Eulo, on the right before the Eulo Queen Hotel, is the famous 'Paroo Track' which is where the world lizard-racing championships are held each August. Called the Cunnamulla–Eulo Festival of Opals, it occurs in late August to early September. The Herbie Trophy is awarded for the fastest time; the world record was set in 1983 by a lizard named 'Spikey' at a time of 1.2 seconds.

Notices to potential participants include the lizard race conditions: 'The lizard race will be conducted under the provisions of the Nature Conservation Act which precludes the private capture, keeping, or racing of lizards other than those covered by the prescribed conservation plan.'

At the left-hand side of the track is a piece of granite with a plaque which reads:
'Cunnamulla–Eulo Festival of Opals. "Destructo" champion racing cockroach accidentally killed at this track (24.8.1980) after winning the challange (sic) stakes against "Wooden Head" champion racing lizard 1980. Unveiled 23.8.81'.

the period, including a kitchen cupboard made out of piano cases, and there is also an extensive collection of dolls.

7 THE AUSTRALIAN WORKERS HERITAGE CENTRE

Return west along Bauhinia St past Maple, Beech and Willow sts to Box St (Capricorn Highway). Turn right here and drive the seven blocks to Ash St. Turn right again and you will find the Australian Workers Heritage Centre which is located in Ash St.

Barcaldine is divided over the issue of the Australian Workers Heritage Centre, which was opened in May 1991 to commemorate the centenary of the Shearers' Strike. It claims to be a celebration of Australia's labour history but many residents feel that because it was an initiative from outside the local community, it lacks local appeal.

This is perhaps best demonstrated by the fact that the exhibitions presently include 'Labour in Politics', an initiative from the State Archives and Queensland Library, and a 'Recreation of the Legislative Assembly' which has been provided by the parliament of Queensland. There are also other exhibits such as 'The Powerworkers' (an initiative of the Queensland Electricity Commission) and 'The One-Teacher School' (from the Department of Education). Visitors who are interested in seeing the way working people have shaped the history of Australia (and particularly Queensland) will find much of interest in this unusual site, including a film showing in the Australian Bicentennial Theatre and a photographic display.

8 ARAMAC

Leave the Australian Workers Heritage Centre and turn right into Willow St. Continue to the Landsborough Highway (Oak St). Cross the highway and railway line and the road becomes the main Barcaldine–Aramac Rd. Travel 67km to Aramac.

Aramac is a tiny little settlement which supports the surrounding pastoral industries and sustains a small local community.

The area around Aramac was first explored and settled in the 1850s. The town was named after Robert Ramsay Mackenzie who became Queensland's first treasurer and later, premier.

William Landsborough who explored the area in 1859 called a nearby watercourse Aramac Creek. In a letter he explained: 'The Aramac, as many wrong reasons for the name have been given, I may say here I named, in honour of the late Sir R R Mackenzie, "Ar-Ar-Mac", who was so well known in Queensland, and who had acted in a very friendly way to me'. The name stuck.

The area was settled in the 1860s and the town, which seems to have had the alternative name of 'Marathon' for a brief period, acquired a pub, a grocery and drapery.

The town was surveyed in 1875 but by that time the wide streets had already been established (apparently one of the locals had been impressed by the streets in Melbourne and had decided to copy them) and the surveyor simply confirmed the strangely disproportionate design.

9 ARAMAC'S TRAMWAY

Entering Aramac the railway sidings are located to the right about 100m from the road.

In 1909, Aramac Shire Council, still isolated from the surrounding area, borrowed £66 500 and built a tramway connecting the town to the main railway line at Barcaldine. It operated until 1975 and is now one of the town's few tourist attractions. The display of rolling stock is located in a large shed on the southern side of town. It is open from 9:00–16:00 each day and a key can be obtained from the Shire Council Offices.

10 MUTTABURRA

Leave Aramac, heading north-west for about 85km to reach Muttaburra.

The small town of Muttaburra was the scene of one of the most daring acts of cattle duffing ever performed in Australia. In fact, the Mount Cornish homestead was built as an outstation to Bowen Downs to prevent any further cattle duffing.

The history of Muttaburra is really the history of Harry Redford: a tale of daring, chicanery and the outback's admiration for a criminal bushman. Redford was born in the Hawkesbury River district of New South Wales in 1842. By the time he was a teenager, he was working as a drover and by 1870 he was in central western Queensland working on the vast Bowen Downs station which then covered 1.75 million acres. The area upon which modern-day Muttaburra stands was at one end of this vast holding.

At the time Bowen Downs was running a herd of about 70 000 cattle and Redford felt that the station owners would never know if they were a thousand short on muster. He devised a plan to drove the cattle down the Coopers Creek into South Australia. He drove the cattle 1300km to the Blanche Water station in northern South Australia where he sold them for £5000. But the loss was noted and in February 1871 Redford was arrested and taken to Roma to be tried. Locals packed the courtroom. Of the 48

THE MUTTABURRASAURUS

Besides the story of Harry Redford, the dashing cattle duffer, Muttaburra's other claim to fame is the discovery in a nearby waterhole of the remains of a dinosaur, the *Muttaburrasaurus langdoni*. Discovered in 1963 by local grazier Doug Langdon during mustering work, it is by far the most complete dinosaur skeleton ever found in Australia. Related to the family Iguanodontidae (which is found on many continents), the Muttaburrasaurus is unique to the east of Australia and outback Queensland. A 10m-high replica of this 100-year-old dinosaur has been erected outside the Muttaburra Motors and Cafe.

Main Street, Muttaburra.

people called as possible jurors, 41 were dismissed because they were prejudiced. The evidence against Redford was overwhelming yet the jury, admiring his bushcraft, acquitted him. In April 1873 the governor of Queensland ordered that the criminal jurisdiction of the District Court at Roma be withdrawn for two years.

Leave Muttaburra heading west for 7km. The road to Longreach (see Tour 40) then turns south for 17km until it reaches a fork in the road. Take the left fork and continue for 105km on mostly dirt road to Longreach.

The Old Railway Station, Aramac.

CHAPTER 7
AROUND ROCKHAMPTON

42 HISTORIC ROCKHAMPTON

■ WALKING TOUR ■ 2KM ■ 2 HOURS ■ CULTURAL AND COMMERCIAL CENTRE

Rockhampton is one of the most impressive cities in Queensland. Wealth flowed into the city as a result of the goldmines in Mount Morgan. This walking tour of the city centre is a feast of great buildings.

Rockhampton's central business district, particularly the area around Quay Street (which is part of the National Estate) and also East Street, is one of Australia's most elegant streetscapes. The high concentration of beautiful old buildings, the tree-lined streets, the malls, the lazy Fitzroy River which flows beside Quay Street, all make this a delightful area.

Initially, the concentration of buildings in the area tends to overwhelm the visitor. The Rockhampton's Heritage brochure (available at the Tourist Information Centre in East Street Mall) lists 26 buildings of historical significance in three blocks of Quay Street and East Street, including Customs House, the Criterion Hotel and the former headquarters of the Mount Morgan Gold Mining Company. However, the reality is far more manageable. Before inspecting these superb buildings it is necessary to place the city in context.

Rockhampton is the unofficial capital of Central Queensland. The area around Rockhampton was first explored by Charles and William Archer who discovered and named the Fitzroy River (after Governor Charles Fitz Roy) on 4 May 1853. The Archers were actually of Scottish descent but their family had moved to Norway in 1825 and it is from their adopted country that they took the names Eidsvold and Berserker after which they named the local mountains. Charles Archer moved into the area in 1855 and the following year the New South Wales Government decided to establish a settlement near the mouth of the Fitzroy River. The site chosen was the rocky, upper navigable limit of the river. This offered an obvious, if somewhat unimaginative, name to the town. 'Rock' was quite simply attached to the English suffix 'Hampton' which denotes 'a place near water' (as in Northampton, Wolverhampton, and Southampton) to produce a name which meant 'place near the rocks in the river'.

The town grew rather slowly with the first store being built in 1856 and the first inn appearing about six months later. The discovery of gold at Canoona in 1858 resulted in a sudden influx of miners and prospectors. Although the rush was short-lived, it did ensure quite a dramatic increase in the local population; some people stayed to work on the surrounding cattle properties while others found work in the town. It is worth noting that when Queensland became an independent colony in 1859 the people of Rockhampton were eager to establish the area as an independent state.

Rockhampton continued to grow throughout the 19th century. It was very fortunate to be involved in a series of industries which ensured its continuing growth and prosperity. Wool gradually gave way to cattle, and today Rockhampton proudly declares itself the 'Beef Cattle Capital of Australia', with herds in the region numbering over two million. Reminders exist at both the northern and southern ends of town where the visitor is greeted by life-size statues of bulls in the median strip, and there is also a huge 'big bull' on top of a shopping complex at the southern end of town.

The city's early wealth was built on the gold which was discovered in the hinterland. The first wave of miners in the 1860s did not really have a major impact on the development of the city. It was the later discoveries, particularly those at Mount Morgan, that created the wealth out of which the city's stately buildings were constructed. In recent times Rockhampton has been sustained by the mining activities in the Bowen Basin where towns like Blackwater, Dysart and Moura produce vast quantities of coal, which is transported to the coast by rail and shipped overseas.

1 HARBOUR BOARD BUILDING

Start this walking tour of Rockhampton on Quay St between Stanley and Derby sts. The first and most impressive building, at the easterly end of the block, is the Harbour Board Building.

This elegant neo-Classic Revival building, designed by local architect J W Wilson and featuring elliptical arches and elaborate parapet detailing, was completed in 1896. The plainer buildings in the street highlight its grandeur and elegance.

2 BETWEEN DERBY AND WILLIAM STREETS

Continue along Quay St and on the corner of Quay and Derby sts are the Walter Reid Apartments.

The Walter Reid Apartments, completed in 1894, are an example of a typical Victorian building. Nearby is the Heron, Todd & White Valuers building which was completed in 1893 in a neo-Classic style and further along are the Colonial-style Avonleigh Chambers which were built in 1885. At 236 Quay Street is the neo-Classic Revival ABC building which was originally built in 1897 for the Mount Morgan Gold Mining company. These four buildings are all located between Derby and William streets on Quay Street.

Located on the corner of Quay and William streets is the Heritage Tavern. Built in 1898 as Mrs L Johnson's Commercial Hotel, the architect J W Wilson adopted a colonial style which is best exemplified by the superb iron columns and lacework on the three-storeyed narrow verandahs.

3 CUSTOMS HOUSE

Cross William St and on the next block you will find the Customs House.

Customs House in Quay Street is another example of Classic Revival architecture which was all the rage in Rockhampton around the turn of the century. Built between 1898 and 1901 of Stanwell sandstone, the building has an enormous copper dome and an elaborate semi-circular portico with a Corinthian colonnade. Customs House was designed by the Queensland Government architect, A B Brady, and is a powerful reminder of the importance that Rockhampton enjoyed as the major central-coast port around that time.

4 REES R & SYDNEY JONES – SOLICITORS

Continue west across Denham St and on the corner is the Rees R & Sydney Jones building.

Rees R & Sydney Jones – Solicitors was built in 1880 to a neo-Classic Revival design by the architect, F D Stanley. Originally constructed for the Queensland National Bank, its cast-iron balustrades and Corinthian columns make it a very distinctive and prominent corner building.

5 UNION TRUSTEE CHAMBERS

Passing Luck House (1862, extended 1880), Cattle House (1864, rebuilt 1898) and Medical Chambers (1886), you will reach The Union Trustee Chambers at 170 Quay St.

The Union Trustee Chambers (built in 1877) is one of the earliest of the elegant riverside buildings. Designed by the Rockhampton architect, J W Wilson, as a residence and surgery for Dr Callaghan, it is an important example of the Classic Colonial style with an interesting combination of Classic columns and cast-iron balustrading. It is regarded by the National Trust as a building of exceptional historical significance.

6 CRITERION HOTEL

After the Rockhampton Club (1887) and opposite the Fitzroy Bridge is the Criterion Hotel.

This prime site at the end of Quay Street near the Fitzroy Bridge was originally the location of Rockhampton's first hotel, the Bush Inn, which was built in 1857 and owned by Robert Parker. Such was the wealth which poured into Rockhampton in the 1880s that Parker's daughter, a Mrs Curtis, commissioned the architect J Flint to build this extraordinary and ostentatious three-storeyed neo-Classic Revival building in 1889. The colonnaded verandahs have hoods to protect the rooms inside from the harsh Queensland sun.

7 SUPREME COURT

Turn left along Fitzroy St and take the first left into the East Street Mall. On your right is the Supreme Court.

The Supreme Court is a typical dour, geometrically correct, Classic Revival building designed by G Connolly, the Government Architect. Set back from the street, the combination of the fine wrought-iron gates, the palm trees in the forecourt, the solid Ionic columns, and the pale sandstone make it a particularly impressive public building. It has been in continuous use for over 100 years, having been built in 1887.

8 ROCKHAMPTON POST OFFICE

Continue along East St and, on your right-hand side, at the intersection with Denham St, is the impressive Rockhampton Post Office.

Customs House on the banks of Fitzroy River.

This huge two-storeyed Classic Revival building which dominates the streetscape was also designed by G Connolly and constructed of Stanwell sandstone by Collins and McLean in 1895. The most striking features of the building are the superb colonnades, clock tower and belfry. The interior has been modernised but the facade and clock tower are a reminder of a time when Rockhampton could legitimately claim to be the capital of central Queensland.

9 MUNRO'S BOOKSHOP

Head west from the Post Office along East St Mall. Cross Fitzroy St (the Bruce Highway) and continue for another half block; Munro's Bookshop is on the left-hand side of the road.

The history of European settlement in Australia is so short that we often ignore the small achievements of families who establish businesses which become part of the local landscape. Within a decade of the establishment of Rockhampton there was a Munro's Bookshop in East Street. It was established in 1861 and the original owner, William Munro, was also the publisher of the first Rockhampton *Almanac* in 1865. There is still a Munro's Bookshop in East Street (it passed out of the family hands in 1924).

The walking tour is now complete. The city's tourist information office is in Quay St; the staff are very helpful and have numerous brochures on the important sites in the city and the surrounding region.

Historic William Street.

The Criterion Hotel, a heritage-listed building.

The Heritage Tavern, Quay Street.

43 EXPLORING BEYOND ROCKHAMPTON

■ DRIVING TOUR ■ 75KM ■ 1 DAY ■ PARKS, GARDENS AND CHURCHES

Beyond Rockhampton city there are a number of significant attractions including some important historic buildings, an Aboriginal cultural centre and several particularly attractive natural sites.

1 MATER HOSPITAL

Start your journey from the city centre, follow Fitzroy St south to George St and turn left. After 400m take the right branch along Gladstone St (the Bruce Highway) for 1.5km and turn right into Prospect St. The cemetery is on the left. At the end of the road turn left into Dawson St and take the first right into Ward St. Some 350m down the road is the Mater Hospital.

The Mater Hospital is a wonderfully ostentatious late-Victorian building. It was constructed in 1890 for John Ferguson (a local member of the Legislative Council) by the architect James Flint and boasts an elaborate tower, an impressive grand staircase and decorative rendering.

2 YUNGABA CENTRE

Continue a little further along Ward St. On the right, at the corner of Jessie St, is the Yungaba Centre.

The Yungaba Centre is another piece of Victorian overstatement and was also designed by James Flint. This time the owner was John Ferguson's daughter. Built in 1897, its grand colonial design and elaborate lacework make it one of the most interesting and dramatic residences in Rockhampton. Nearby is the home of the Boland family now known as Mr and Mrs Jeha's Residence, a classic Queensland colonial house elevated from the ground to let the cool summer breezes reduce the heat. The elaborate timberwork is a reminder of the superb craftsmanship which existed in central Queensland around 1898 when the house was built.

3 THE BOTANIC GARDENS, JAPANESE GARDENS AND ROCKHAMPTON ZOO

Turn left into Agnes St and take the first right into Spencer St, at the end of which is the entrance to the Botanic Gardens.

The Botanic Gardens were first developed in 1869 and boast a wide range of tropical and warm-climate plants. In 1982 separate Japanese Gardens were established. Across the road is the zoo which has monkeys, birds, emus, kangaroos and koalas.

The lush Rockhampton Botanic Gardens.

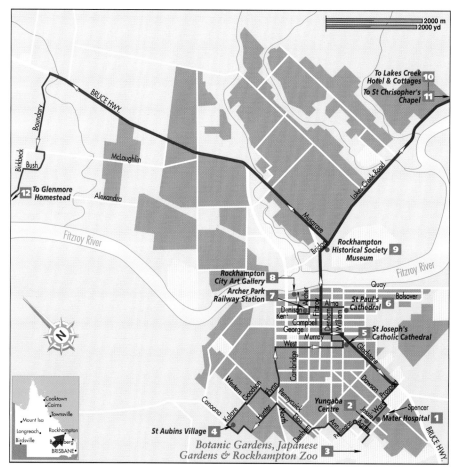

4 ST AUBINS VILLAGE

Leaving the grounds at Spencer St, take the first left into Agnes St. Turn left at the roundabout into Penlington St and drive to the end of the road. Turn right into Ann St, take the first left and follow Denham St, ignoring the left branch into Clarke St. Cross Pennycuick and Harrow sts. Turn right at Eton St and follow it for 800m. After crossing North St, take the immediate left into Hunter St. Follow the road until the intersection with Canoona Rd. Turn right into Canoona and keep following the road; the airport is on your left. After 1km, on the right-hand side, just before Kalare St is St Aubins Village.

St Aubins Village is a collection of five cottages set amongst the trees. It is run as an historical village. The centrepiece of the complex is a grand Spanish Colonial residence, designed and built in the 1870s by a German bricklayer named Roderkirchen who owned the local brickworks. He enthusiastically used bricks from his pit, resulting in walls of up to 18in thick.

This house has the distinction of being the first house in Rockhampton to be listed by the National Trust. The historical village is open from 9:00–18:00 daily.

5 ST JOSEPH'S CATHOLIC CATHEDRAL

From here, turn into Kalare St and then right into Western St. Take the first left turn into Goodson St. At the end, turn right and take the first left into Flynn St. Turn left into North St. After about 1km turn right into West St and follow it to its end. On the corner of West and William sts is the cathedral.

St Joseph's Catholic Cathedral was built of Stanwell sandstone in Victorian Gothic style in 1889–1890. A beautiful twin-spired building, its interior is characterised by a dramatic, large-scale timber-vaulted roof and some particularly lovely joinery work.

6 ST PAUL'S CATHEDRAL

Head north along William St and turn left into Murray St. Take the first right turn into Denham St. Cross over George, Campbell, Kent and Denison sts. Turn right into Alma St and at the intersection with William Street is St Paul's Cathedral.

St Paul's is another one of the Rockhampton buildings constructed out of Stanwell sandstone. Built between 1879 and 1883 in Classic Gothic style it was constructed in response to criticisms levelled against the previous, somewhat modest, church which

St Joseph's Cathedral, Rockhampton.

St Christopher's Chapel, built by American servicemen during World War II.

the locals felt was inferior to cathedrals in other Queensland towns. Building actually started as early as 1874 but came to an abrupt halt due to lack of funds. It commenced again in 1879 when Bishop Stanton laid the foundation stone and it was finally consecrated in 1883.

7 ARCHER PARK RAILWAY STATION

Turn back along Alma St, cross Denham and Fitzroy sts, and then turn left into Archer St. Take the first right turn into Denison St and on the right you will find the Archer Park Railway Station.

Archer Park Railway Station is an interesting old timber railway station (1899). It has a long front verandah with cast-iron columns, some attractive lace ironwork and an elaborate entry porch. There are plans to turn it into a railway museum.

8 ROCKHAMPTON CITY ART GALLERY

Continue along Denison St and take the first right into Cambridge St which intersects with Victoria Parade. On the left corner is the Rockhampton City Art Gallery.

It is claimed that this gallery has one of the best collections of Australian art outside the major state capital city galleries. The collection includes major works by Fred Williams, Jeffrey Smart, Sidney Nolan, Clifton Pugh and John Perceval. There is also a collection of contemporary Australian ceramics.

9 ROCKHAMPTON HISTORICAL SOCIETY MUSEUM

Head back along Cambridge St and take the first left into Bolsover St. After crossing Archer St turn left into Fitzroy St, cross the bridge and take the right fork into Bridge St. On the right, at the corner of the first crossroads, is the Rockhampton Historical Society Museum.

This delightful colonial building was completed in 1885 for the North Rockhampton Borough Council. The Museum contains an interesting collection of memorabilia from the area and is open from 10:00–14:00 on Tuesdays and Thursdays and also from 14:00–17:00 on Sundays.

10 LAKES CREEK HOTEL AND COTTAGES

Continue along Bridge St and cross Musgrave as it becomes Lakes Creek Rd. Follow the road for about 5km crossing the bridge over Lakes Creek. Continue on the road, past Vestey and Hill sts, turn to the right past the railway station, cross over the railway tracks and follow what is now the Emu Park–Yeppoon Rd for about another kilometre.

On the left is the Lakes Creek Hotel, a typical central Queensland pub dating from the turn of the century. Just up the road, to the left and right, are the interesting Lakes Creek Cottages which were built for local meatworkers in the 1880s.

11 ST CHRISTOPHER'S CHAPEL

Continue along the road for about 4km then turn to the right at the signpost to St Christopher's and follow the road until you reach the banks of the Fitzroy River and St Christopher's Chapel.

St Christopher's Chapel is an unusual open-air, non-denominational church which was built in 1943 by American servicemen stationed in the area. Built from bush timber with a concrete floor and corrugated-iron roof, it is a modern church made from simple, inexpensive materials. A special memorial service is held each year on the closest Sunday to the 4th of July, American Independence Day.

12 GLENMORE HOMESTEAD

Return along Lakes Creek Rd to the Historical Society Museum and then turn right into Musgrave St. After about 1.5km the street joins with the Bruce Highway. About 4km along the highway is a left turn into Boundary Rd. At the end of this road, turn left into McLaughlin Rd and take the first right into Bush Crescent. At the end turn left into Birkbeck Dve. This road becomes Alexandra St. Follow it for a short distance and then turn left into Belmont Rd where you will find the Glenmore Homestead on the left.

Glenmore Homestead is one of the many interesting old buildings in the rural hinterland around Rockhampton. Classified by

the National Trust, the homestead complex consists of the original log cabin (built in 1858) which is an excellent example of the primitive style of construction adopted by the early settlers. It boasts log walls, slab flooring and a shingle roof. There is also a slab house which was once a bush inn and a stone and adobe house built by a Mexican stonemason in 1862.

Glenmore homestead has won a number of awards and has been turned into a tourist complex which is so much more than a collection of old buildings and memorabilia: it serves damper, hosts wedding receptions, and also holds bush dinner-dances every Saturday night. There are daily guided tours at 11:00, 13:00, 14:00 and 16:00 from Sunday to Thursday. For more details contact tel: (079) 36 1033.

Return to Rockhampton via the Bruce Highway.

The verandah, Glenmore Homestead.

Interior, Glenmore Homestead.

44 THE COAST EAST OF ROCKHAMPTON

■ DRIVING TOUR ■ 186KM ■ 1 DAY ■ SINGING SHIPS AND ABORIGINAL HERITAGE

The coast to the north-east of Rockhampton is not only exceptionally beautiful, it can also, with the area around Yeppoon, claim to be the site of one of Australia's first tourist resort developments.

1 EMU PARK

To reach Emu Park, leave Rockhampton along Fitzroy St, cross the Fitzroy Bridge, take the right-hand fork and travel along Lakes Creek Rd for 45km.

Emu Park is a quiet little resort south of Yeppoon that was established in 1888. The first European to visit this attractive spot was Captain James Cook who sailed past the area some time between 25 May and 27 May 1770. He experienced some difficulty with the shallowness of the water. During this time he named Great Keppel Island and Keppel Bay (after Admiral August Keppel) as well as Cape Capricorn.

Today Emu Park is passed through by travellers who take the circular scenic route from Rockhampton to Yeppoon. The town itself is relatively undeveloped with only a couple of motels and a few shops. Even the tourist attractions are somewhat limited.

2 SINGING SHIP

Coming into Emu Park from Rockhampton, pass the golf club on your right and then the State School on your left. You will cross Fountain St and find yourself in what is now Hill St. Drive virtually to the end of this street, taking the last right into Emu St. Turn left at the end of the road. A short distance from the parking lot is the Singing Ship.

The great attraction of Emu Park is the remarkable Singing Ship sculpture in Kele Park on the headland south of the main beach. It is dedicated to James Cook who named Keppel Bay on 27 May 1770.

The Singing Ship sculpture really works. It sings almost constantly because of the on-shore breezes. The effect, particularly on

a clear day when the white ship gleams in the sun, is quite stunning. The design was the idea of Mrs C M Westmoreland who won a local competition aimed at commemorating the 200th anniversary of Cook's discovery of Australia. The construction was by S W Kele, a Rockhampton steel and concrete contractor after whom the park is named, and the specific engineering and acoustic problems were handled by George Cain and David Thomas from the Capricornia Institute of Advanced Education. It is a notable and very interesting landmark.

3 KINKA BEACH AND THE CORAL LIFE MARINELAND

Drive back along Emu St and turn left into Hill St. Take the first right into Pattison St and follow it north until it becomes the Emu Park Rd (sometimes known as the Scenic Highway). Continue along the road for 5km.

On the southern outskirts of Kinka Beach is the Coral Life Marineland which is one of the few 'tourist attractions' in the area. Kinka Beach is delightfully peaceful and unspoilt. The surrounding country is well known for its mangoes, bananas, lychees,

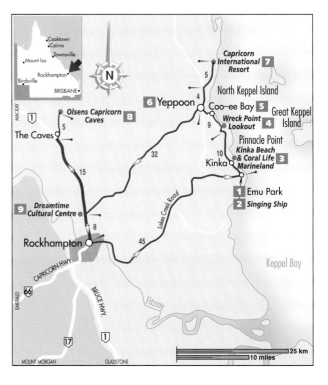

pineapples, macadamia nuts and paw paws. The beach itself has excellent camping facilities and Causeway Lake, situated at the northern end of the beach, not only has canoes and paddle boats for hire but is also the ideal location for windsurfing, swimming and fishing.

4 WRECK POINT LOOKOUT

Continue heading north along the Scenic Highway. After driving for about 5km turn right into Matthew Flinders Dve. Approximately 700m further on, the drive reaches the ocean at Wreck Point Lookout.

At various points along the Scenic Highway there are excellent views across to Great Keppel and North Keppel islands. There are easy walks to the shoreline at Pinnacle Point (situated just north of the causeway), at Bluff Point National Park and at Rosslyn Head and Double Head National Park which lie at the southern end of Yeppoon. Wreck Point Lookout affords magnificent views of all the major islands which lie off the coast from Yeppoon, including Great Keppel and North Keppel.

5 COO-EE BAY

Follow Matthew Flinders Dve for another 500m then take the right-hand branch into The Esplanade. On the right are Coo-ee Bay and Coo-ee Beach.

Each year at Coo-ee Beach there is a coo-ee-ing competition. This rather extraordinary event also includes such all-Australian

Causeway Lake near Kinka Beach.

The Singing Ship, Emu Park.

View along the coast from the Singing Ship.

activities as gum-leaf blowing, husband calling, bottle-top flicking, and a myriad equally unusual activities.

However, for all the apparent appeal of the area it is worth remembering that it is prone to the dangers of the tropics. A sign on the Yeppoon beaches declares:

WARNING. Swimmers are warned that potentially deadly marine stingers may be present in these waters particularly between November and March.

People may be able to build beautiful resorts but this doesn't change the fact that during the summer months they can't swim in the dangerous waters.

6 YEPPOON

At the northern end of The Esplanade is a left-hand turn into Cliff Lane. Follow this back into Matthew Flinders Dve and turn right. This takes you back to Scenic Dve. Turn right, cross the bridge and continue through the roundabout; follow the bend to the right until it ends in Anzac Parade and turn left.

It is hard to imagine that the Ross family, the first settlers, arrived in 1865 and that the area, for well over 100 years, was really nothing more than a fruit-growing (pineapples), timber and cattle area. The town of Yeppoon was surveyed in 1867 but the road from Rockhampton was only completed in the 1870s. The Yeppoon Sugar Company was established in 1883 and by 1910 the railway had arrived.

Today, Yeppoon is a holiday resort which has grown in popularity due to the extraordinarily successful advertising campaign associated with Great Keppel Island, and the growing awareness that Yeppoon is surrounded by attractive beaches where, for most of the year, the swimming is good and the living is easy. It is basically a series of flat, firm-sand, well-developed beaches accessed via good roads.

In spite of this apparent holiday atmosphere there is also a real sense that Yeppoon is a commuter belt for Rockhampton. With more than 8000 permanent residents it is obviously much more than a holiday resort.

The first holiday homes in the Yeppoon area were built by Rockhampton people eager to escape the city or by people from the south who found the peace and quiet of the area refreshing.

7 CAPRICORN INTERNATIONAL RESORT

Head north along Anzac Parade – this road becomes the road to Byfield. About 4km from Yeppoon there is a very clearly signposted road which will take you north-east to the Capricorn International Resort.

Yeppoon first came to the attention of Australians when the Capricorn International Resort was established nearby. It was one of the first exclusive Japanese resorts on the Queensland coast and was the idea of businessman Mr Iwasaki, who saw the potential of the site as early as 1972 but his application for development was opposed and building did not start until 1979. Used mainly by honeymooning Japanese couples, it is planned to become a 12 000-room complex, complete with golf courses, swimming, parklands and animal sanctuaries. It covers 8500ha and has 15km of beach.

8 OLSENS CAPRICORN CAVES

Return to Yeppoon the way you came. Once back on Anzac Parade, turn right into James St, opposite the Surf Life Saving Club, then turn left just before the end of the street, into Park St. At the street's end, turn right into Rockhampton Rd. After 32km you will reach the

Bruce Highway. Turn north away from Rockhampton and continue for 15km. Follow the signs to Olsens Capricorn Caves, turning right off the highway through the small Caves township, with the school on your left, and follow the road for 5km.

The 16 above-ground dry caves were first discovered by John Olsen, a Norwegian migrant, in 1882 and have the distinction of being the oldest tourist attraction in Queensland. The Capricorn Caves were opened to the public two years later. Formed from an ancient coral reef some 380 million years ago, the caves are privately owned and are therefore used for such unlikely activities as weddings and parties. They are refreshingly cool on hot days and surrounded by a fauna sanctuary where you are likely to see ducks, wallabies and kangaroos. There is also a swimming pool. There are daily 60-minute walking tours every hour on the half hour between 8:30 and 16:30.

9 THE DREAMTIME CULTURAL CENTRE

Return to the Bruce Highway and head south until you reach the Yeppoon turn-off to your left. Opposite this is the Dreamtime Cultural Centre.

This is one of the most interesting and unusual of all the attractions at Rockhampton. Set in beautiful gardens, which include a small waterfall and pond, the centre aims to introduce visitors to the culture of Central Queensland Aborigines and the peoples of the Torres Strait Islands. This is not done through the customary displays of corroborees and didgeridoo playing but rather through conducted tours which explain the way the Aborigines used the plants of the area and how they built their dwellings. The stories of the Darumbal peoples are also told, and some of the artefacts from the surrounding area are displayed.

The building at the centre of the park was constructed to recreate a cave in the Carnarvon Gorge National Park which, according to Aboriginal legend, is haunted by an old Aborigine who only appears to women. He apparently lost his wife to a young man and is doomed to spend eternity trying to find her again. The centre is open from 10:00–17:30 daily except on Sundays.

Return to Rockhampton along the Bruce Highway, travelling south for 8km to the city centre.

Rosslyn Bay Boat Harbour, Yeppoon.

45 HISTORIC MOUNT MORGAN

■ DRIVING TOUR ■ 78KM ■ 1 DAY ■ EXPLORING A GOLDMINING TOWNSHIP

The elegance and style of Rockhampton's historic buildings is a direct result of the wealth that flowed into the city from Mount Morgan, one of the finest of Australia's 19th-century goldmining towns.

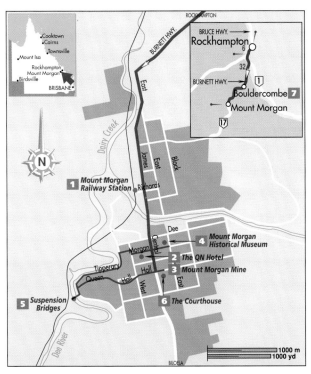

The well-maintained Mount Morgan Courthouse.

Mount Morgan must surely be the most charming mining town in Australia with a history which reaches back to the late-19th century. Its wooden houses are scattered over the hills and valleys and its eccentric character is preserved in the huge timber pubs (the QN, or Queensland National, is a real joy) and the mining relics in the median strips: outside the museum is a railway signal and some railway lines from the rack railway; around the corner is a steam engine, an old lamp and some dray wheels.

Mining began at Mount Morgan in 1882 and has continued for over 100 years. The town was named after Frederick, Edwin (Ned) and Thomas Morgan who, on 22 July 1882, pegged out a gold-mining claim on Ironstone Mountain (later renamed Mount Morgan). At the time of their lease the Morgan brothers were all living in Rockhampton.

Europeans had been in the area since the 1850s and a local stockman, William Mackinlay, discovered that the Ironstone Mountain was gold-bearing around 1870, but he kept his discovery secret, hoping to sell his knowledge. The Morgans, with some Rockhampton businessmen, formed a six-man partnership to mine the mountain. They all became fabulously wealthy. One of the partners in the syndicate was Thomas Skarrat Hall whose brother's widow donated a portion of the Mount Morgan fortune to a fund which established the famous Walter and Eliza Hall Institute of Medical Research in Melbourne.

The Mount Morgan syndicate lasted until 1886 when the Mount Morgan Gold Mining Company Limited was formed. The town was officially proclaimed in 1890 and in 1898 the railway arrived.

By 1902, gold, silver and copper were being mined. Throughout the 20th century the mine has experienced the fluctuations typical of the industry. Production peaked before World War I but declined after the war and by 1927 the company was in liquidation.

The newly formed Mount Morgan Ltd company bought the mine for the sum of £70 000 in 1929 and started mining by the open-cut method. It was subsequently bought out by Peko Wallsend in 1968 and by the 1970s the mine's production of copper was second only to that of Mount Isa.

The mine was closed down in 1981 – operations nowadays consist only of extracting gold from the tailings.

1 MOUNT MORGAN RAILWAY STATION

Head south out of Rockhampton on the Bruce Highway. About 6km south of Rockhampton, turn west onto the Burnett Highway (Route 17). Proceed along this road for 32km until the highway enters the town of Mount Morgan. Entering the town from the north, take the turn-off to the Railway Hotel and the bridge over the Dee River. The station is located behind the Railway Hotel and is clearly signposted.

Mount Morgan Railway Station (1898) is a charming timber building with a beautiful porch entrance. The railway from the coast had to travel up a gradient of 1:16.5 at the

sharp hill called the Razorback outside the town; consequently a special Abt rack locomotive (the first in Australia) was purchased and a toothed rack rail was built between the two normal rails so that the trains could get extra traction when they were going up and down the Razorback. A section of this special toothed rack railway line is displayed on the median strip in front of the Mount Morgan Historical Museum in Morgan Street. The Mount Morgan Tourist Information Centre is located in the Railway Station. It is the most sensible place to start exploring the town.

2 THE QN HOTEL

Return to the main road and follow it over the bridge and through the town. Turn right into Morgan St; not far along on the left, at No. 28, is the QN Hotel.

The QN Hotel, which is well worth a visit, is the starting point for tours of the mines which are held at 12:45 on Mondays, Wednesdays, Fridays and Saturdays. Before departing, ask the publican of the QN for permission to climb up the hotel's tower which was manned during World War II to keep a lookout for Japanese aircraft. The stairs are rickety but the views over Mount Morgan are impressive.

Site of the old goldmine, Mount Morgan.

RUNNING THE CUTTER

On the corner of Central and Morgan streets there is a statue titled 'Running the Cutter'. It recalls the interesting custom, which was commonplace at the mine between 1900 and 1918, of buying beer in billy cans. The 'cutter' bought the beer and ran it to the miner so that work did not have to stop.

Mount Morgan, an open-cut mine now filled with water.

3 MOUNT MORGAN MINE

The only way to visit the Mount Morgan Mine is with a tour group which departs from the QN Hotel.

The Mount Morgan mine has a number of important historical buildings within its boundaries – the assay chimney, the manager's house, the treatment plant and the mine offices are all of historical importance. Tours of the mine provide an insight into the scale of production when Mount Morgan was at its peak.

4 MOUNT MORGAN HISTORICAL MUSEUM

Down the eastern end of Morgan St, at the intersection with East St, you will find the Mount Morgan Historical Museum.

Mount Morgan Historical Museum is an interesting mining and folk museum. It recalls the history of the town through a display of artefacts and memorabilia.

5 SUSPENSION BRIDGES

Head back along Morgan St until it intersects with West St. Turn right, take an immediate left and then turn left again into Tipperary Rd. Follow this road to its intersection with Queen St.

On the Dee River are two unusual swing, or suspension, bridges which were built in the 1890s to provide access to the mine from the town. During the 1890s there were six suspension bridges across the river but four of them have disappeared.

6 THE COURTHOUSE

Return to the township via Queen St (stop at the lookout). This will run into Hall St and, on your right-hand side, between the main road (Central St) and East St is the Courthouse.

The Courthouse, which was built in 1899, is an example of the formal Classic Revival style which was very fashionable at the time and it stands as a reminder of the status Mount Morgan enjoyed in its heyday. Today it seems much too ostentatious for this quiet, historic township.

7 BOULDERCOMBE

Return along Hall St and then turn right into Central St. Return to the Burnett Highway, heading back to Rockhampton. Bouldercombe is 17km away.

Bouldercombe is a tiny rural retreat which now consists of little more than a few houses with a pub; it is difficult to imagine that it was once quite an important gold-rush township. The only hint of its former glory is a real estate sign which announces the sale of blocks of land on the Goldfields Rural Residential Subdivision.

Bouldercombe was originally known as Crocodile Creek and it was here in 1865 that gold was discovered. Within a year it was a thriving township of 2000 miners, but the fortunes of the town waxed and waned. By 1876 the population had been reduced to 149 but, with the establishment of the Usher Reef mine in 1897, the population increased to over 1000. It dropped back only to be revitalised in 1934 by the establishment of the Crocodile Creek Gold Dredging Company which won 1100 oz of gold from alluvial washing in 1935. It was the largest gold extraction in the history of the field. The dredging operation stopped in 1946 and since then there has been no further mining in the Bouldercombe area. Today the only gold to be made is by the land developers hoping to attract people to live in this pleasant rural retreat.

The return journey to Rockhampton is via the Burnett and Bruce highways.

The main street, Mount Morgan.

Mount Morgan township.

46 COAL AND PRECIOUS STONES

■ DRIVING TOUR ■ 835KM ■ 2 DAYS ■ A WONDERLAND OF PRECIOUS STONES

People are drawn to the hills and plains inland of Rockhampton by the mineral wealth from the Bowen Basin and the allure of towns with romantic names like Sapphire, Rubyvale and Emerald.

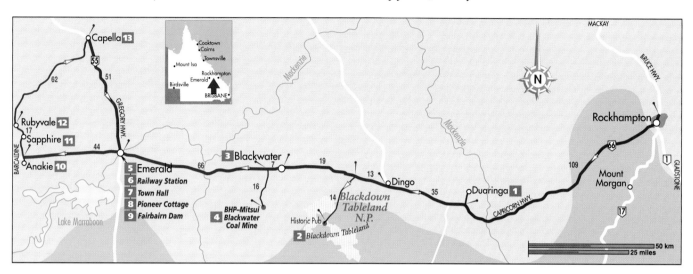

1 DUARINGA

Head south out of Rockhampton along the Bruce Highway (Route 1) and turn off onto the Capricorn Highway (Route 66). Follow this road for 109km. The road to Duaringa branches off the highway. The township itself is 7km along this road.

Duaringa is a tiny settlement of less than 500 people which came into existence as a base camp for railway workers. The town's role in the building of the railway was brief; the camp was set up in 1875, the railway arrived in 1876 and had moved through to Blackwater later that year.

2 BLACKDOWN TABLELAND

Return to the Capricorn Highway and continue west for another 62km to the central attraction in the Duaringa area (apart from the pub, some sections of which date back to the 1880s), the Blackdown Tableland to the south-west of the hamlet of Dingo.

Blackdown Tableland National Park is characterised by waterfalls, dramatic cliffs, excellent bushwalks, and Aboriginal rock art near the upper end of the Mimosa Creek. The park has six major walks including the Mimosa Creek Culture Circuit which passes Aboriginal stencil art, the Rainbow Falls walk and the Stony Creek Gorge walk.

BLACKWATER AIRPORT

For those interested in mining history the Blackwater airport has a display of mining equipment dating from the 1920s and 1930s when the Rangal Mine was in operation. A gas explosion in 1934, which killed four miners, saw the mine close down.

---

3 BLACKWATER

Return again to the Capricorn Highway and turn left. Travel a further 19km from the junction and you will find the township of Blackwater.

The visitor might well think Blackwater consists of nothing more than a few petrol stations and motels as the highway skirts around the southern edge of the town. However, behind the motels and roadhouses lies a town which was originally designed to hold 20 000 people. It currently has a population of around 8000, nearly all of whom work for the five mines located nearby.

The first person to discover the coal deposits at Blackwater was Ludwig Leichhardt who observed the 'beds of coal indistinguishable from those on the Hunter at Newcastle' about 27km from the present site of Blackwater.

The township, named after the local waterholes which seemed to have black water in them, was laid out in 1886 after the railway had come through the area. In 1959–1960 coking coal was found south of the town. A mining lease was granted in 1965, and in 1967 the first mine in the area started operating. It is claimed that in 1962 the town's population was only 25.

4 BHP-MITSUI BLACKWATER COAL MINE

Continue along the Capricorn Highway. About 7km outside Blackwater there is a signpost indicating the road to the BHP Mine to the left. Follow this road for 2km to reach the airport. Another 14km south along this road is the BHP Mine.

Tours of the BHP-Mitsui Blackwater Coal Mine are held every Wednesday at 10:00. It is a good idea to book in advance on tel: (079) 86 0666. There is no point in going out there on other days as the Observation

Deck behind the Administration Building gives no insights into the open-cut mining process – you can't even see the open cut.

5 EMERALD

Return to the Capricorn Highway and turn left. Head west for about 66km to enter Emerald.

Emerald is a typical thriving rural centre with a rural training college, a large number of farm machinery sales outlets, a cotton gin, a huge irrigation dam and an airport. Established in 1879 it has slowly grown to be the major regional centre in the Central Highlands and the gateway to the flatter Central Western region.

In the 1860s both gold and copper were found in the area and there was a brief flurry of interest. The town was established in 1879, but very little is left of its early history as there were major fires in 1936, 1940, 1954 and 1968.

6 EMERALD RAILWAY STATION

Follow the Capricorn Highway across the bridge over the Nogoa River where it becomes Clermont St. The station is on the left, 700m from the bridge.

Of all the buildings in Emerald, and indeed, in the Central Highlands, the most impressive is undoubtedly the Emerald Railway Station in Clermont Street. Classified by the National Trust and made out of chamferboard, the station boasts an elaborate central entry porch with much iron lacework and impressive cast-iron columns.

7 EMERALD TOWN HALL

Just past the station, along Clermont St, is a right turn into Anakie St. The first crossroad is Egerton St and across the road to the right is Emerald Town Hall.

Outside the Emerald Town Hall is a piece of fossilised wood estimated to be around

250 million years old. It was dug up in 1979 when a new railway bridge was being built across the Mackenzie River.

8 EMERALD PIONEER COTTAGE

Continue heading north along Anakie St until it intersects with Harris St and then turn right. The first cross street is Borilla St. Continue along Harris St and take the next left into Centenary Dve. A little up the road on the left is the Pioneer Cottage.

The Emerald Pioneer Cottage was built as a shop on Clermont Street around 1880. Moved to its present site in the 1980s, it is now part of a small historical village which includes the town's lockup (built in 1910 and in operation until 1970), St Mark's Presbyterian Church (built in 1884) and a Communications Museum which has important memorabilia tracing the history of the town's communications.

9 FAIRBAIRN DAM

Return along Centenary Dve, Harris Dve and Anakie St to Clermont St (the Capricorn Highway) and turn right. Continue for just over 1km, past Apex Park and the showgrounds, which are both on the right, and turn left into King St. Cross Douglas St almost immediately. Just across Douglas Street is a right-hand turn into Selma Rd. Head along Selma Rd and follow the signposts to Fairbairn Dam.

Emerald would have remained a small town had it not been for the decision in 1948 by the British Food Corporation to grow sorghum in the area. It was quickly realised that the rich black soils were ideal for crop growing and, to strengthen the agricultural base of the area, the huge Fairbairn Dam, located south of the town on the road to Springsure, was built in 1972. It has helped the area grow so that it now produces over 25 per cent of Queensland's cotton, and has been instrumental in seeing the whole shire move from cattle to crops.

The vast waters of Lake Maraboon, dammed by Fairbairn Dam, are a popular leisure haunt for the Emerald townsfolk.

10 ANAKIE

Return to Emerald. Head west on the Capricorn Highway for about 44km and turn left at the signpost for Anakie, 1km from the main road.

Anakie is a gem-fossicking settlement. The streets, the gardens and houses and the social activities all pale into insignificance when compared to the efforts invested in digging up sapphires and rubies.

Anakie has very little to offer apart from the hotel/motel, a railway station, a few houses (most of which have signs inviting visitors to come and inspect the gems) and a few unimportant roads.

It is generally accepted that Europeans first discovered gemstones in the Anakie region when Archibald John Richardson found zircons at Retreat Creek in 1875. The following year a prospector found sapphires in the area and by 1881 commercial mining operations had begun.

In 1902 the Anakie Sapphire Fields were officially proclaimed a mining area and over the next 30 years the three settlements of

Cotton fields near Emerald.

Anakie, Sapphire and Rubyvale grew to meet the demands of the miners who, when the prices were high, poured into the area.

A boom occurred which lasted from 1906 until the outbreak of World War I. In 1907 over £40 000 worth of gems were mined. By 1953 there were only 21 full-time miners working in the area. Today the fields are a true combination of dreams and hopes with fossickers, tourists and machine operators all vying for the beautiful stones. It is indicative of the harshness of the area that electricity only arrived in 1977.

11 SAPPHIRE

To reach Sapphire, turn right off the Capricorn Highway. Travel north for 9km to this tiny settlement. The road winds past a number of miners' residences.

On the way to Sapphire the trees are emblazoned with signs advertising such exotic places as 'Luke's Sapphires', 'Old Mick's Gem Shop' (located on the marvellously named Goanna Flats Road), 'Pat's Gems', 'Rainbow Treasure', 'Cut-a-slice Lapidary Supplies', 'Ransom Mine – Find Your Own Sapphires' all promoting themselves as *the* place to visit while on the gem fields.

Sapphire consists of a playing field, a few isolated homesteads, a general store, a caravan park, and a few shops selling gems. It has a wonderfully temporary and transient feel suggesting that it might only exist for the next few minutes.

12 RUBYVALE

Continue a further 8km north to Rubyvale.

Between Rubyvale and Sapphire are the large-scale sapphire operations that use heavy equipment and convert the countryside into a bizarre moonscape as they dig relentlessly for the precious jewels.

Rubyvale is a slightly more substantial settlement with a small shopping centre and a pub. One of its major attractions is the Bobby Dazzler Mine (located beside the road into town) where visitors can go underground to search for gemstones.

13 CAPELLA

Travel north to Capella. The distance on an adequate road is approximately 62km.

The tiny township of Capella is located on the Gregory Highway. It is the headquarters of the Peak Downs Shire Council and the centre of the region's agricultural activity which includes the growing of a variety of grains (predominantly sorghum and wheat), sunflowers and beef cattle. There are also several coalmines in the area.

The Peak Downs area was settled by graziers in the early 1860s and the town of Capella came into existence with the arrival of the railway line in 1883.

From Capella, head south along the Gregory Highway (Route 55) for about 51km and then turn left to get back on to the Capricorn Highway It is about 263km back to Rockhampton.

'Pat's Gems', Sapphire.

Emerald Railway Station.

47 THE GLORIES OF CARNARVON GORGE

■ DRIVING TOUR ■ 469KM ■ 2 DAYS ■ BUSHWALKING AND ABORIGINAL HERITAGE

The Central Highlands of Queensland offer some of the state's most rewarding bushwalking, several spectacular displays of Aboriginal art and some of the most unspoilt scenery anywhere in Australia.

The Carnarvon Gorge area was first explored by Europeans when Major Thomas Mitchell passed through it in 1846, but such was the ruggedness of the terrain that it wasn't until around 1900 that cattlemen moved into the area. The local cattle duffers, the Kenniff brothers, used it as a suitable hideout but their occupation was brief. In 1932 the bulk of the Carnarvon Gorge National Park (65 000 acres – about 26 300ha) was proclaimed with another 1480 acres (600ha) being added in 1954. Today the park has been extended to cover over 223 000ha.

The centrepiece of the national park is the spectacular Carnarvon Gorge itself which runs for over 30km, varying in width from 40–400m. The gorge has vast stands of spotted gum, cabbage palm and cycads as well as ferns, elkhorns and lichens near the waterfalls.

The caves and cliff walls were a popular place for Aboriginal art and contain some of Australia's finest examples of paintings of hands, axes, emu tracks and boomerangs. Using the technique of blowing pigment over a stencil, the Aborigines painted on the walls in red ochre, and white, black and yellow pigments. The biggest displays of art are found in areas known as Art Gallery and Cathedral Cave.

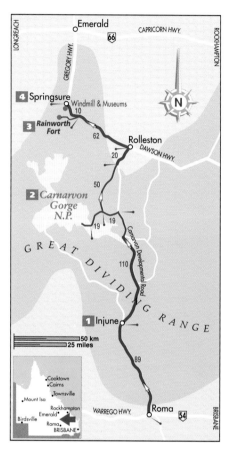

1 INJUNE

This journey starts at Roma, located some 479km west of Brisbane on the Warrego Highway. From Roma take the Carnarvon Developmental Rd and head north for 89km until you reach the tiny township of Injune, generally recognised as the southern entry point to the Carnarvon Gorge National Park. There is a dirt road from Injune less than 1km north of the town which heads north-west for 179km to the western Mount Moffatt section of the park. It is the most difficult entry and is not part of this journey, which basically provides access to the main Carnarvon Gorge area.

Injune is one of those quaint central west townships where it seems as though time has stood still. The signpost at the southern end of Injune announces that the town has an elevation of 1274 (which must be feet – it's certainly not metres), a population of 600, and lots of 'menities' including electricity (1955), water (1956) and sewerage (1962).

Historically the town is well known throughout the area as the home of some of the best cattle duffers in all of Australia. The Hidden Valley, nearby, was a place of some notoriety.

Virgin Rock, behind Springsure stockyards.

2 CARNARVON GORGE NATIONAL PARK

Travel north from Injune on the Carnarvon Developmental Rd for about 110km. Turn west on a winding dirt road and after a journey of 38km you will reach the Ranger's Lodge at the eastern edge of the park.

A visit to the Carnarvon Gorge National Park is a labour of love. It is also one of the most rewarding experiences for people looking for dramatic scenery, unspoilt Australian bushland and some of the best Aboriginal art in the country.

Both the Queensland National Parks and Wildlife Service and the RACQ (the Royal Automobile Club of Queensland) have brochures on the park. National Parks and Wildlife have described the area as a 'tangle of peaks, gorges, and sandstone cliffs ... one of the wildest regions of the central western section of Queensland'.

Camping is allowed and must be arranged in advance with the Park Ranger at tel: (079) 84 4505 or, for those requiring more creature comforts, there is the Carnarvon Gorge Oasis Lodge with both camping and cabin-style accommodation and a licensed dining room. Contact tel: (079) 84 4503 for more information.

There is a rich variety of walks in the area from the Lodge and the camping area to various amphitheatres, art galleries, caves and narrow side gorges. The most popular is the main walk up the gorge and, although it crosses the Carnarvon Creek 20 times between the Ranger Station and Big Bend, most of the crossings are made from stepping stones and the track is well established. Of particular interest on the walk is Wards Canyon which has a small waterfall cascading into a green gorge. The vegetation is

remarkable, and the gorge is home to the kings fern which is only found here, on Fraser Island and far to the north in the Daintree Forest. The fern is a survivor of a time when Queensland was much wetter and areas like the gorge were densely covered in rainforest. It is unreasonable to expect to spend only one day at the gorge, so if you are driving from Roma or Injune you should plan to spend the night and explore the gorge the next day.

3 RAINWORTH FORT

From the Ranger Lodge return 19km along the main dirt road out of the national park. When you come to the turn-off take the road to the north. Continue along this road for 50km and you will reach the final sealed section of the Carnarvon Developmental Rd. Take this road for a further 20km and you will reach the small township of Rolleston. Leave Rolleston on the Dawson Highway heading north-west towards Springsure. You are moving through an area which, in the 1860s, became famous for the violent conflicts between the newly arrived white settlers and the local Aborigines. About 62km north of Rolleston turn west and follow the signs to Rainworth Fort. This will mean continuing on the road for about 3km, turning right and continuing north for about 1km before turning west on Wealwandangie Rd. The sign to Rainworth Fort is on your right. Open the gate and continue towards the property for a couple of kilometres; the owners will see you approaching across the paddocks and will come to greet you.

Rainworth was one of the properties which came under continuous attack from the local Aborigines throughout the 1860s. The most famous property in the district is Cullin-la-ringo which is not open to visitors.

The Aboriginal resistance to the encroachment of Europeans was courageous and violent. At Cullin-la-ringo a group of Kairi warriors killed 19 people in the largest recorded massacre of whites in Australian history. It is likely that the massacre was prompted by a combination of frustration at the loss of land and as an act of revenge for the atrocities which were being committed with monotonous regularity by both the whites (who were eager to rid themselves of the Aborigines) and the dreaded native police who had stolen tribal women.

It is still possible to see the mass grave in which the victims were buried but the residents of the station discourage visitors because of their bad record of disturbing the livestock and being exceedingly careless with rubbish and fire. Ask at Rainworth Station for more details.

The massacre at Cullin-la-ringo occurred before any kind of permanent building had been constructed. However, this is not the case at Rainworth where it is still possible to see the slits where the original settlers mounted their guns during attacks.

It is not clear whether, as is suggested by the name 'fort', it was built to resist Aboriginal attack. Certainly it was designed as a storehouse, not a home. It is ironic that the massacre at Cullin-la-ringo was probably a result of an attack made on the local Aborigines by Jesse Gregson who, at the time, was manager of Rainworth Station.

A visit to Rainworth is well worthwhile. The owners are knowledgeable about local history and the property now includes both the Cairdbeign School (dating from 1896) and the Cairdbeign Homestead (a superb seven-roomed slab homestead dating from the 1870s) which were transferred from Nat Buchanan's Cairdbeign property lying to the south of Rainworth.

4 SPRINGSURE

Return to the main road from Rainworth Station and head north for 10km until you arrive at the outskirts of Springsure. On the way, if the season is right, you will notice vast fields of sunflowers which have become an important crop in the area in recent times. Before you enter the town you will notice a large windmill on the left-hand side of the road. Stop here, it is the Historical Association Museum.

Springsure is a typical and rather charming Queensland country town nestling below the Capricorn Highlands. The well-known local landmark, Mount Zamia, of which Virgin Rock is the most prominent feature, looms above the town.

The area around the town of Springsure was first explored by Ludwig Leichhardt during his 1844–1845 journey through central Queensland. Leichhardt's glowing reports of the area around the Comet River prompted graziers to move there.

Some kind of rather haphazard settlement sprang up at Springsure as early as 1859 although it wasn't until 1879 that it was surveyed and gazetted.

For people interested in finding out more about the local history, Springsure boasts two museums. The Historical Association Museum is at the southern end of town. It is simply an old slab hut which is unattended but open for inspection throughout the day (displays are behind strong netting).

In nearby Jaycees Park is a huge Pattern Comet Windmill which was built by the Sidney Williams Company of Rockhampton in 1935. The windmill has a diameter of 24ft (just under 7.5m) and the head weighs 2.4 tonnes. It was originally erected at Johnnies Bore on Cungello Station, near Springsure.

Continue into the township itself. The second museum, the Flyin' Horse Shoe Museum, is located in William Street. It has interesting displays of early memorabilia from the region.

The area around Springsure has quite a number of parks; the most notable is Virgin Rock which can be visited by travelling approximately 4km out of town on the Emerald road. There is also the Mount Zamia Environmental Park 4km to the west of the town on the Tambo road.

Continue north out of the town past Virgin Rock. After about 66km you will arrive in Emerald. If you want to continue, this trip joins with Tour 42.

Crossing 13, Carnarvon Creek.

Aboriginal art, Carnarvon Gorge.

The spectacular Carnarvon Gorge National Park.

48 AROUND GLADSTONE

■ DRIVING TOUR ■ 560KM ■ 2 DAYS ■ INDUSTRY, EXPORT AND HISTORICAL ATTRACTIONS

Gladstone is one of the largest and busiest ports in Australia. In the last three decades this once sleepy little port has become a busy centre with some of the most sophisticated loading facilities in the country.

The Gladstone area was first explored in 1770 by Captain Cook who, sailing north along the coast, sighted and named Bustard Head to the south of the city. Cook was followed in 1802 by Matthew Flinders, who named Port Curtis, and in 1848 Owen Stanley surveyed the entrance to the port.

The first settlement of Gladstone occurred in 1847. It was named after William Ewart Gladstone, British Colonial Secretary at the time; he would later become Prime Minister of Great Britain. Basically a penal colony, Gladstone was closed down less than a year later and it wasn't until 1854 that it was opened to free settlers.

The town's first wharf was built at Auckland Point in 1885 and it was connected to Brisbane by rail in 1897. By 1960 it still only had a population of 7200 and its economy was dependent on its importance as a port. Although it had the advantage of a superb natural harbour (Port Curtis), Gladstone remained a relatively small port serving the local cattle industry until 1961, when the export of coal from the Moura fields to the west resulted in a huge increase in both population and port activity.

Today Gladstone is Queensland's largest port and the second-largest port on the Australian east coast. It is also the home of the world's largest alumina plant. The production of aluminium requires huge amounts of electricity and thus the Queensland Electricity Commission's power station (fuelled by coal from the mines at Blackwater, Moura and Callide) produces more than half of the state's electricity. There is also a large cement and lime works.

In addition, the port of Gladstone exports vast quantities of coal and grain. The new grain-loading terminal moves over 1 million tonnes of grain each year and the coal-loading facilities are some of the most advanced in the world.

Having experienced most of its development since World War II, Gladstone's premier attractions tend to be either modern or scenic.

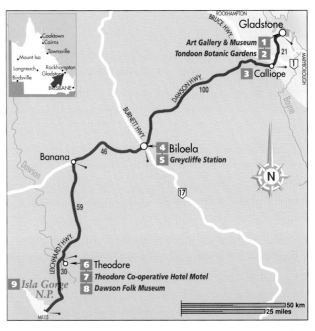

Gladstone Harbour from Auckland Hill.

1 ART GALLERY AND MUSEUM

The Art Gallery is located in the Old Town Hall at the roundabout, on the corner of Bramston and Goodoon sts, in the city centre.

The Gladstone Art Gallery and Museum is housed in an attractive Georgian-style Colonial building. It was opened in 1985 and hosts travelling art exhibitions as well as purchasing local art works and artefacts for an expanding collection.

2 TONDOON BOTANIC GARDENS

From the Art Gallery, drive through the roundabout south-west along Bramston St for 200m and turn left into Glenlyon St. Follow it for 6.5km to the Tondoon Botanic Gardens on the right.

The beautiful Botanic Gardens are located south of the city centre along Glenlyon Street. Completed as recently as 1982 they cover 55ha and include lakes, cascades, an herbarium and arboretum, and an interpretive nature trail.

3 CALLIOPE

Return north for about 3km along Glenlyon St to the large roundabout where Glenlyon meets Philip St and turn left. When Philip St reaches the Dawson Highway (Route 39), turn left and follow the highway for about 21km to Calliope.

Calliope is a small settlement located at the entrance to the Boyne Valley, that was Queensland's first officially proclaimed goldfield in 1863. It went through a period of decline, but in recent times has experienced a minor boom as a result of the increasing importance of Gladstone.

The town was named after the HMS *Calliope* in 1854. It was around this time that settlers moved into the area and alluvial gold was found. The goldfields were short-lived: the miners moved in during the early 1860s but the gold had been completely dug out before the end of the decade. After that the town continued as a service centre for the local beef industry.

Today the town of Calliope still attracts gold and gemstone fossickers and there are local deposits of petrified wood, chalcedony, porphyry and green jasper as well. The Diggers Arms pub was built during the gold boom and stands today as a reminder of the town's colourful past.

4 BILOELA

Travel a further 100km south-west along the Dawson Highway to reach Biloela.

Biloela – said to mean '(white) cockatoo' in the language of the local Aborigines – acts as a service centre for the surrounding area (it is also home to most of the miners at the nearby Callide coalmine). Its importance stems from its location at the point where the Dawson and Burnett highways meet.

The area around Biloela was first explored by Charles Archer in 1850 and the first settlers in the area established the Prospect Station in 1852 where the town now stands.

Coal was discovered in the region during the 1890s but it wasn't developed until 1944 when an open-cut mine was established on the site of the old Callide Station.

The town's economy is driven by the nearby mines and a healthy agricultural base which includes the cultivation of crops such as sorghum, wheat and cotton. It is also the centre of a cattle-breeding area.

5 GREYCLIFFE STATION

Entering Biloela, the Dawson Highway becomes Gladstone Rd. Pass parkland on the right and left. Just past the cemetery, on the left, before Lawrence St and the High School is Greycliffe Station.

Greycliffe Station, which is built of timber slab with a fine encircling verandah, has been re-sited from Rannes outside the town. It is a beautifully preserved slab hut dating back to the 1870s and has been converted into a museum by the local historical society.

6 THEODORE

Travel a further 46km west along the Dawson Highway to reach Banana. From here travel south along the Leichhardt Highway for 59km to Theodore, which lies 1km from the highway.

Theodore must be one of the most luxuriant-looking towns beyond the Great Divide. The first thing the visitor notices are the palm trees and tropical bushes growing in the broad median strip which runs down the Boulevard and which culminates in a large and gracious roundabout edged by a series of attractive, wooden buildings, including the local police station. This is no ordinary Queensland country town.

It is a town of considerable elegance and originality. But then any town which started its life as Castle Creek and ended up, by its own choice, being named after one of Australia's most controversial politicians, E G 'Red Ted' Theodore (Premier of Queensland 1919–1925 and Treasurer and Deputy Prime Minister 1929–1930), should be different from other places.

Castle Creek grew up as a tiny settlement serving the needs of the large properties in the Dawson Valley. In 1923 many of the larger properties in the area were taken over by the government, which planned to develop an elaborate irrigation system and sell smaller blocks of land for more intensive agriculture. The dream was to create a model garden city in the Dawson Valley wilderness and an area where 5000 irrigable farms would produce vast amounts of food for Australia and the rest of the world.

Theodore would be 'planned on the most modern lines ... Traversing the township from north to south is a spacious garden boulevard, intersected at intervals by avenues which have also been planted with palms and shade trees in such a manner as to lend a restful appearance to the scene ... in the centre of the town is an oval around which has been erected the residences for the accommodation of members of the Commissioners local staff ... the oval is laid out in lawns, in the centre of which stands a picturesque water tower 50 feet high, from

Queensland Alumina, the world's largest bauxite refinery, Gladstone.

which the town water supply is reticulated. The floor of the tower is arranged as a bandstand.' A new tower now supplies the town with treated water and, sadly, the bandstand has long since departed.

Theodore's irrigation project was officially opened in 1924. The plan was to build a dam over the Natham Gorge, but this was never constructed, and the water in the region was contained behind a number of smaller weirs. The Glebe Weir, about 30km east of the town, can be seen from the road and is a popular and attractive picnic spot. Theodore was the first irrigation project in Queensland and the government, determined to succeed, had built a settler accommodation house for all new arrivals to the area. The settlers moved out to the holdings and gradually the town became the centre of a successful experiment.

Today Theodore continues to succeed because of the rich black soils of the area and the irrigation which is provided from the Dawson River. Apart from sheep and cattle, the area also produces sorghum, wheat and cotton.

There are quite a number of interesting buildings in the town. The Catholic Church and residence, located in the main street just before 7th Avenue, is an example of Queensland vernacular wooden architecture; as is one of the few reminders of the town's original name, the Castle Creek Theatre, also on the Boulevard between 5th and 6th Avenues.

7 THEODORE CO-OPERATIVE HOTEL MOTEL

Continue along the Boulevard, past 3rd Ave. The Co-operative Hotel Motel is to the right, heading south.

Theodore Co-operative Hotel Motel is literally owned by the townsfolk. The profits from the hotel are still used to fund community activities and projects.

8 DAWSON FOLK MUSEUM

Continue along the Boulevard to 2nd Avenue and turn right. The Dawson Folk Museum is located in the street behind the hotel.

The Dawson Folk Museum has a huge collection of memorabilia from the area, including the old telephone exchange, pieces of farm and domestic equipment, and photographs recalling the town's early history.

9 ISLA GORGE NATIONAL PARK

Return north up the Boulevard and continue to the Leichhardt Highway. Turn left and head along the highway for another 30km, to Isla Gorge National Park.

Located on the eastern section of the central Queensland highlands, the main gorge can be conveniently reached on a 1.4km dirt road which runs off the main Theodore–Taroom road. It is very beautiful and unspoilt with dramatic cliffs, deep sandstone gorges and some fine examples of Aboriginal hand paintings. There is a campsite at the entrance of the park.

Return to the Leichhardt Highway and follow it north for approximately 90km until it rejoins the Dawson Highway at Banana. It is 167km north-east along the highway to Gladstone.

The Gladstone Power Station.

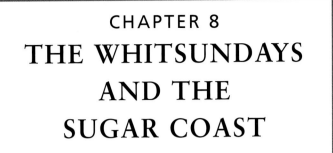

CHAPTER 8
THE WHITSUNDAYS
AND THE
SUGAR COAST

49 CRUISING THROUGH THE WHITSUNDAYS

■ BOAT TOUR ■ 185KM ■ 1 DAY ■ EXPLORING THE GLORIES OF THE GREAT BARRIER REEF

The Whitsundays, a network of 74 islands, some of which have become luxury tourist resorts, are part of the Great Barrier Reef Marine Park.

Geologically, all the Whitsunday Islands are drowned mountains. Prior to the last ice age they were connected to the mainland and would all have been prominent mountains in the region. The melting of the polar caps drowned the valleys between the mountains, creating a network of 74 islands of which only seven have resort facilities. Beyond the resorts, the whole area is part of the Great Barrier Reef Marine Park and the uninhabited islands are all controlled by National Parks and Wildlife.

The first European to explore the area was Captain James Cook who travelled through the islands on his journey up the eastern coast of Australia in 1770. He passed through Whitsunday Passage on Sunday 4 June which happened to be Whit Sunday (the seventh Sunday after Easter) – hence the name.

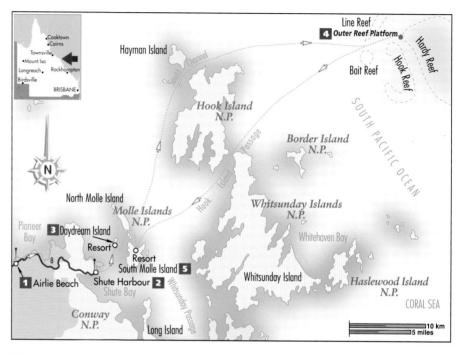

1 AIRLIE BEACH

This is a boat trip which starts in Shute Harbour at Airlie Beach and travels to the edge of Hardy Reef, 50 nautical miles from the mainland.

Airlie Beach is at the heart of the complex of islands, villages and resort towns that is the Whitsunday Group. The centre of the town has a myriad gift shops, eating places ranging from fast foods to quality restaurants, pubs and bars, and shops catering for the needs of holiday-makers. The whole township has a distinctly tropical flavour.

2 SHUTE HARBOUR

Pass through the town and continue on Shute Harbour Rd which, after winding its way around the foreshores, crosses the hills, then passes the airport and the National Parks Office, located in the Conway National Park. There are camping and picnic facilities in the area as well as a number of clearly marked bushwalking paths. The road then drops down into Shute Harbour. Continue to the end of the road where there is a parking lot and wharves from which the boats and ferries depart to the islands. The distance from Airlie Beach to Shute Harbour is 8km.

Shute Harbour is reputedly the second-busiest harbour in Australia after Sydney's Circular Quay. Many boats and cruise vessels depart from the harbour for journeys to the Whitsunday Islands; one of the most appealing of these would have to be the *Gretel*, Australia's first challenger for the America's Cup (it lost 4–1 to *Weatherly* in 1962). It now sails daily from the harbour. For bookings call tel: (079) 46 6184.

Undoubtedly the greatest attraction in the area is the Conway Range National Park which covers over 19 000ha and is the largest coastal national park in Queensland. A short 1km walk which starts at the camping ground and passes through rainforest is ideal for birdwatchers, particularly at dawn and dusk. Another 2km walk (more strenuous) heads up Mount Rooper and offers excellent views of the whole area from Mount Rooper Lookout, while there is a 2km walk known as the Swamp Bay Track which leads down to the coral beach at Swamp Bay. Detailed maps and information on all these walks can be obtained from the National Parks Office at tel: (079) 46 9430.

The major commercial operator to the Outer Reef is FantaSea Cruises – their boats depart daily from Shute Harbour.

3 DAYDREAM ISLAND

The FantaSea JetCat leaves Shute Harbour at 8:30 and stops at Daydream Island to pick up any passengers from the island's holiday resort. The JetCat has seating on two levels. Depending on the weather you can sit

Sailing is a popular pastime at Airlie Beach.

Shute Harbour, near Airlie Beach, is the gateway to the Whitsundays.

outside or in the protection of the large cabin areas. There is a bar downstairs which sells alcohol as well as soft drinks. Tea and coffee are provided. The vessel's journey across Shute Harbour is slow.

Daydream Island is sometimes called the 'Honeymooners' Isle' because it has luxury accommodation but on a small, intimate scale as opposed to the large luxury resorts on Hamilton and Hayman islands. It is only 20 minutes from Shute Harbour.

4 OUTER REEF PLATFORM

Daydream Island is the last stopping point for the JetCat before it makes the journey to the outer reef. Depending on weather conditions the boat travels up the west coast of South Molle Island and swings east, either passing north of Hayman Island or passing through the channel between Hayman Island and Hook Island. The journey is uneventful unless the weather is bad, when the waters between the outer reef and the Whitsundays can become choppy. However, even in the roughest weather, the reef ensures calm waters at the reef platform.

It takes around two and a half hours to travel from Shute Harbour to the Outer Reef Platform – this includes the brief stopover at Daydream Island. The platform is a large, permanent structure on the western side of Hardy Reef. It is specifically designed to enable visitors to explore all aspects of the reef. The cruise usually spends about three and a half hours at the platform which is more than enough time to go snorkelling, to travel along the edge of the reef in the *Reefworld* sub (a semi-submersible vessel which allows visitors to sit in a large cabin underwater and watch as the sub passes over sections of coral at the edge of the reef), to go swimming, visit the platform's under-water observatory and enjoy a delicious smorgasbord lunch which is included in the price of the tour.

Upon arrival at the platform each passenger is provided with a sealed snorkel mouthpiece. For those eager to go swimming, flippers, snorkels, wetsuits and life vests are provided and there are conveniently located decks at water level on either side of the platform. For an additional cost it is possible to hire scuba-diving equipment and take either an introductory lesson or enjoy scuba diving on the reef if you are a certified diver.

Perhaps the most spectacular way to see the reef (although it is not cheap) is to take a five- or ten-minute joy flight in a helicopter. The helipad is moored about 200m from the platform and the number of flights is determined by the demand.

Travellers are struck with awe at the sheer enormity of the Great Barrier Reef. This great natural phenomenon covers a total area of around 215 000km^2 and stretches along the coast for about 2000km. It has been created by a unique set of circumstances. The stony corals that produce reefs grow best in sea water which doesn't drop below 22°C or rise above 28°C. They need lots of sunlight, should grow in relatively shallow water (below 60m there is often not enough light) and survive and prosper where there is little muddying of the water by rivers or, more recently, by human pollution. This environment has existed for millions of years off the Queensland coast.

It is thought that the first reefs off the Queensland coast developed about 25 million years ago when sea levels rose. However the main development of the reef probably occurred as recently as 1.8 million years ago and the modern coral reef may be only about 8000 years old.

In the area of the Whitsundays the continental shelf is no more than 9–16m deep and this has produced ideal circumstances for the coral to continue to grow and develop.

5 SOUTH MOLLE ISLAND

The JetCat leaves the Outer Reef Platform around 13:30 and makes the journey back to Shute Harbour, swinging around Hayman Island and cruising down the western coastline of South Molle Island. There is a brief stopover at South Molle Island to let people staying at the resort depart and to pick up people from the resort wanting to go to Shute Harbour.

South Molle Island boasts facilities for over 600 guests and provides the usual range of Whitsunday activities from golf, tennis and squash to bushwalking, scuba diving, cycling and just lazing on the beaches.

The National Park areas of the island, with grasslands, eucalypts and some rainforest areas, have graded walking trails to facilitate easy access to the more remote parts of the island. South Molle, which is hilly and has a lot of small bays and inlets, is ideal for walking.

From Shute Harbour there is only one route back to Airlie Beach. The journey is 8km. If you want to explore the hinterland, take any one of the walking paths which are clearly signposted on either side of the road.

Looking out to the Whitsunday Islands from Airlie Beach.

50 EXPLORING THE SUGAR COAST

■ DRIVING TOUR ■ 117KM ■ 1 DAY ■ SUGAR MILLS AND QUIET SEASIDE TOWNS

Some say that the journey between Townsville and the Whitsundays is of little interest. This is not true. Bowen is a delightful town with lovely beaches and Proserpine is also worth a visit.

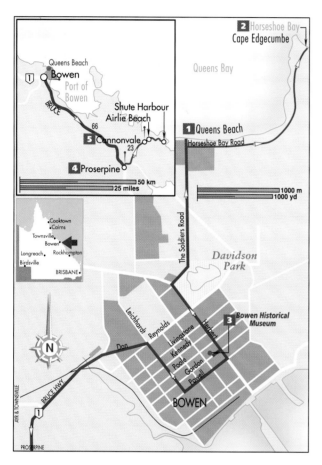

Waterlilies bloom on a dam near Proserpine.

Bowen is a classic Queensland town. The wide streets, the easiness of the lifestyle and the languidness of a city slowly melting under a hot tropical sun contribute to the charm of this old-style town. The great appeal of Bowen lies in the unspoiled bays to the north which boast some of the most beautiful beaches in the tropical north. There is Horseshoe Bay, Murrays Bay (which only has access down a narrow dirt track), Rose Bay, Grays, Kings and Queens beaches, the Town Beach and Dalrymple Point.

The first European to sight present-day Bowen was Captain James Cook who named Cape Gloucester after William Henry, the Duke of Gloucester. Cook passed within 9km of the coast.

The town of Bowen really dates back to 1859 when Captain Henry Daniel Sinclair sailed from Rockhampton in the 9-ton ketch *Santa Barbara* in search of a suitable port north of Rockhampton. He found a good harbour which he named Port Denison and returned south to claim a reward, only to find that Queensland was about to become a separate colony and neither the old colony nor the new one was prepared to reward his discovery.

At the same time, the explorer George Elphinstone Dalrymple had left Rockhampton looking for suitable grazing land further to the north. He recognised the potential of the area but failed to find a suitable port. Hoping that the mouth of the Burdekin River would be a port he persuaded the new Queensland government to send a party to investigate. They found that the mouth of the Burdekin was useless but, in the process, confirmed the accuracy of Sinclair's initial analysis of Port Denison.

In March 1861 the Queensland government declared Port Denison an official Port of Entry, allowing for the future development of the region. Dalrymple arrived on 11 April 1861 and with due ceremony and lots of cheering from the 111 people who had made the journey by sea and land, he raised the Union Jack and declared Bowen (named after the first Governor of Queensland) the northernmost town in Queensland.

Within a year there were 20 cattle stations in the area and hotels and stores had been established in the infant settlement.

The year 1862 saw the North Australia Hotel get its liquor licence; it now has the longest-running continuous liquor licence in north Queensland. However, it is only the licence that is old, as the original pub (on the site of the Commonwealth Bank) has long since gone. Today the North Australia is a modern, single-storeyed hotel with attached motel facilities.

Perhaps the most interesting moment in the early history of Bowen occurred in 1863 when James Morrill appeared out of the bush and announced 'Don't shoot mates, I'm a British object'. He had been shipwrecked 17 years earlier and had spent the intervening time living with the local Aborigines. He went to Brisbane where he became something of a celebrity but he eventually returned to Bowen and worked in the Customs House.

The town has retained its importance although in recent times it has been bypassed by the establishment of the huge coal-loading facilities at Abbot Point and by the tourist bays to the north.

1 QUEENS BEACH

Head north out of Bowen along the main street, Herbert St. After crossing Reynolds St, Davidson Park is on the right. Take the next right-hand turn into The Soldiers Rd, on the far side of the park. At the end of the road is Queens Beach.

Within a few kilometres of Bowen there are eight beautiful beaches of which Horseshoe Bay is the most attractive, although Queens Beach, which is the largest, is probably the most popular. The success of Queens Beach seems to be based largely on the fact that it is the most highly developed. It has tennis courts, a nine-hole golf course, bowling green, an old-style cinema and other social activities whereas the other beaches are strictly for swimming.

2 HORSESHOE BAY

Return a very short distance south along The Soldiers Rd and take the first left into Horseshoe Bay Rd, adjacent to the caravan park. If you drive along this road to the end you will find yourself at the bay itself.

There is a very pleasant walking trail which runs from Horseshoe Bay via a lookout to Murray Bay (about 870m away) and Rose Bay (2.5km away).

The bays are really Bowen's tourist *raison d'être*. Without them, modern-day Bowen would be little more than a coal-loading facility, a harbour, a saltworks, a few pubs and old buildings and a reasonably substantial community.

Behind Queens Beach in the hinterland, and stretching for maybe 50km up the coast is the vegetable-growing area for which Bowen is famous. Tomatoes are grown throughout the year in these fertile soils and some 4 million cartons are shipped south.

3 BOWEN HISTORICAL MUSEUM

Return to the city centre along Horseshoe Bay Rd. Turn left into The Soldiers Rd and left again into Herbert St. After crossing Reynolds, Livingstone, Kennedy and Poole sts, turn right into Gordon St and on the right, before you reach the next intersection, is the Bowen Historical Museum at 22 Gordon St.

The Bowen Historical Museum has a fine collection of memorabilia and historical artefacts including Captain Sinclair's waterman's badge, photostats of the early maps of the township and a map of the arduous Old Bowen Downs Road over the Leichhardt Ranges which took up to three months to traverse. It also contains old newspapers and Aboriginal artefacts from the area. The Bowen Historical Museum is widely regarded as one of the best local museums in Central Queensland.

Another place of interest in the surrounding area is the Bowen Courthouse (1883), a large impressive building in Herbert Street. To get to Flagstaff Hill Lookout and the Captain Cook Memorial (the foredeck and foremast of Cook's *Endeavour*), head down Herbert Street to the harbour, turn left into Santa Barbara Parade, drive past the caravan park and Hay Street to your left, and take the next left turn into Dalrymple Point Road, which will lead you to the lookout and some fine views.

4 PROSERPINE

The road from Bowen to Proserpine is very poor. It has constantly been repaired and patched so that now there are bumps over bumps and patches over patches. Starting from the harbour end of Herbert St turn left into Powell St, take the third right into Leichhardt St and, after the fifth cross street (Reynolds St), take the left diagonally opposite, into Don St. Continue south along Don St as it becomes the Bruce Highway (Route 1), ignoring the turn-off to the right signposted for Ayr and Townsville. Proserpine lies some 66km south along this route.

There are a number of towns along the Queensland coast which came into existence specifically to serve the sugar industry in the region. They are towns characterised by dozens of small railway tracks all leading towards the sugar-crushing mills.

Proserpine is located about 8km from the mouth of Repulse Bay and stands 12m above sea level. It is distinguished by the endless fields of sugarcane which surround the town and the sugar mill.

The region was named by the explorer George Dalrymple who passed through the area in 1859 on his way north. He named the whole area Proserpina after the Roman name for the Greek goddess of fertility, Persephone. It was his way of declaring the richness and fertility of the area which he was eager to develop.

The area was first settled by Europeans in 1861 and the Proserpine sugar mill opened in 1897. The mill became a cooperative in 1931 and is now recognised as one of the most modern sugar mills in the world.

This is a region where gardens give way to sugarcane; the town's major attractions are a sugarcane tour run by the local bus company which, between July and October, takes visitors from the sugar fields through the entire process of sugar making, including a tour of the sugar mill. Contact Sampsons Bus Service on tel: (079) 45 2377. It is also possible to have a guided tour of the Proserpine Sugar Mill. For more information contact tel: (079) 45 1755.

The main street, Bowen.

Boats in the harbour, Bowen.

If you are already in the area, St Paul's Anglican Church in Faust Street (the main street) is an interesting rounded A-frame building and worth a visit.

5 CANNONVALE

Return north along the Bruce Highway (Route 1) in the direction of Bowen, but just out of town take the turn-off to the right along the Proserpine–Shute Harbour Rd. Cannonvale lies 23km along this road.

The road winds through Cannonvale with its residential area and substantial industrial area. This holiday retreat is close to the main centre of Airlie Beach but far enough away to be removed from the bustle of tourism.

Of particular interest at Cannonvale is the molten volcanic rock at the end of Cannonvale Beach which gives an insight into how the area was geologically created.

If you wish to visit Airlie Beach and Shute Harbour (see Tour 45), continue travelling north-east along the Proserpine–Shute Harbour Rd.

The sugar mill dominates the township of Proserpine.

51 MACKAY AND THE HIBISCUS COAST

■ DRIVING TOUR ■ 120KM ■ 1 DAY ■ BEACHES, BUILDINGS AND BULK SUGAR TERMINALS

Mackay is one of Queensland's major coastal cities. It has everything from good beaches, motels, hotels and restaurants to excellent boating facilities and trips into the hinterland.

The first European to pass by the Mackay area was Captain James Cook as he sailed up the eastern coast of Australia in 1770. He named Cape Palmerston, failed to recognise the mouth of the Pioneer River and, quite sensibly, was more concerned about avoiding running aground on the reef than he was about the potential of the land to the west.

The area remained isolated for over 70 years after the settlement of Port Jackson. The first person to explore the area was Captain John Mackay, after whom the town is named. In 1861, Mackay brought cattle and horses overland from Armidale in New South Wales. The following year the tiny settlement of Mackay was established on the banks of the Pioneer River. The area around Mackay remained predominantly a cattle-breeding one until 1865 when John Spiller planted the first sugar. Sugar mills were built in the area around Mackay in 1867 and the first sugar was exported that year.

Mackay became increasingly important because of its location as a major transport node. The railway arrived in 1922 and in 1939 an artificial deepwater harbour was built with the largest sugar terminal in the southern hemisphere jutting out to load ships with the produce from the hinterland.

More recently, the discovery and development of the huge coal deposits in the Bowen Basin (particularly at Blair Athol, Dysart and Moranbah) has led to the construction of the Hay Point Coal Terminal which, when it was built, was the world's largest coal-loading facility. In 1983 it was added to when the Dalrymple Bay coal loader was opened.

Mackay is a very gracious tropical city. Its wide streets are characterised by beautifully kept median strips with royal palm trees and flowering tropical plants. The town's current pièce de résistance is the huge Mackay Civic Centre complex.

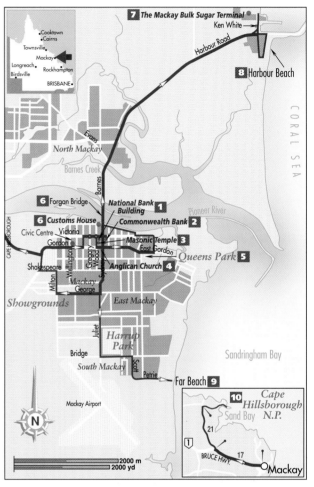

1 NATIONAL BANK BUILDING

The Civic Centre is located in Gordon St, just past the intersection with Wellington St. From the Civic Centre head east along Gordon St and turn left into Macalister St. At the next intersection turn right into Victoria St. This is Mackay's main street and there are a number of outstanding old buildings along its length. Just past Wood St, on your right, is the National Bank.

This imposing building, built in 1922, was originally the Queensland National Bank but is now no longer used as such. It is an interesting mixture of Corinthian columns with ornate corners and plaster arches.

2 COMMONWEALTH BANK

Continue east along Victoria St. Cross Sydney St and on the right, at 63 Victoria St, the Commonwealth Bank (1880) is situated.

The Commonwealth Bank features huge Doric columns on the ground floor with cast-iron columns and balustrades on the first floor. It is an impressive part of the streetscape and indicative of the wealth of Mackay in the late 19th century.

3 MASONIC TEMPLE

Return west along Victoria St. Cross Sydney St and then turn left into Wood St. Halfway along the block on the left is the Masonic Temple.

Mackay's Masonic Temple, built in 1927 at a cost of £6500, is a huge ornate building. The style is basically Classic Revival which was all the rage in the 1920s.

4 ANGLICAN CHURCH

Continue along Wood St and then turn left back into Gordon St. On the right-hand side of this block, near Sydney St, is the Anglican Church.

The current Mackay Anglican Church is the third to stand on this site. The first was built in 1867 and actually fell down; the second was destroyed by a cyclone in 1918. The present building displays some of the stained glass windows from the 1918 building.

5 QUEENS PARK

Continue along Gordon St for 750m as it bends to the right across the railroad tracks. Keep left as the road becomes East Gordon St. Queens Park is on the right.

Queens Park is a delightful place for a walk or a picnic with its avenue of palm trees, manicured lawns, band rotunda, children's playground and excellent displays of over 180 species of tropical orchids in the Orchid House. In summer, cricket is often played at the Oval and sometimes a band will perform at the rotunda.

6 FORGAN BRIDGE AND THE CUSTOMS HOUSE

Continue east on East Gordon St; take the first left and the road will almost immediately bend to the left again along the bank of the Pioneer River. The seventh road on the left is Sydney St which crosses the river at the Forgan Bridge. On the corner of the river and Sydney St is the Customs House.

On the way out to the Mackay Bulk Sugar Terminal the visitor has to cross the Pioneer River. The Forgan Bridge was constructed in 1938 and replaced an earlier bridge (dating from 1886) which was rammed and quite seriously damaged by an ocean-going vessel during the cyclone of 1918.

The port of Mackay is home to one of the southern hemisphere's largest sugar terminals.

On the town side of the Forgan Bridge is the superb Customs House which was built in 1901 to collect interstate excise on the local rum production.

7 THE MACKAY BULK SUGAR TERMINAL

To get to the Bulk Sugar Terminal, cross the bridge on Barnes Rd and continue north, ignoring the left branch along Evans Ave just after the Barnes Creek Bridge. Take Harbour Rd out to Mackay Harbour. Turn left before the water along Ken White Ave which leads past the Mackay Bulk Sugar Terminal.

The Mackay Bulk Sugar Terminal is reputedly the largest in Australia and is capable of holding over 700 000 tonnes of sugar. The sugar-loading facilities offer conducted tours in the crushing season between July and November. Contact the Tourist Information Office at tel: (079) 52 2677 for details.

8 HARBOUR BEACH

Return to the Harbour Rd and turn left towards the water, then take the last right along Mulhern Dve. On your left is Harbour Beach.

Harbour Beach is a delightful, quiet location removed from the more popular Town and Illawong beaches which lie to the south of Mackay. Beside the beach is an excellent children's park with a huge variety of activities, including a large replica of Fred Flintstone to play on, as well as distinctively novel fish garbage bins. The beach is perfect for people wishing to sunbathe and the small harbour nearby is very popular with local fishermen and women.

9 FAR BEACH

Return to the city centre via Harbour Rd and Forgan Bridge. Follow Sydney St to the south all the way to George St. Turn right into George St and then take the immediate left into Juliet St. Some 1.2km down the road, just past Harrup Park which is on the left, turn left into Bridge Rd, then take the second turn to the right into Scott St. This bends to the left, becoming Petrie St; at its end is Far Beach.

At Far Beach there is a monument to the 29 people, most of them school children, who were killed in 1960 when a Fokker Friendship crashed in the sea while it was approaching Mackay Airport.

10 CAPE HILLSBOROUGH NATIONAL PARK

Head back towards the city. Turn left into Bridge Rd and right into Juliet St. At George St, just across the railroad tracks, turn left and after 800m turn right into Milton St. Take the second left into Shakespeare St (the showgrounds are on the right) and the first right turn into Nebo Rd. Then take the first left into Rockleigh Rd (the Bruce Highway, Route 1). About 17km north-west along the Bruce Highway is the turn-off called Seaforth Rd. Follow this almost to the coast for 21km but turn off to the right at the sign for Cape Hillsborough National Park and Andrews Point.

The park covers an area of 850ha and is a combination of rugged hills, rhyolite boulders from the old volcanic plug known as Pinnacle Rock, and sandy beaches where, in the late afternoon, kangaroos can be seen. The area is predominantly rainforest and the chief activities are bushwalking, swimming and sunbathing. There is a camping area at Smalleys Beach and at Cape Hillsborough. For further information contact the Queensland National Parks and Wildlife Service in Mackay at tel: (079) 59 0410.

To return to the centre of Mackay follow the route back along Seaforth Rd and the Bruce Highway. When the highway reaches the T-junction at the Mackay showgrounds, turn left and you are back on Gordon St which will lead you directly to the city centre.

The Customs House, Mackay.

Mackay's Civic Centre.

52 FROM COAST TO RAINFOREST

■ DRIVING TOUR ■ 168KM ■ 1 DAY ■ A WORLD OF SUGARCANE AND RAINFORESTS

West of Mackay the mountains rise to some of Queensland's most beautiful and tranquil rainforest areas. A day spent travelling from Mackay to Eungella is a day of great contrasts.

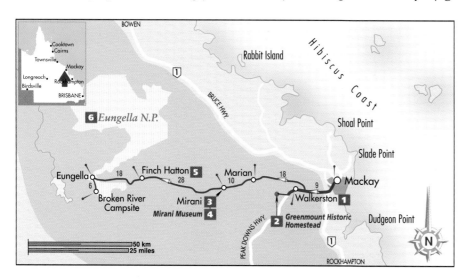

1 WALKERSTON

Head west out of Mackay along Gordon St, following it as it bends south at the showgrounds and becomes Nebo Rd. After 3km, just past the parkland to your right, turn right onto the Peak Downs Highway and follow it for 9km to Walkerston. This journey from Mackay along the Peak Downs Highway is perhaps the most interesting.

Walkerston is 20m above sea level and lies in the heart of a rich sugar-growing area. The first settler here was John Mackay but then in the late 1860s John Walker (after whom the town is named) took over Mackay's properties which, following his death in 1879, were sold to the Colonial Sugar Refining Company.

The principal attraction at Walkerston, which is now not very much more than a commuter suburb for Mackay, is Greenmount Historic Homestead.

2 GREENMOUNT HISTORIC HOMESTEAD

After passing through Walkerston the road to Greenmount is clearly signposted. Continue to the southwest along the Peak Downs Highway for 3km and turn off to the right onto Greenmount Rd.

This gracious old house is located a couple of kilometres from the highway and is beautifully situated amidst gardens of tropical splendour on the top of a hill overlooking the surrounding sugar plantations.

The land was originally owned by John Mackay but he was forced to sell it and it then passed through a number of hands before Albert Cook purchased it in 1912. By this time, the Cook family had established themselves as one of the Pioneer Valley's premier land holders. Albert Cook built the present home in 1915; it was left to the Pioneer Shire Council by his son Tom

in 1981 and it is currently leased by the Mackay Historical Society and Museum Inc.

A visit to the home is a rare opportunity to experience the lifestyle of a successful cattle grazier in the late 19th century. Each room has been restored to its original condition and the furniture, even down to the large dining room table with the individual place settings, is all original. All items in the homestead belonged to the Cook family. It is open Mondays to Fridays from 9:30–12:30 and Sundays from 10:00–15:30.

3 MIRANI

Return to the Peak Downs Highway and about 1km east of Walkerston is a branch to the left. The road goes west to Marian which is 17km away. A further 10km along the road is Mirani.

Although Mirani is a small sugar town, it lies at the heart of the beautiful Pioneer Valley which the brochures, with some justification, call the 'Showcase of North Queensland'. Mirani, with a population of over 5000, is the centre of a shire which contains some of the most densely grown sugarcane anywhere in Queensland (it is commonplace to see sugarcane forming a wall around the garden of a small house), two sugar mills (at Pleystowe and Marian), the beautiful Finch Hatton Gorge Falls and the cool rainforest beauty of Eungella National Park State Forest.

No one knows how Mirani got its name. It may have an Aboriginal origin or it may, as local folklore has it, be a combination of the names 'Mary' and 'Annie' but there is no real evidence for this fanciful explanation.

The Mirani area was first settled by John Mackay in May 1860. On 27 August 1872, 149 acres were reserved and gazetted as Mirani town site; in the early days the area was known as Hamilton. In 1884 the township was surveyed and in 1885 a railway line, connecting Mirani to Mackay, was completed. The following year a school was established there and in 1889 Eungella was proclaimed a goldfield.

Perhaps Mirani's most famous citizen in these early days was David Mitchell who arrived in Mackay in 1881. He was contracted to build the first sugar mill at Marian. Mitchell came with his two daughters, Anne and Helen. Helen was to change her name and become known throughout the world as the great opera singer, Dame Nellie Melba.

In December of 1882, Charles Nesbit Frederick Armstrong married Helen Porter Mitchell. In April 1883 the couple returned to Marian and Armstrong became the manager of the sugar mill.

The general store, Mirani.

The Eungella Honeyeater is only found in the rainforest areas of Eungella.

Cyathea tree ferns in Eungella National Park.

Although it was Helen (Nellie) who became world famous, it was Charles Armstrong who left his mark on the area. He blazed a trail up into the Great Dividing Range behind the sugar towns.

4 MIRANI MUSEUM

The Museum is located next to the Shire Council Offices on the southern side of the main street.

A nice historical vignette of the town is provided in the 1889 edition of *Pugh's Almanack* which records:

MIRINI (sic) – A township at the terminus of the Mackay and Hamilton Railway 23 miles from Mackay and situated on the south bank of the Pioneer River about 200 feet above sea level. There's one hotel, also a boarding house and a butcher's shop. There are a number of settlers in the neighbourhood and the ground is very rich alluvial suited for the growing of sugar and other tropical produce. Scenery is beautiful and Mirani [they got it right this time] is a favourite resort of pleasure seekers from Mackay. There is a Post Office at the Hollow (the residence of Mr Rawson) a quarter of a mile from the township and another at Hamilton, a cattle station owned by Dalrymple and Murray across the river two miles away.

What is remarkable about this brief sketch of Mirani is that, in most details, it is an accurate description of the town as it is today. It is still surrounded by sugar, it is still small and it still has only one pub.

All this information, as well as a fascinating collection of artefacts, can be inspected by the curious visitor at the town's modern museum. The museum is open from 10:00–16:00 on Tuesdays, Thursdays and Fridays and from 9:00–16:00 on Sundays.

In recent times the Mirani Museum has added the Juipera Walk, providing an insight into the Aboriginal culture of the district which also contains a range of bush-tucker plants and bushes.

5 FINCH HATTON

A further 28km west of Mirani is Finch Hatton.

Finch Hatton is a charming, sleepy little township. The main attractions include Jack Wilms Cedar Gallery, noted for its sculptures and carvings in wood, and the Finch Hatton Gorge which lies north of the township at the bottom of the mountain range. It is part of the eastern extremity of the Eungella National Park. There is a track up the creek bed which leads to the waterfalls.

6 EUNGELLA NATIONAL PARK

It is another 18km to the township of Eungella. The Eungella National Park headquarters, camping ground and picnic facilities are 6km to the south at Broken River. Contact tel: (079) 584 552 for camping permits and further information.

Eungella National Park is the largest rainforest national park in Queensland. It covers a total area of over 50 000ha and is noted especially for its beautiful waterfalls, clear streams and the many pools in the rainforest in which the weary walker can have a refreshing swim on hot summer days.

The park has over 25km of walking paths and boasts proudly that, for the patient watcher, there is a rare opportunity to see platypus in the wild. The Broken River is a well-known platypus habitat.

The Queensland National Park Rangers are located at Broken River near the entrance to the park. Their office provides detailed information about the fauna and flora in the park and they are happy to answer questions and to provide details about the variety of walks available. There

is also a Eungella Display Centre which is open every day from 7:00–17:00.

The walks range from a short 1km rainforest stroll at Broken River to a full-day 16km hike which encompasses most of the park's most important attractions.

Walkers will find a great diversity of fauna in the rainforest including such rare indigenous creatures as the Eungella Honeyeater, the gastric brooding frog and the orange-sided skink.

This area, with its dramatic views and dense forest, is a must for anyone wanting to experience the wonderful beauty of the Central Coast rainforest.

Return to Eungella and follow the road east back through Finch Hatton, Mirani and Marian until you rejoin the Peak Downs Highway. Continue east back into Mackay, turning left into Nebo Rd just past the racecourse on the outskirts of Mackay.

The Mirani Bridge over the Pioneer River.

129

53 SUGARCANE AND COAL

■ DRIVING TOUR ■ 178KM ■ 1 DAY ■ LONELY BEACHES AND HEAVY INDUSTRY

So much of the northern coast of Queensland is covered in sugarcane that the traveller begins to believe that the world is a narrow road surrounded by one continuous wall of cane.

B y the 1870s Mackay and the Pioneer Valley to the west of the township were so sugar-rich and productive that there were 16 sugar mills in the area.

Sugar is Mackay's reason for existence. Even today it is hard not to be overwhelmed by the magnitude of sugar production in the area. Once outside the city it seems that every road is flanked by endless fields of sugarcane. It has been estimated that the Mackay region produces over 25 per cent of all Australia's sugar.

In Mackay today sugar is everywhere, but this modern, attractive city has reached beyond its major industry to create an active tourist trade and, to the south at Hay Point and Sarina, to develop a huge coal terminal and a specialist factory producing commercial alcohol.

1 NEBO ROAD

From the Forgan Bridge which crosses the Pioneer River, head to the south along Sydney St for two blocks, passing the Police Station and the Town Hall on the left, to reach Gordon Rd (known also as the Mackay–Slade Point Rd). Turn right into Gordon Rd and head west for 1km where the road turns to the south after passing the showground. Continue past the south end of the showground which is bordered by Shakespeare St. Nebo Rd (the Bruce Highway) continues south-west for the next 3km.

Mackay has one thing in common with many cities in America. It has a clearly defined area of fast-food outlets and motels on the outskirts of town. Nebo Road, on the south side of the city, is a solid wall of good quality motels which are only booked out during the school holidays and when the Mackay Cup and other major festivals (including the Festival of the Arts, the Greenmount Fair, the Maltese Festival and the Sugartime Festival) are being held in the town. At the southern end of this accommodation complex is the Tourism Mackay Information Centre.

2 TOURISM MACKAY INFORMATION CENTRE

The Information Centre is located at the southern end of Nebo St on the western side of the road, about 200m north of the intersection of the Bruce Highway and the Peak Downs Highway.

When visitors arrive in Mackay they should first stop at the unusual Tourism Mackay Information Centre, contact tel: (079) 52 2677, which features a replica of the chimney from the old Richmond Sugar Mill. The centre provides excellent maps and can book trips to the Great Barrier Reef as well as advise on accommodation and sightseeing in the area. There are one-day or overnight trips to places such as Brampton Island, the Great Barrier Reef, and Hamilton and Lindeman islands.

The best known, and most accessible, of these islands is Brampton. Most of the island is a National Park, with typical tropical rainforest vegetation. It is an ideal day out with a 7km walking trail which winds around the side of the island offering the visitor excellent views over the Great Barrier Reef and the opportunity to take tracks down to the beaches. The journey across from Mackay takes only 45 minutes.

3 HAY POINT

From the southern end of Nebo Rd head south into Broadsound Rd (the Bruce Highway). Follow the Bruce Highway to the south passing through Bakers Creek and Rosella. About 14km south of Rosella take the turn-off to Alligator Creek and Hay Point heading in an easterly direction. Continue through Alligator Creek to reach Hay Point on the coast

The discovery and development of the huge coal deposits in the Bowen Basin (particularly at Blair Athol, Dysart and Moranbah) has led to the construction of the Hay Point Coal Terminal which, at the time it was built, was the world's largest coal-loading facility. In 1983 it was expanded when the Dalrymple Bay coal loader was opened.

Today this facility, with its two wharves, is still the largest coal-loading facility in the southern hemisphere. It has a capacity of over 50 million tonnes per year.

The coal is brought to the port by electric trains which can be up to 2km long. The major mine at Blair Athol reputedly has the largest seam of steaming coal in the world – it is apparently 29m thick. By 1984 coal from Blair Athol was being exported and today it is one of the largest and most successful mines in Queensland.

4 SARINA

Take the same road out of Hay Point heading west back through Alligator Creek and onto the Bruce Highway. Turn left onto the highway and continue south for 12km to Sarina.

One of the truisms about Queensland is that if a town, by luck or good fortune, is located on the coast, it can become a major tourist attraction. If, however, it is located in the coastal hinterland it remains underdeveloped and driven by the sugar industry which created it. Sarina is a perfect example. Located 13km from Sarina Beach it is a small sugar town with very little to interest the average visitor apart from the industrial alcohol distillery at the local sugar mill.

Mackay Harbour.

The town is split by the Bruce Highway which runs down the main street. There is a pleasant median strip with tropical flowers, trees and bushes. At the northern end is a rock commemorating the fact that John Atherton (after whom the Atherton Tableland was named) was the first European to reach this area travelling overland from Rockhampton. When he was only 20, Atherton and his brother James overlanded sheep to Rockhampton from the New England district of New South Wales.

Sarina Inlet was named by a Greek surveyor in the early 1860s and by the 1870s sugarcane plantations had been established in the area.

Today the heart of the town's economy is Plane Creek Mill and the Australian National Power Alcohol Company Pty Ltd (Sarina Distillery), which opened in 1927 and processes molasses bought from the sugar mills in the surrounding area. It was the first alcohol distillery in Australia and is now one of the biggest.

While Sarina is primarily a town driven by its local industry, it does lie in the centre of a number of important local attractions.

The Pioneer River, Mackay.

5 CAPE PALMERSTON NATIONAL PARK

From Sarina head south along the Bruce Highway for 22km to Koumala. Continue along the highway for another 10km where a turn-off to the north-east leads to Cape Palmerston National Park.

Although the area around Sarina is known for its industry, there are sections of the coast which have remained unspoilt. Cape Palmerston is one such area. However, it is necessary to obtain a permit from the National Parks and Wildlife Service in Mackay and, because it is a genuinely unspoilt and undeveloped park, the roads are so rough that access is only possible for 4WD vehicles. For more information contact the Queensland National Parks and Wildlife Service in Mackay on tel: (079) 59 0410. There are basic camping and picnic facilities in the park.

Cape Palmerston is of particular interest as it covers 32km of coastline and has areas ranging from mangrove swamps and wetlands to thickly vegetated sand dunes and the volcanic Mount Funnel Range.

The area is noted for its superb views across both the hinterland and the ocean towards the Great Barrier Reef. Its melaleuca forests are the habitat of a wide range of birds and the lonely beaches give the visitor the opportunity to experience what this beautiful stretch of coastline was like before Europeans arrived.

6 SARINA BEACH

Return from Cape Palmerston National Park to the Bruce Highway and drive about 32km north to Sarina. The road to Sarina Beach heads north-east out of town. The road reaches the coast after some 13km and splits in two with Campwin Beach to the north and Sarina Beach to the south.

The industrial urgency of Sarina, Hay Point and Mackay seems so far away when the visitor makes the journey to the coast east of Sarina. Here is a run of quiet beaches, the most popular of which are Campwin and Sarina. Others include Half Tide, Salonika and Grasstree. This is a relatively underdeveloped area of the coast specialising in family holidays and relaxing activities such as fishing, walking and swimming.

At the southern end of Sarina Beach, Coral Point Lookout offers excellent views over the ocean and north along the beach. There are excellent fishing places (consult the locals) around Sarina Inlet where there are ready supplies of flathead, whiting, bream, grunter, salmon and estuary cod. Offshore fishing, for those with access to a boat, will yield catches which may include coral trout, red emperor, sweetlip and cod. The winter months, which are generally the best time to visit the area, see the waters rich in mackerel and snapper.

7 CAMPWIN BEACH

Return less than 1km towards Sarina and then take the turn-off to the north towards Campwin Beach.

While Campwin Beach, to the north of Sarina Beach, is not as beautiful as its southern neighbour it does have the novelty of the Beach Prawn Farm. This farm claims to be the only commercial prawn hatchery in Australia which is open to the public. There are regular tours explaining the breeding cycle of prawns.

Return to the Bruce Highway which is about 13km west of Sarina Beach and drive north for 38km in order to return to Mackay.

The Racecourse sugar mill, near Mackay, surrounded by cane fields.

CHAPTER 10
THE GULF COUNTRY

59 ACROSS THE EMPTY PLAINS

■ DRIVING TOUR ■ 772KM ■ 2 DAYS ■ A WORLD OF DINOSAURS AND BORE WATER

There was a time, millions of years ago, when the Gulf Country of northern Queensland was a vast inland sea. Fossils abound, the skeletons of dinosaurs are on display and the road goes on forever.

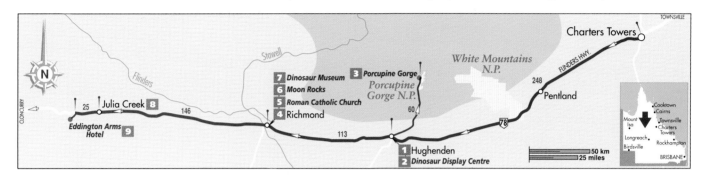

1 HUGHENDEN

Leaving Charters Towers, drive east along Gill St (the main street) past the Catholic School on your right and take the next right into High St. Follow it to its end, turn left into Rainbow Rd and take the first right into Thompson Rd, just across the railway tracks. This becomes the Flinders Highway. It is 248km along this route (Highway 78) to Hughenden.

Hughenden owes its existence to the railway line and the surrounding cattle grazing land. It is a functional town that is eager to capture the attention of tourists but it is somewhat restricted in what it can offer them.

Fortunately, it is located at a point experts consider to be the edge of Australia's ancient inland sea and consequently there have been several important fossils found in the area. Undoubtedly the most important discovery was that of a Muttaburrasaurus (named after the town of Muttaburra where remains

A replica of the Muttaburrasaurus' skeleton.

The Roman Catholic Church, Richmond.

of this dinosaur were first found), a cast of which is displayed prominently in a building in the centre of town. (See also Tour 41.)

2 DINOSAUR DISPLAY CENTRE

As you enter Hughenden the Flinders Highway becomes Gray St just past the small Rotary Park. Cross over the railway line just before you reach Moran St. This is followed by Mowbray and Stansfield sts. Just past Stansfield St you will find the Display Centre for the Muttaburrasaurus.

The dinosaur display gives one an insight into the nature of life on the edge of the 'inland sea' about 100 million years ago. The dinosaur itself is only a cast of the original bones which now are located in the Brisbane museum. This, however, should not detract from the convincing reproduction located in a building which looks as though it were purposely designed for the huge creature. There are explanatory boards which tell of the discovery of the skeleton and place the dinosaur in a larger historical context. One of the boards explains:

The Hughenden area 100 million years ago was on the edge of a shallow inland sea that extended from what is now the Gulf of Carpentaria through to South Australia. Australia was joined to Antarctica, but there were no polar ice caps at this time and the world climate was quite warm. Large marine reptiles called Icthyosaurus and Plesiosaurus swam in the inland sea while on land dinosaurs such as Muttaburrasaurus and the long-necked Austrosaurus browsed on the vegetation amongst conifers, cycads and ferns. Most of the remains of Muttaburrasaurus came from two individuals. The first was found in 1962 near Muttaburra where it derives its name and the other in 1987 near Hughenden. Their bones were preserved because the carcasses had been washed into the sea and became buried in the mud which protected them from destruction.

The area was settled in 1864 by Ernest Henry. Henry named his property Hughenden Station after the English home of his maternal grandfather, Hughenden Manor in Buckinghamshire. When the town was surveyed in 1877 it was decided to name the town after the station.

In 1905 the railway arrived in the town. This ensured the continuing prosperity of the area. Today the town is a service and administrative centre for the surrounding Flinders Shire which, at over 41 000km², is one of the largest shires in Queensland.

3 PORCUPINE GORGE

Continue north along Gray St across the Flinders River to the Kennedy Developmental Rd. The journey to Porcupine Gorge is 60km.

The area's premier attraction is the exceptionally beautiful and dramatic Porcupine Gorge. Sometimes known as the 'little Grand Canyon', the gorge drops 120m from the surrounding countryside. It is not possible to enter it from the lookout (which is clearly signposted) but another 10km further to the north is the small monolith known as the Pyramid; at this point there is a path which leads down into the gorge. The bottom of the gorge is especially notable for its deep pools, which are inhabited by tortoises, and its flora, which includes paperbarks and casuarinas.

There are rudimentary (water and toilet) camping facilities at the Pyramid end of Porcupine Gorge. It is possible in the dry season that the water (rainwater collected off the roof of a shed) will have been used up and visitors are therefore advised to bring their own supplies.

4 RICHMOND

Return to Hughenden via the Kennedy Developmental Rd. Once across the river take the third turn-off right into Stansfield St, which again becomes the Flinders Highway. Head west; it is 113km to Richmond.

Richmond is one of those tiny centres whose sole reason for existence is that it services the surrounding pastoral community.

The flat landscape of the Gulf Country.

The Richmond area was first explored by William Landsborough who came through in 1862 while looking for Burke and Wills. Landsborough's report on the area was such that within the next decade the area had been settled by pastoralists. The discovery of gold at the Woolgar fields 113km north of the town resulted in a rush to the district and Richmond became an important point for the Cobb & Co coaches which moved miners through the town. A superbly preserved Cobb & Co coach in Goldring Street (the main street) recalls this historic link.

In 1904 the railway reached the town, making it the terminus and railhead for the Gulf Country. For the next four years (until the railway pushed on to Julia Creek) cattle were brought to Richmond to be shipped out to the coast. The arrival of the railway meant the hasty demise of Cobb & Co.

5 ROMAN CATHOLIC CHURCH

Enter Richmond from the direction of Hughenden on the Flinders Highway. This becomes Goldring St. On the right-hand side of the road you will find the very unusual Roman Catholic Church.

Although today the town of Richmond is only a shadow of its former self, this church is one of a number of old buildings which are a reminder of its past. It is a remarkable example of a west Queensland timber church which has been constructed to look like a stone structure.

6 MOON ROCKS

Continue for another 100m down the main street and on your right near the highway you will notice a park with a small collection of stones.

In the Lions Park is a strange monument made of different shaped rocks positioned on top of each other. It looks like the sort of plasticine model that pre-school children would make. In fact the rocks are a local phenomenon known as 'moon rocks' which often contain the fossilised remnants of fish and shells. The monument, opened in 1976 by then Queensland Premier, Joh Bjelke-Petersen, celebrates the completion of the bitumen sealing to the Flinders Highway.

7 STRAND THEATRE – DINOSAUR MUSEUM

Further down the main street, on the right, is the old Strand Theatre, recently converted into a Dinosaur Museum celebrating the area's rich fossil deposits.

The old Strand Theatre, made out of corrugated iron and looking like a Nissen hut, makes the visitor wonder what it must have been like going to the movies on a hot summer night in Richmond.

Richmond came to the attention of all Australians in 1989 when the skeleton of a 100 million-year-old Pliosaur was discovered near the town. It was the second major discovery of an important fossil in the Richmond area. The famous *Kronosaurus queenslandicus* was discovered at Army Downs north of Richmond in 1929 by a team of palaeontologists from Harvard University. In 1995 the Strand Theatre became an important tourist attraction when it was officially opened as a Dinosaur Museum.

8 JULIA CREEK

From Goldring St turn south into Larsen St. This street again becomes the Flinders Highway and it is about 146km to Julia Creek.

Julia Creek was the first European settlement in north-western Queensland. Donald Macintyre arrived in the area in 1862 – only a year after the ill-fated Burke and Wills expedition had passed through the region on the way north to the Gulf. Macintyre didn't come as a result of the explorations of Landsborough or Frederick Walker (who opened up the area while searching for Burke and Wills) but rather on his own initiative. He travelled up the Darling River and established the property Dalgonally about 70km north of the present town.

The creek upon which the town is located was originally named Scorpion but, in 1870, it was changed to Julia Creek in honour of Donald Macintyre's niece. Julia Creek's moment of importance came with the arrival of the railway in 1908 which meant that the town became the railhead for north-western Queensland. The transport industry became the town's main economic *raison d'être* until the railway later moved on to Cloncurry and Mount Isa.

Julia Creek achieved some small level of fame in Neville Shute's *A Town Like Alice* when the hero, Joe Harman, overlands 1400 cattle from the Gulf to the town. He stays at the fictional Post Office Hotel, which was obviously based on Gannon's Hotel located across the road from the Post Office. The fact that there is a Post Office Hotel in Cloncurry may mean that Shute was fictionally blending the two towns.

The main industries in the area around Julia Creek are beef and wool production. It is, like so many of the towns in the Gulf, a service centre. There is the Macintyre Museum in Burke Street (the main street) but it is largely a collection of shire records, old photographs and equipment relating to the early sheep and beef industries.

9 EDDINGTON ARMS HOTEL

Continue west along the Flinders Highway. About 25km from Julia Creek is a turn-off to the south and one of the shire's genuine curiosities is just a few kilometres further on.

The Eddington Arms Hotel at Gilliat is an old corrugated-iron pub which has remained virtually unchanged since its construction in 1908. The hotel is one of the most authentic pubs in western Queensland – anyone who is at all interested in what western Queensland was like at the turn of the century should drop in for a drink.

Return to the highway and head west for another 112km to Cloncurry (see Tour 61).

60 IN THE STEPS OF BURKE AND WILLS

■ DRIVING TOUR ■ 1138KM ■ 2 DAYS ■ EXPLORING THE DESOLATE GULF COUNTRY

It was in the isolated Queensland Gulf Country that Burke and Wills managed to reach the Gulf, thus becoming the first Europeans to cross the continent from north to south.

1 FREDERICK WALKER'S GRAVE ON FLORAVILLE STATION

Travelling from Cloncurry (see Tour 61), take the Flinders Highway to the west. On the outskirts of the town take the Burke Developmental Rd north. Travel 45km and pass through Quamby. Burke and Wills Roadhouse is 136km north of Quamby on the Burke Developmental Rd. At the roadhouse take the Wills Developmental Rd north-west for about 77km to the Nardoo–Burketown Rd turn-off. Take the Nardoo–Burketown Rd north for 69km to Floraville.

Frederick Walker was one of the many explorers who, while looking for Robert O'Hara Burke and William Wills, opened up the whole of the Gulf area. His grave is located on Floraville Station. To get to the grave site, travellers turn south off the Burketown–Normanton road at the sign which says 'Floraville Station' and then travel towards the station buildings. Before reaching the station turn left to find the grave which is located on the far side of a dry creekbed. The inscription beside the grave includes the observation:

Frederick Walker was in many ways a remarkable man. His exploration of the Gulf assisted in opening up the region and his maps were considered accurate. Walker did not find Burke and Wills but he did find Camp 119, the last Burke and Wills camp before they turned south on their return journey.

Frederick Walker's grave became a mystery as to its location for many years until discovered by Mr. Walter Camp of Floraville Station after many years of searching.

The Purple Pub, National Hotel, Normanton.

The Gulflander train, Normanton Station.

2 BURKETOWN

From Floraville follow the road north-west for 72km to Burketown, passing Armraynald at the half-way point.

Burketown rather proudly announces to the world that it is 'The Barramundi Capital of Australia'. This small town on the flat plains of the Gulf near the Albert River is now very little more than a school, a pub, a couple of service stations, a council office, and three general stores.

The first Europeans into the area were Burke and Wills who reached the coast near Normanton in 1861. Both Frederick Walker and William Landsborough explored the area while looking for them.

Landsborough was impressed with the land between the Albert and Nicholson rivers and named it the Plains of Plenty, which was enough to cause a minor flurry of interest. In 1865 the town site was established when Landsborough arrived in the tiny settlement with a number of native police. He had recently been appointed police magistrate and commissioner of Crown lands in Carpentaria.

3 EDKINS BROTHERS BOILERS

Travel north through the town, pass the pub, drive past the hospital which is on your right, go across a grid and follow the main dirt road until you reach a sign which says 'Historic Sites'.

In the late 1860s a boiling works was set up on the banks of the Albert River by the Edkins brothers. All the equipment was shipped up from Sydney.

By March 1867 the Edkins brothers were exporting cured beef and barrels of tallow to Batavia and Singapore and were sending horns, hooves and hides to Brisbane and Sydney for secondary processing. It looked as though Burketown would become prosperous. However in 1866 Gulf Fever hit the settlement and decimated the population. Those who did not die of the fever moved to Normanton. Today the boiling works is nothing more than a few boilers and rusting machinery beside a dry river bed.

4 POST OFFICE

Return to the town. The Post Office is located in the main street.

One of Burketown's first buildings, the Post Office, was constructed in 1887 and retains many of its original features. It is typical of the Post and Telegraph offices which were built in Queensland in the late 19th century.

5 ARTESIAN BORE

Head to the south on the Normanton Rd. You will see an artesian bore on your right approximately 500m from the Post Office.

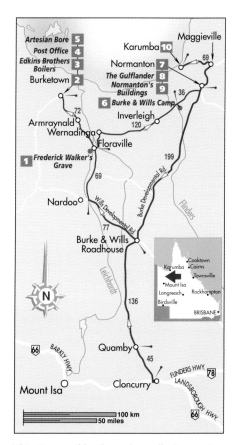

This is arguably the only really interesting bore in Queensland as it has been running for over a century and the minerals in the water have built up so that now it looks more like a piece of modern sculpture than a tap to an underground supply of hot water. The pond which has formed around the bore has also been coloured by the minerals.

6 BURKE & WILLS CAMP

Leave Burketown by the Nardoo–Burketown Rd heading south-east; pass through Yarram and Armraynald to reach Floraville after 72km. From Floraville proceed north-east to Normanton. After 14km pass through Wernadinga, and after 73km, Inverleigh. Cross the Bynoe River 33km beyond Inverleigh and continue a short distance to find the signposted turn-off to the Burke & Wills Camp on the southern side of the road. There is a dirt road which takes you 1.5km into the bush to a couple of plaques.

The dedication on the main plaque reads:

This monument marks the site of Camp No: 119 of the 1860–61 Burke and Wills expedition occupied on Saturday 9 February 1861 by Robert O'Hara Burke, William John Wills, John King and Charlie Gray. On Sunday 10 February Burke and Wills left on the attempted journey to the

Vast cattle stations are found throughout the Gulf Country.

Gulf of Carpentaria returning on Tuesday 12 February. All four abandoned the camp the next day for the return journey to Coopers Creek, Depot No: 75, and home to Melbourne. During the return journey all died with the exception of King who survived with the assistance of a friendly Aboriginal tribe. This monument was provided through, and with thanks, to the generous donation of Mr. Douglas Jolly of Brisbane and the historical advice of the State Library of Victoria and was erected in 1978 by the Normanton Lions Club.

7 NORMANTON

From the Burke & Wills camp rejoin the road to Normanton and proceed north-east for about 31km passing through Magowra. Upon reaching the Burke Developmental Rd turn north toward Normanton which is 5km further on.

Normanton is a genuinely delightful town with a lot of old-world charm. It started life as a port for the Gulf of Carpentaria's cattle industry and grew in importance with the discovery of gold at Croydon in 1885.

The area was first explored by Ludwig Leichhardt on his epic journey from the Darling Downs to Port Essington. The next Europeans through the area were Burke and Wills who made their final dash to the Gulf (or, more correctly, to the mangrove swamps somewhere near the edge of the Gulf) only 26km west of the town.

It was Frederick Walker, one of the many explorers who went out looking for Burke and Wills, who discovered and named the Norman River after the captain of a ship named *Victoria*.

In 1867 William Landsborough sailed up the Norman River and chose the site for the settlement of Normanton. Over the next decade it became an important port. The large Burns Philp building at the end of the town's main street is evidence of its importance at this time.

The town experienced a major boom with the discovery of gold at Croydon; by 1891 the population had reached a total of 1251. However the gold diggings were short-lived and although the Normanton–Croydon railway line was opened by 1907 the whole area was on the decline. By 1947 the town's population had dropped to only 234. It has since picked up with the development of prawn fishing at Karumba and the increasing interest in tourism.

8 THE GULFLANDER

From the main street turn left and you will reach the Normanton Railway Station.

The town's greatest tourist attraction is The Gulflander. The railway line was originally planned to service the beef industry by running from Normanton to Cloncurry but the discovery of gold at Croydon redirected it.

The station itself is now listed by the National Trust. It is an unusual building which is made distinctive by the decorative patterns on the cross-braces which hold up the corrugated-iron roof. It has become one of Normanton's most distinctive landmarks.

The demise of the Croydon goldfield occurred in 1906. Since then The Gulflander has not made any profit. Today it runs a once-weekly service leaving Normanton at 8:30 on a Wednesday and then returning from Croydon at 8:30 the next morning. It is occasionally also booked to make the tour at other times.

9 NORMANTON'S BUILDINGS

Return to the main street of Normanton. There are several interesting buildings worth inspecting.

The town's most interesting buildings include the distinctive Purple Pub, the Albion Hotel where Captain Percy Tresize drew a series of humorous paintings on the bar room walls, and the Bank of New South Wales which is now a listed National Trust Building. Designed by Richard Gailey in 1896 it is an extraordinarily beautiful timber building with cross-bracing on the verandah and a fashionable exposed frame; it looks more like a house than a bank.

10 KARUMBA

From Normanton take the road out of town which goes to Maggieville 29km on. At Maggieville head west along the road to Karumba 40km away. The journey to Karumba passes over very flat Gulf Country. The land is alive with birdlife and it is common to see flocks of cranes and brolgas feeding beside the road.

Karumba is a small fishing town and consists of a port, a few shops, a pub, a lot of inexpensive accommodation for fishermen and a river front which abounds with slipways, wharves, refrigerated storage areas and engineering services.

In the 1870s a telegraph station was built on the site of the present town. It was known simply as Norman Mouth. Karumba first came to importance in the 1930s when it became a stopover point for flying boats on the run from London to Australia. By the 1950s it had become a popular spot for people eager to go fishing in the Gulf of Carpentaria. The town went through something of a boom period in the 1960s and 1970s when it became the centre for the Gulf fishing industry. Today the prawn and barramundi fishing industries earn over A\$130 million each year. In spite of this there is something quite beautiful about the place. Karumba Point, near the entrance to the town, has a magnificent view over mangroves in the foreground and the Gulf waters disappearing into the horizon.

To return to Normanton, travel via Maggieville. Leave Normanton via the Burke Developmental Rd heading south for Cloncurry.

Sunset over the Norman River, Karumba.

61 OUTBACK MINING TOWNS

■ DRIVING TOUR ■ 262KM ■ 1 DAY ■ VISITING THE LARGEST CITY IN THE WORLD

Mount Isa (the largest city in the world), Mary Kathleen and Cloncurry are three of the most interesting towns in outback Queensland and represent the diversity of the region.

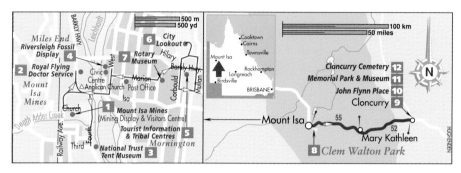

Mount Isa, the largest and most impressive township in western Queensland, has an air of self-confidence and sophistication that is rare in the outback. It proudly claims to be the largest city in the world, a fact born out by its accreditation in the Guinness Book of Records. The city extends for 40 977km², and the road from Mount Isa to Camooweal, a distance of 189km, is also the longest city road in the world.

Mount Isa was first mined for copper as early as the 1880s but during the 1920s the price of copper slumped and the settlement virtually had to be closed down. However, the town came back to life in February 1923 when Mount Isa's vast silver, lead and zinc deposits were discovered by the prospector John Campbell Miles who named the site after Mount Ida, a Western Australian gold mine. Mount Isa Mines Ltd was formed in 1924 and by 1925 it had taken over all the leases to the field. At the request of the Australian Government copper production began in the early 1940s and parallel production of both lead and copper ores began in 1953.

Mount Isa Mines plays a major role in this inland oasis.

1 MOUNT ISA MINES

From the Post Office in Marian St head west to the intersection with West St. Turn left here, and then proceed south for one block where you turn right to cross the Leichhardt River. Continue west to Railway Ave, head south and take the first left into Church St. The Mining Display and Visitors' Centre is on the right.

Today Mount Isa Mines Ltd is one of the most highly mechanised and cost-efficient mines in the world. It is the world's biggest single producer of silver and lead and is among the world's top ten for copper and zinc. Mount Isa is also one of the few areas in the world where the four minerals – copper, silver, lead and zinc – are found in close proximity. As Australia's largest underground mine, it has a daily output of around 35 000 tonnes of ore. The underground workings are approximately 4.5km long and 1.3km wide.

The highlight of any visit to Mount Isa is a comprehensive tour of the mines. It is necessary to book well in advance; at the height of the season tours are quite often booked out as long as two months ahead.

Bookings can be made on tel: (077) 49 1555 or by writing to the Information Centre, Marian Street, Mount Isa, 4825.

2 ROYAL FLYING DOCTOR SERVICE AND SCHOOL OF THE AIR

Rejoin Railway Ave at the end of Church St. Head north for a block where the road becomes Camooweal Rd (Barkly Highway). Continue for approximately 250m to the Royal Flying Doctor base which is situated just past the Anglican Church.

The Royal Flying Doctor Service (open between 9:00 and 15:00) and the School of the Air (10:00–12:00 during school term) are fascinating facets of outback life. Both provide vital services for property owners far removed from townships.

3 NATIONAL TRUST TENT MUSEUM

From the Royal Flying Doctor base turn left onto the Barkly Highway and drive south, passing the Anglican Church. Take the first left and then turn right into Fourth Ave which runs along the west bank of the river. Head south along Fourth Ave passing the basketball courts and Kruttschnitt Oval on the right. Cross

Death Adder Creek past First Ave on the right. The next street is Third Ave. The National Trust Tent House is on Fourth Ave opposite Third Ave.

In 1932 Mount Isa Mines began building low-cost accommodation to attract miners to the area. Miners had been living in very primitive conditions and J L Urquhart, who had gained a substantial interest in the mining company, began to develop Mount Isa as a company town. One of his first acts was to establish reasonable quality low-rent housing. The blinds to keep the heat out and the simple design were a vast improvement on the primitive quarters the miners had been living in. These houses made with canvas were vital to the growth of Mount Isa.

4 RIVERSLEIGH FOSSIL DISPLAY

From the Tent Museum head north up Fourth Ave, crossing Death Adder Creek to reach the main intersection leading to the Isa St Bridge. Turn right and take the bridge to the other side of the river. Turn into West St, the second street on the left. Continue past Marian St and the Riversleigh Fossil Display is on the left just past the Civic Centre, behind the city library.

The Riversleigh Fossil Display is located under an amphitheatre. It is a small collection of fossils from Riversleigh Station, about 250km north of Mount Isa. The fossils include everything from bat's teeth to the bones of a huge flightless ancient bird known as the Dromornorthis – the precursor of the emu.

5 TOURIST INFORMATION AND KALKADOON TRIBAL CENTRES

From the Fossil Museum head east along Marian St (Barkly Highway) for four blocks; the road angles to the left and then straightens out again after 250m. The next cross street is Corbould St. The Tourist Information Centre is on the right in the block bound by Corbould and Mullan sts. Kalkadoon Tribal Centre and Cultural Keeping Place is next to the Tourist Centre.

The very helpful Tourist Information Centre can provide visitors with maps and directions. The Kalkadoon Tribal Centre and Cultural Keeping Place contains interesting Aboriginal artefacts from the area.

6 CITY LOOKOUT

From Kalkadoon head east for half a block and take the first left which is Mullan St. Travel north for one block along Mullan St and turn left into Hilary St. The turn-off to the City Lookout is next on the right.

An overview of Mount Isa can be had by going up to the City Lookout. At night the lookout is a popular vantage point as the streetlights and lights of the mines give the city an attractive appearance.

7 FRANK ASTON ROTARY UNDERGROUND MUSEUM

From the lookout return to Hilary St and turn right. At the next intersection take Corbould St to the left and proceed to Marian St at the next intersection. Turn right into Marian St to find the Frank Aston Rotary Underground Museum, just behind K-Mart.

Built into the hill, the museum has good displays of old mining equipment and some

A mighty road train near Cloncurry.

The open-cut mine, Mount Isa.

interesting Aboriginal artefacts. It has been designed to give a sense of what the old mines at Mount Isa must have been like. The museum actually enters the hill from the top and goes down into a series of underground chambers and rooms. It was originally the city's reservoir.

8 CLEM WALTON PARK

From the museum return to Marian St (Barkly Highway) and follow it east. The Barkly Highway is the main route to Cloncurry. Clem Walton Park is outside of Mount Isa on the southern side of the Barkly Highway with a signposted turn-off.

Most of the Gulf lands are flat but the road to Cloncurry is uncharacteristically hilly and dramatic. The reason for this is that the Selwyn Ranges are mountains which have been so eroded that their bedding is exposed, twisting erratically in a thousand different directions. The people of Mount Isa will tell you that these mountains are the oldest exposed landmass on earth. The Clem Walton Park includes a remarkable lake with lots of birdlife.

9 CLONCURRY

From Clem Walton Park rejoin the Barkly Highway and travel east. Mary Kathleen is 55km east of Mount Isa. From Mary Kathleen travel 52km east along the highway to reach Cloncurry. Cross the Cloncurry River over the Ernest Henry Memorial Bridge. As the highway leads through the centre of town it is referred to as McIlwraith St.

There is real skill involved in finding Mary Kathleen these days as the famous mining town is now only a bitumen road leading into the bush.

It was at Cloncurry that copper was first discovered in western Queensland and it was here that the first regular Qantas flight landed and John Flynn established his first Flying Doctor Base.

The first Europeans in the area were Burke and Wills who passed through the rugged country between present-day Cloncurry and Mount Isa on their way to the Gulf of Carpentaria. Robert O'Hara Burke gave the town its name by calling a nearby river after his cousin, Lady Elizabeth Cloncurry.

In 1867, pastoralist and prospector Ernest Henry discovered the rich deposits of copper upon which the settlement of the area was based. Henry is Cloncurry's founding father; not only did he find the first copper in the area but he also established the Great Australian Mine.

10 JOHN FLYNN PLACE

After crossing the Cloncurry River follow the Flinders Highway. Rotary Park is on the left. After three blocks the highway turns to the right, but keep going straight ahead into Courthouse St, passing the school on the left and the swimming pool on the right. John Flynn Place is in the next block.

Perhaps Cloncurry's most important museum is that dedicated to Rev. John Flynn (Flynn of the Inland) who established the Royal Flying Doctor Service at Cloncurry in 1928. John Flynn Place moves progressively

The interior of John Flynn Place, Cloncurry.

Kalkadoon Tribal Centre, Mount Isa.

from an image of outback conditions at the turn of the century to the history of Flynn himself. The display includes some interesting personal memorabilia and explanations of how the whole Flying Doctor system worked in the early days.

11 THE MARY KATHLEEN MEMORIAL PARK AND MUSEUM

From John Flynn Place head south down Station St for two blocks. Turn left into McIlwraith St (Flinders Highway) and travel east. Cross the railway line and continue for 750m. The Cloncurry Mary Kathleen Memorial Park and Museum is on the right.

When Mary Kathleen was sold the Museum obtained a number of buildings and some important relics from the site. The sign which once stood on the road into the town is prominently displayed. The site includes a kiosk, tourist information centre and caretaker's residence, and there is an outdoor museum of historical machinery including steam engines and farming and mining equipment. The museum also houses an excellent collection of rocks and minerals from the area. Its prize possession is Robert O'Hara Burke's waterbottle.

12 CLONCURRY CEMETERY

From the Memorial Park and Museum head west along the Flinders Highway back to town. Cross the railway line, travel a further two blocks and follow the highway around to the right into Sheaffe St. Remain on Sheaffe St for the next five blocks to reach Alice St. The cemetery is on the left.

The town's Chinese and Afghan cemeteries are of interest. The Afghan Cemetery on the fringes of the town's old cemetery contains only one marked grave (with the headstone pointing towards Mecca) and a number of unmarked graves indicated by numbers.

Take the Flinders Highway back to Mount Isa.

62 THE LAND OF CROCODILE DUNDEE

■ DRIVING TOUR ■ 603KM ■ 1 DAY ■ THE PLACE OF AUSTRALIAN FOLKLORE

The road between Cloncurry and Winton is part of Australia's mythology – McKinlay's pub was the setting for scenes in Crocodile Dundee *and in Winton 'Banjo' Paterson composed 'Waltzing Matilda.'*

1 MCKINLAY

Head east out of Cloncurry on McIlwraith St (Flinders Highway). After 14km turn off the Flinders Highway onto the Landsborough (Matilda) Highway. Continue south-east for 90km to McKinlay. Turn right at the only street in McKinlay and continue for about 100m to the Walkabout Creek Hotel.

McKinlay's great claim to fame is that the local pub, now known as the Walkabout Creek Hotel, was featured in the original *Crocodile Dundee* as the location where Dundee regularly drank. Known initially as the Federal McKinlay Hotel, it was sold for $290 000 after the movie had been made and the current owners, while maintaining the rough and tumble feel of the original, are committed to promoting it as the town's one tourist attraction.

McKinlay was named after the river which was discovered and named by the explorer John McKinlay. He arrived in New South Wales in 1836 and by 1861 had become such an adept bushman that he was chosen to lead the South Australian Burke Relief Expedition to search for the missing Burke and Wills.

There was no immediate rush to the McKinlay area. Captain James Henry, the founder of Cloncurry, passed through the area in 1866. Gold was discovered on the McKinlay–Cloncurry road in 1872, and in 1883 a letter-receiving office was opened in the small settlement.

It wasn't until 1888 that lots of land in McKinlay were sold and 17 people bought half-acre blocks. The town grew as a service

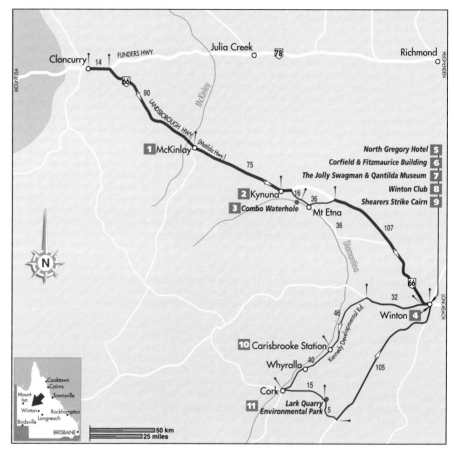

Corfield & Fitzmaurice, Winton.

Walkabout Creek Hotel, McKinlay.

centre for the surrounding pastoralists but it never became a major centre. Even today, with the interest generated by *Crocodile Dundee*, it is really nothing more than a couple of stores, a few houses and a pub.

2 KYNUNA

Leave McKinlay via the Landsborough Highway heading south-east for 75km to reach Kynuna.

A simple service centre for the surrounding stations, Kynuna's current importance is based on its location on the Matilda Highway. Most travellers will stop at one of the service stations to fill up with petrol, but there is little else to cause them to pause.

3 COMBO WATERHOLE

Leave Kynuna by the Matilda Highway heading east. The turn-off to the Combo Waterhole is on the south side of the highway, about 4km out of town. Follow this road south for 2km to reach another dirt road which follows the Diamantina River. Take this road for 10km to reach the waterhole.

Undoubtedly the region's greatest claim to fame is its association with 'Banjo' Paterson and particularly with the writing, and first performance, of 'Waltzing Matilda'.

4 WINTON

From the Combo Waterhole continue south-east along the road which follows the Diamantina River for about 19km to Mt Etna. From there a road leads 17km east back to the Matilda Highway. Once at the highway, travel south-east for 107km to Winton.

Winton is the centre of an important cattle- and sheep-raising region. Originally known as Pelican Waterhole, Winton owes its existence to the abortive Burke and Wills expedition and the subsequent expeditions which scoured central Queensland looking for the missing explorers. In the early 1860s a number of explorers including Frederick Walker, John McKinlay and William Landsborough all passed through the area. It was as a result of their reports that the area was first settled in the mid-1860s.

In 1875 Robert Allen arrived in the Winton area and became the postmaster at Pelican Waterhole. The following year the waterhole flooded and he was forced to move to higher ground. It is said that he got tired of writing the long 'Pelican Water-hole' on letters and so he renamed the town after the suburb in Bournemouth, England, where he was born.

5 NORTH GREGORY HOTEL

Enter the township of Winton via the Matilda Highway which at the southern end of town is called Elderslie Rd. At the beginning of the main median strip on Elderslie Rd note the statues of the pelicans at a watering hole. Further along the same road is the North Gregory Hotel.

Whatever the real origins of the events and images that 'Banjo' Paterson used when he wrote 'Waltzing Matilda', it is definitely known that it received its first public performance at the North Gregory Hotel. The current hotel is the fourth North Gregory (the other three either burned down or were destroyed) but it is still located on the site of the original pub. Judging from old photographs, the first North Gregory Hotel was a modest building with little more than bark walls and a corrugated-iron roof.

6 CORFIELD & FITZMAURICE BUILDING

Continue heading down the main street on the same side as the North Gregory Hotel and you will find the Corfield & Fitzmaurice Building.

Winton has a number of tourist attractions but none quite compare with a visit to the store of Corfield & Fitzmaurice. Corfield arrived in the area in the late 1870s and established a general store. The original store was replaced in 1916 and the current building, now listed by the National Trust, is one of the most perfectly preserved old-style general stores in Australia. Of particular interest is the 'flying fox' which is used to process cash transactions. It is now one of only two left in Australia, but in the 1940s and 1950s it was commonplace in rural stores all over the country.

7 THE JOLLY SWAGMAN AND QANTILDA MUSEUM

The Swagman Statue is on Elderslie St, in front of the swimming pool, on the block bounded by Oondooroo and Manuka sts. The Qantilda Pioneer Place Museum is across the road.

'Banjo' Paterson's jolly swagman has been immortalised for posterity, albeit in fibreglass, and appropriately he sits near a very healthy-looking coolibah tree.

The Qantilda Museum includes displays of old machinery, a dressed-up mannequin of Christina Macpherson playing 'Craiglea' and an extensive display of Qantas material. The museum is run by voluntary labour and there is always someone who can answer the questions of even the most curious of visitors. It is open from 9:00–16:00.

8 WINTON CLUB

From Qantilda Pioneer Place Museum head west along Elderslie St and take the first right into Oondooroo St. Head north to the end of the block. The Winton Club is on the corner of Oondooroo and Vindex sts.

The town of Winton is the birthplace of Qantas. On 16 November 1920 the Queensland and Northern Territory Air Service was registered as a company with its headquarters located in the town. The first official meeting of Qantas took place at the Winton Club on 10 February 1921. The Club is open to visitors.

9 SHEARERS STRIKE CAIRN

From the Winton Club head south along Oondooroo St for one block to Elderslie St. Turn left into Elderslie and next right into Manuka St. Head south for 8km following signs to the Shearers Strike Cairn.

This memorial cairn records the town's involvement in the famous shearers' strike of 1891. Over 500 shearers camped south of the town for four months during the dispute and, although Winton was not greatly affected by the strike, the mounted police arrived from Charleville to keep order.

10 CARISBROOKE STATION

From Winton head west along the Matilda Highway for 6km to the Kennedy Developmental Rd turn-off. Follow the Kennedy Developmental Rd for 32km to the Carisbrooke Station turn-off, then follow the signs for another 46km to the station.

Today Carisbrooke Station is a wildlife sanctuary and, with its wonderful Aboriginal rock paintings and its dramatic scenery, is regarded by many of the Winton locals as a place which richly deserves to be ranked with some of Australia's most interesting outback reserves.

11 LARK QUARRY ENVIRONMENTAL PARK

From Carisbrooke Station head south-west for 22km to Whyralla. From Whyralla take the road to Cork which is 18km to the south-west. From Cork head east for 15km to reach Lark Quarry Environmental Park.

Lark Quarry Environmental Park with its famous Dinosaur Stampede depicts life in western Queensland 95 million years ago.

The Qantilda Museum, Winton.

This is the largest group of footprints of running dinosaurs uncovered anywhere in the world. First discovered in the early 1960s, the site was completely excavated in 1976–1977 by the Queensland Museum. The evidence gathered showed that three species of dinosaur made the 1200 tracks – a large flesh-eating carnosaur and many small coelurosaurs and ornithopods.

The brochure on Lark Quarry explains the footprints: 'Most of the footprints were made when a carnosaur trapped groups of coelurosaurs and ornithopods on the muddy edge of a lake.' There was general panic and the small dinosaurs fled in a stampede across the lake. The triangular-shaped area is now protected from the weather by a permanent roof; clear signs on a 650m track explain the events. The footprints make up an area of about 210 square metres

From Lark Quarry Park return to Winton; the journey is 110km. The road should be reasonably good as it is now regularly graded.

WALTZING MATILDA

No one knows exactly what prompted Paterson to write his tale of the swaggie who, rather than surrender to the police, decided to commit suicide by jumping into a billabong. The origins of the verse have been the subject of debate virtually ever since it was written. However the blurry pieces of the puzzle are intriguing.

On 4 September 1894 the *Brisbane Courier* reported: 'Information has been received at Winton that a man named Hoffmeister, a prominent unionist, was found dead about two miles from Kynuna. The local impression is that he was one of the attacking mob at Dagworth and was wounded there. There were seven unionists with Hoffmeister when he died. These assert that he committed suicide.'

It is now widely believed that this story was the inspiration for the song, although the Winton town history offers a more romantic version. Paterson was staying at Dagworth Station in 1895 when Christina Macpherson played the tune 'Craiglea' for the guests. Paterson liked the tune and inquired about the words. Macpherson explained that she did not know them. This was enough to inspire Paterson. The lyrics which he wrote were an intermingling of a series of events that occurred while he was staying at Dagworth Station. During his stay Paterson saw a sheep which appeared to have died but on closer examination it had been killed, presumably by a swagman, and portions of it carefully removed to give the impression of natural death. This was possibly the inspiration for 'the crime'.

A second strand to the story focuses on Combo Waterhole at Belfast Station which is clearly the setting for the poem. It is argued that Paterson used the setting after he had been told the story of Hoffmeister at Combo Waterhole by Robert Macpherson. It is also claimed that the expression 'Waltzing Matilda' was first mentioned to Paterson at Dagworth Station by a jackeroo named Jack Carter.

CHAPTER 11
THE FAR NORTH

63 ATTRACTIONS OF CAIRNS AND KURANDA

■ DRIVING AND RAIL TOUR ■ 44KM ■ 1 DAY ■ NORTH QUEENSLAND'S PREMIER DESTINATION

Cairns is the premier holiday and tourist destination in north Queensland. A town steeped in history, it has in recent times attracted millions of dollars in tourist development.

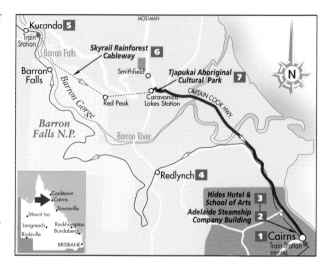

Cairns lies at the centre of a tropical paradise. To the north of the city are palm-fringed beaches; to the east are spectacular rainforests, exotic fauna and flora, and dramatic waterfalls. Captain Cook was the first European to see the site which is now modern-day Cairns. In June 1770, Cook sailed into an inlet which, because it was Trinity Sunday, he named Trinity Bay. A little further north, Cook's ship *Endeavour* ran aground on the reef and he was forced to beach the vessel at the site now known as Cooktown.

On 6 October 1876 the *Porpoise* arrived in Trinity Bay with a postmaster and customs officers aboard. The public servants cut out an area for themselves near where The Esplanade in Cairns now stands. At the time the whole of the area was covered with dense scrub. On 1 November, Trinity Bay was declared a port of entry and clearance and was named Cairns after the then Governor of Queensland, Sir William Cairns.

In spite of these official actions the region around Smithfield to the north of the present city was much more popular. By November its population had reached 150 and it was growing quite rapidly. The following year, however, Smithfield was completely destroyed by a freak flood on the Barron River. Following the destruction of Smithfield, most of the population moved to Port Douglas rather than Cairns and in so doing immediately took the bulk of the maritime business away from it.

The town's revival occurred with the establishment of the sugar plantations in the Mulgrave and Russell river valleys in 1882. This was followed by the building of a railway from Myola (just beyond Kuranda) in 1886. The combination of a rail terminus and port sustained Cairns. It became the terminus for the Brisbane railway line in 1924. It was an important air and naval base during World War II and in 1984 the airport was upgraded to international standard, thus giving the city the boost it needed.

1 HISTORIC CAIRNS

Drive south along The Esplanade, turning left towards the shoreline where The Esplanade becomes Abbott St. The Esplanade veers to the right just past Spence St and becomes Wharf St.

There is enough of the old Cairns left for the astute visitor to imagine what the city was once like. The most interesting buildings are in the Wharf Street, Abbott Street and Lake Street areas. The famous Barbary Coast collection of buildings is most vividly portrayed by two hotels – the Barrier Reef and Oceanic on Wharf Street – which recall the shipping origins of Cairns. Their location close to the wharves and their wide verandahs and awnings make them an important part of Cairns' streetscape.

The Hides Hotel, Cairns.

2 ADELAIDE STEAMSHIP COMPANY BUILDING

From the corner of Wharf and Sheridan sts, drive in a north-easterly direction along Wharf St and turn left into Lake St opposite the cruise liner terminal. Drive north along Lake St for three blocks to City Place.

The old Adelaide Steamship Company Building on the corner of Lake and Aplin streets is now owned by Quaids Real Estate, however it has retained its distinctive charm. The relief image of a steamship on the Lake Street side recalls its previous owners.

3 HIDES HOTEL AND SCHOOL OF ARTS

Hides Hotel is located on the corner of Lake and Shields sts at City Place.

Stalls at Kuranda Markets.

Hides Hotel is a typical north Queensland grand hotel dating back to the 1920s. Built out of a combination of timber and brick, it used to dominate the corner and was an important gathering point for the people of Cairns before World War II.

Opposite Hides is the elegant School of Arts building. Constructed in 1907, it now houses the Cairns Historical Museum which has a good display of memorabilia relating to Cairns and the region. Its documentation of the town's history from Cook through to the building of the railway is complemented by good displays of Aboriginal artefacts and a very interesting video on the Great Barrier Reef. The building itself, with its wide verandahs, is an excellent example of the kind of architecture which made Cairns an elegant city before World War I.

4 REDLYNCH

From The Esplanade travel south to Spence St and turn right. Drive five blocks before turning right into McLeod St. The train station is located on the left. Trains from Cairns to Kuranda run at 8:20 and 9:00 on Mondays and Tuesdays; at 8:20, 9:00 and 9:40 on Wednesdays, Thursdays, Fridays and Sundays; and at 9:00 on Saturdays. The trip takes 1 hour.

Redlynch, only a couple of kilometres from Freshwater on the Kuranda railway line, is famous in the literary life of Australia. The great novelist, Xavier Herbert, lived here for 34 years during which time he worked at the local pharmacy (on Saturday mornings) and wrote the mammoth *Poor Fellow My Country*. Published in 1975, it is the largest novel ever written in Australia. Herbert lived opposite the railway station and wrote the novel in a shed behind the house.

5 KURANDA

From the Kuranda Railway Station it is only a short walk up the hill to the town's main street with its gift shops and eateries.

Kuranda is awash with shops and activities which are all designed to entice the tourist dollar out of the tourist pocket. There are the inevitable arts and craft shops; seemingly endless eateries, from pie shops to coffee lounges and restaurants; and a market – the kind of place where candles, jewellery, leather goods, T-shirts, tropical fruits and woodwork are sold.

The town boasts three genuine tourist attractions – a Butterfly Sanctuary where some of the rainforest's most beautiful creatures are on display, the markets which are deservedly popular and successful, and the Kuranda Wildlife Noctarium. The wide range of items at the markets – particularly some of the interesting handicrafts made by the 'alternative lifestyle' people who live in the area – is remarkable and there are some really good bargains. The Noctarium offers a lovely display of nocturnal wildlife in a simulated night-time rainforest setting. Carpeted ramps allow the visitor to follow the 'Forest Alive at Night' display.

6 SKYRAIL RAINFOREST CABLEWAY

Straight across the road from the Kuranda Railway Station is the Skyrail Terminal.

This spectacular 7.5km journey over rainforest from the top of the escarpment to Caravonica Lakes Station north of Cairns must rate as one of Australia's most memorable tourist experiences. There is nowhere else on earth where you can travel across a tropical river, beside a huge waterfall and across untouched tropical rainforest without damaging the landscape.

The Skyrail became a reality after years of on-going battles with environmentalists (it was argued that its construction would irreparably damage the rainforest). The result is beyond criticism; the Skyrail blends into the environment and offers a once-in-a-lifetime experience as it moves silently over the top of the rainforest canopy.

The first stop is the Barron Falls Station which offers a glorious panorama of the Barron Gorge. It is then possible to alight from the cable car and walk to the cliffs for a better view of the Barron Falls.

Returning to the cableway, the Skyrail passes over the top of the rainforest before arriving at Red Peak Station where, again, it is possible to break the journey and inspect the rainforest from a wooden walkway. The wonderful diversity of the vegetation is evident with palms, ferns, epiphytes and towering rainforest trees surrounding the station. The journey then descends the escarpment to the Caravonica Lakes Station.

7 TJAPUKAI ABORIGINAL CULTURAL PARK

The Tjapukai Aboriginal Cultural Park is located next to the Caravonica Lakes Station.

The Park is a unique attempt to explain Aboriginal culture (in this case the society of the Djabugay and Yirrgandyji peoples) in a thematic way. There is a Cultural Village (complete with boomerang and spear throwing), a Creation Theatre (in which the story of creation is told in the Tjapukai language – with headset translations), a History Theatre (an overview of the past 120 years) and a Magic Space where people can view the giant murals. Visitors can experience all the performances in a 2-hour period.

The Cultural Park is a powerful statement of what it means to be an Aborigine. The effectiveness of the experience rests on a mixture of the educational (each dancer explains a particular aspect of Aboriginal life, ranging from the boomerang and didgeridoo to songsticks, spears and clothing), the blending of the ancient and the modern in both dancing and singing, the enactment of a tribal legend which is easy to follow, a genuine rapport with the audience, a buoyant sense of humour, and a constantly reiterated theme of 'Proud to be an Aborigine'. The result of all this is entertainment which leaves the audience both elated and educated.

From the Skyrail and Tjapukai Aboriginal Cultural Park head south on the Captain Cook Highway. The highway becomes Sheridan St which leads into the centre of Cairns. Several bus companies offer regular transfer services from the Skyrail and Tjapukai Theme Park to Cairns station. Package deals for the Kuranda Railway, the Skyrail and the bus back to Cairns are available.

THE KURANDA RAILWAY

The journey on the Kuranda train is delightful. The Kuranda railway line is probably the most scenically beautiful in Australia with one section running across the face of the Stony Creek Falls and other sections winding around the hillside and through no fewer than 15 tunnels. At various points there are views across the Coral Sea. It was built by John Robb between 1886 and 1891 and is recognised as a masterpiece of railway engineering. In 1915 the railway station at Kuranda was completed.

Perhaps the perfect symbol of the town's unswerving commitment to tourism is the way the Barron Falls are used. In the dry season the water over the falls reduces to a trickle. However, to provide the tourists with good photographs, just before the tourist train arrives at Barron Falls Station someone opens one of the floodgates and, quite miraculously, the falls begin to fall. This phenomenon is also worth watching if you travel to Kuranda by car.

Dancers at the Tjapukai Aboriginal Cultural Park, north of Cairns.

64 THE CORAL CAYS AND THE OUTER REEF

■ BOAT TOUR ■ 270KM ■ 1 DAY ■ EXPLORING THE GREAT BARRIER REEF

This tour offers visitors an opportunity to explore the outer sections of the Great Barrier Reef and to enjoy snorkelling, swimming or scuba diving on the western side of Agincourt Reef.

1 MARLIN MARINA

Cruises to the Great Barrier Reef leave Cairns from either Marlin Marina, located at the end of Spence St, or Trinity Wharf in Wharf St. Access to the Marlin Marina can be gained either by travelling south along The Esplanade (which runs along Cairns' main beach) or by travelling south along any of the main roads in the city centre and turning left into Spence St. There is parking available nearby. Trinity Wharf is situated just south of Marlin Marina.

The *Wavepiercer* transfer vessel leaves the Marlin Marina at 8:00 every morning. You can arrange for a courtesy bus to collect you from your accommodation in Cairns. The journey up the coast from Cairns to Port Douglas is about 65km and takes around one and a half hours. The transfer catamaran travels close enough to the shore to allow travellers to watch the coastline with its necklace of tropical beaches lying under the escarpment which rises sharply behind.

2 OUTER REEF PLATFORM

The cruise to Agincourt Reef at the outer eastern extremity of the Great Barrier Reef is run by the Australian-owned company Quicksilver. The journey from Port Douglas starts at the Marina Mirage which is located on Wharf St, Port Douglas. Travel north into Port Douglas and turn right into Port St near the Chinese restaurant. Port St becomes Wharf St. Quicksilver is located next to the Marina Mirage parking lot and the booking office is in the marina's arcade.

It takes around one and a half hours to travel from Port Douglas Marina Mirage Jetty to the Outer Reef Platform. The same destination can also be reached in two and a half hours from Shute Harbour. (See Tour 49

for a description of the Outer Reef Platform.)

The *Wavepiercer* leaves the Outer Reef Platform at around 15:00 and makes the journey back to Port Douglas, arriving at the Mirage Marina around 16:30. The connection to Cairns takes another one and a half hours. Travellers can expect to be back at the Marlin Marina no later than 18:00. Courtesy buses are always on hand to take people back to their accommodation.

3 LOW ISLES

The trips to the Low Isles are also organised and run by Quicksilver. See above for detailed instructions on how to get to the Marina Mirage at Port Douglas. This trip to the Low Isles, though much shorter than the journey to the Outer Reef, leaves the Marina Mirage at the same time and also returns at the same time. Thus, all the connections with Cairns are the same.

The Low Isles lie 13km north-east of Port Douglas. First discovered by Captain Cook in 1770 they offer an interesting alternative to the longer but faster journey to the Outer Reef. A cruise leaves the Marlin Marina at Port Douglas each day at 10:00. The journey to the Low Isles sails past the rocky headland to the north of Port Douglas township and provides views of Four Mile Beach. Visitors can sit on the beach, walk around the island (the coral cay is only 1.5ha although it is surrounded by 22ha of coral

Basking in the sun, Green Island.

Cruise boats moored at Cairns Harbour.

The coral cay of Green Island near Cairns.

reef), view the coral gardens from a glass-bottomed boat, inspect the island's historic lighthouse, and go on guided snorkelling and scuba-diving expeditions on the reef. The 30m catamaran, called the *Wavedancer*, is moored at a platform at the edge of the coral cay's reef.

4 FITZROY ISLAND

Great Adventure Tours, located at The Pier Market-place, offers daytrips to Fitzroy Island which depart from Trinity Wharf in Cairns at 8:30 every morning and then return at 17:30 in the afternoon. These trips are far less organised than those to the Outer Reef. The size of the island allows visitors to go walking in the rainforest, hike to the lighthouse, lie on the beach or go snorkelling on the reef.

Unlike Green Island and the Low Isles, Fitzroy Island is a mountainous continental island covered with dense vegetation. It is a favourite spot for travellers, as some 324ha of this 666ha island is covered by tropical rainforest and is almost completely surrounded by fringing coral reef. The island's main peak rises 271m above sea level.

Fitzroy offers a serious bushwalking alternative to exploring the reef while still providing excellent beaches and easy access to the Great Barrier Reef. Also available is a guided tour of the local clam farm.

5 GREEN ISLAND

Tours of Green Island operate from The Pier Market-place in Cairns. Quite a number of tours are available. Big Cat Green Island Cruises offer full-day packages including snorkelling, glass-bottomed boat tours of the reef around the island, a barbecue lunch, and an opportunity to visit the island's Marineland Melanesia zoological gardens. Reef-Jet Cruises offer a variety of trips to the island including a morning trip which departs from The Pier Marketplace at 8:45 and returns at 12:30, an afternoon trip which departs at 13:00 and returns at 17:00, and a full-day trip which departs at 8:45 and returns at 17:00.

For several years the coral cay of Green Island was one of Cairns' prime unspoilt Barrier Reef tourist attractions. This small uninhabited island once had nothing more than a jetty with a marine-viewing point at its end. In recent times a resort offering a wide range of attractions has been established so that tourism has taken over from its rather primitive charm.

The island now has the Marineland Melanesia zoological gardens, an aquarium complex which holds the two largest saltwater crocodiles in captivity (their names are Oscar and Cassius). Also on display are shipwreck artefacts and antique diving equipment. There are glass-bottomed boat and semi-submersible coral-viewing tours, snorkelling trails, an underwater observatory, a range of excellent eating facilities and a Barrier Reef Theatre.

Green Island was the fictional setting for an innocent pre-marital holiday for Joe Harman and Jean Paget in Neville Shute's novel *A Town Like Alice*.

Accommodation at the Green Island Reef Resort can be arranged by contacting the resort on tel: (070) 31 3300.

The aquamarine waters of the Great Barrier Reef.

65 NORTHERN BEACHES AND TRINITY BAY

■ DRIVING TOUR ■ 164KM ■ 1 DAY ■ SWIMMING AND WALKING NEAR CAIRNS

A pleasant daytrip is a journey up the beaches linking Cairns with Port Douglas. Between Yorkeys Knob and Port Douglas there are special shelters to protect swimmers from stingers and sharks.

Although Captain James Cook was the first European to reach Cairns, it wasn't until October 1873 that the area began to attract settlers. The discovery of gold at Palmer River meant that port facilities were created at Cooktown. In the next few years there were a number of gold discoveries in far north Queensland. Cooktown was the only port servicing the area and the miners in the south, particularly those on the Hodgkinson field, began to look for a new and shorter route to the coast.

One miner named Bill Smith had worked around Trinity Bay as a bêche-de-mer fisherman before becoming a prospector and he was convinced that Trinity Bay could become a suitable port. In 1876 he successfully cut a track from Trinity Bay across Freshwater Creek and the Barron River to the Hodgkinson River goldfields. Smithfield to the north of Cairns was named after him.

At the same time the local policeman on the Hodgkinson field, an Inspector Douglas, was instructed to cut a track down to the coast. Douglas joined Smith on his return to Trinity Bay but he came down the south side of the Douglas River. Within the space of two months there were two tracks from the goldfields to the coast.

A small township was established at the present site of Cairns in late 1876, but it was short-lived because the land was swampy. Smithfield became the more important centre and within a year it had blossomed. It soon had a reputation as 'the wickedest town in Australia' and legend has it that the town's publican made so much money from the goldminers that he had his horse shod with gold.

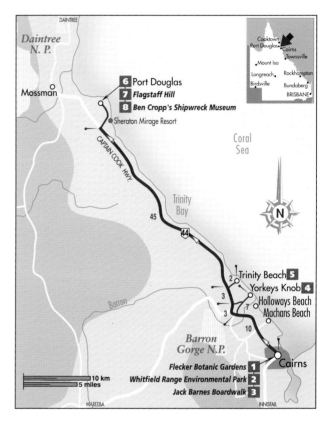

1 FLECKER BOTANIC GARDENS

Drive to the North Cairns end of the Esplanade. Turn left into Lily St, crossing Lake and Digger sts. Turn right into Sheridan St and drive two blocks north to Collins Ave, turning left into it. The entrance to the Flecker Botanic Gardens is 500m further on the right.

The Flecker Botanic Gardens at Edge Hill are widely regarded as the most impressive botanical display in north Queensland with over 10 000 plant species as well as excellent views over Cairns. The gardens were started in 1886 and take their name from Dr Hugo Flecker, a very keen botanist and biologist, who established the North Queensland Naturalists Club. Of particular interest is the Aboriginal Plant Use Garden which contains plants used by local Aborigines for medicine, food, weapons and shelter. There are also forests of palms and paperbark trees which are typical of the original vegetation of the Cairns district.

2 WHITFIELD RANGE ENVIRONMENTAL PARK

Travel back along Collins Ave for 200m to the Whitfield Range Environmental Park.

The Whitfield Range Environmental Park provides a number of walking trails through the rainforest which lies between Mount Whitfield, Mount Lumley Hill and the Cairns International Airport. The tracks are very clearly marked and there are a number of lookouts which provide excellent views over Cairns Harbour.

3 JACK BARNES BICENTENNIAL MANGROVE BOARDWALK

Return along Collins Ave to Sheridan St. Turn left into Sheridan St and travel 100m to Airport Ave. Turn right into Airport Ave and drive 1km to the Jack Barnes Bicentennial Mangrove Boardwalk.

In 1988 another very interesting botanical expedition was included in the city's sights with the opening of the Jack Barnes Bicentennial Mangrove Boardwalk. Located off Airport Avenue it allows visitors to inspect and explore the mangrove swamps from elevated boardwalks.

4 YORKEYS KNOB

Return along Airport Ave to Sheridan St and turn right. This road becomes the Captain Cook Highway. Drive north across the Barron River. Pass the turn-offs to Machans Beach and Holloways Beach and turn right onto Yorkeys Knob Rd. Travel north for 7km to Yorkeys Knob where the road becomes Varley St. At the end of Varley St veer left into Buckley St which leads to Sims Esplanade and the beach.

The beaches to the north of Cairns are a delight. Once separate communities, they are now commuter suburbs for the city. Of all the beaches Yorkeys Knob has the most interesting history. It was named after a one-armed bêche-de-mer fisherman who used the point as a base for his fishing activities at the turn of the century. During World War II it became a popular haunt for American servicemen on R & R leave. Today it is one of Cairns' more exclusive areas.

5 TRINITY BEACH

Return along Yorkeys Knob Rd for 3km to Dunne Rd and then turn right. Follow Dunne Rd to McGregor Rd. Turn left and travel 1km to the Captain Cook Highway. At the roundabout, turn right onto the Captain Cook Highway. Travel approximately 3km north to the next roundabout and turn right into Trinity Beach Rd. Travel 2km to Trinity Beach.

Trinity Beach, without doubt the best-kept secret in the Cairns district, is a secluded sanctuary which lies just 15 minutes to the north of Cairns. The beach is palm-fringed and is protected from sharks and stingers. Accommodation is excellent and the eating facilities are outstanding. Whereas Cairns is all hustle and bustle, Trinity Beach is tranquil and extremely beautiful.

6 PORT DOUGLAS

Return along Trinity Beach Rd to the Captain Cook Highway and turn right heading north to the turn-off to Port Douglas, Port Douglas Rd. Travel 2km along Port Douglas Rd to a roundabout. This is the turn-off to the Sheraton Mirage Resort which is located to the right. Continue along Port Douglas Rd, which becomes Davidson St. Turn left into Macrossan St to reach Wharf St, which leads to the shore.

Port Douglas was first established in 1877 when Christie Palmerston cut a road through the rainforest and down the mountain range. Palmerston is one of those fascinating characters who inhabit the early history of Queensland. Born Cristofero Palmerston Carandini in Melbourne, it is claimed that he headed for Queensland in 1873 to join the Palmer River gold rush. It is more likely that he came with his mother's theatre group. Certainly his fame came with the Hodgkinson River gold rush. The track he cut from the goldfields to Port Douglas was his first but in the next decade he blazed at least four trails to the coast.

Palmerston's first track was affectionately known as 'The Bump' and it went from the goldfields on the Hodgkinson River to Island Point (which was the first name for Port Douglas) on the coast. In the early days the settlement at Port Douglas was known variously as Terrigal, Port Owen, Island Point and Salisbury. It was given the name Salisbury after Lord Salisbury, the British Prime Minister at the time. However this name was changed following a visit by government officials. The town was then renamed after John Douglas, the Queensland Premier during the period.

Within weeks of its establishment the town was booming. There were an estimated 50 tent pubs, a bakery, a general store and rough accommodation. People poured into the town on their way to the diggings. It took the town less than a year to establish itself. By mid-1878 there were 21 permanent hotels and a local newspaper, the town had

been surveyed, lots were for sale, and the mail was being delivered from Port Douglas to Thornborough on the goldfields.

By the early 1880s the town had a population of around 8000 and had overtaken Cairns as the most important port on the north Queensland coast.

Its decline was rapid. The gold started to run out by about 1886 and the miners moved on to Papua and New Guinea. Cairns became the major railhead for the whole of the region with lines running south along the coast and inland to the mining fields. Port Douglas, however, remained the port for the sugar mill at Mossman until 1958.

Looking at Port Douglas now it is hard to imagine that it was once a wild frontier town filled with itinerant seamen and gold prospectors. Today it is a luxury holiday resort. The Sheraton Mirage Hotel complex, with its golf course, neat rows of palm trees, and huge apartments, has generated an industry in the town. The once-sleepy little village which remembered its roaring days is now a major tourist-resort centre with fashionable arcades.

The town is positively awash with elegant holiday apartments and motels, all sporting their beautifully manicured lawns; there are private golf courses, lavish tennis courts and fashionably expensive restaurants; every conceivable tour to the Great Barrier Reef is offered and day bus tours and safaris operate to the lush hinterland.

7 FLAGSTAFF HILL

Turn right into Wharf St which curves sharply to the right and heads up Flagstaff Hill.

Flagstaff Hill (also known as The Lookout) can be reached by turning right at the end of the main street and following the signs. It offers an excellent view over Four Mile Beach and superb views over the Coral Sea.

Four Mile Beach has a reputation as one of the most attractive beaches in the area. It is characterised by hard white sands but,

Four Mile Beach, Port Douglas.

as always, it is not safe to swim there during the summer months when the poisonous box jellyfish arrive in the area.

8 BEN CROPP'S SHIPWRECK TREASURE TROVE MUSEUM

Return along Wharf St, turn right into Dixie St and at the northern end of the jetty is Ben Cropp's Shipwreck Treasure Trove Museum.

One of the town's highlights is local adventurer Ben Cropp's Shipwreck Treasure Trove Museum on the wharf at Port Douglas. The collection of material from shipwrecks includes everything from ballast to 'pieces of eight' coins; a section of the decking has been opened up so that visitors can view reconstructed pieces of wreckage in the sea below the wharf and, of course, there is a continuous video featuring Cropp's remarkable underwater photography. It is well set out and presented.

Return along Dixie St to Wharf St. Continue south along Wharf St to the marina which is located about 500m further on the right, next to the Bally Hooley rail terminal. The marina is both a shopping mall and the main point of departure for cruises to the coral cays and outer reef. To return to Cairns head south on Wharf St, which veers to the left and becomes Port St. Turn right onto Davidson Rd, which becomes Port Douglas Rd. Continue south to reach the Captain Cook Highway. Travel south for 61km to reach Cairns.

The Shipwreck Museum, Port Douglas.

The interior of the Shipwreck Museum.

Marina Mirage at sunset, Port Douglas.

66 FROM SUGARCANE TO RAINFOREST

■ DRIVING TOUR ■ 208KM ■ 1 DAY ■ EXPERIENCING UNSPOILT RAINFOREST

This tour is an indication of the rich diversity of coastal tropical Queensland. The road passes through fields of sugarcane before entering the beautiful Daintree rainforest.

Mossman, the most northerly sugar town in Queensland, lies at the foot of rainforest-clad Mount Demi (1158m) and under the gaze of the unusual rock formation of Good Shepherd Rock. The rock is said by the local Aborigines to keep watch over Mossman and the town will be prosperous as long as it stands. The nearby Mossman Gorge on the edge of the Daintree National Park is a magnificant tropical wilderness area.

The town of Mossman was named by the explorer George Dalrymple in 1873 after the minerals explorer Hugh Mosman. Mosman's great moment of fame came when he (or, rather, his 11-year-old Aboriginal servant, Jupiter) found gold at Charters Towers in 1872. The boom which followed the discovery did much to help the development of north Queensland.

The name of the town was changed from Mosman to Mossman to avoid any confusion with the suburb in Sydney. A village was established in 1876 and in 1896 the first sugarcane plantation was established in the area; the following year the Mossman sugar mill was opened.

The mill, the first in Australia to crush over 100 000 tonnes of sugarcane in one season, is now the town's largest employer. From June to October, the cane-crushing season, cane trains are a familiar sight along the main street.

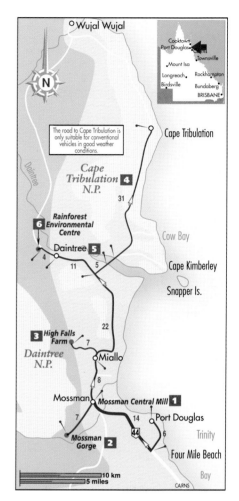

1 MOSSMAN CENTRAL MILL

From Port Douglas head east along Macrossan St and then turn right into Davidson St. Continue heading south along Davidson St which becomes Port Douglas Rd. Continue for a further 6km to the Captain Cook Highway and then head north-west for 14km to Mossman. Leading into Mossman the highway becomes Alchera Dve and then Front St. The next right past the Post Office is Mill St, which leads to the Mossman Central Mill, 500m from the main street.

The town's main attraction, the Mossman Central Mill, has been the focus of a very enterprising exercise in tourism known as

The shopping precinct, Port Douglas.

Mossman Gorge.

the Bally Hooley Rail Tour. Each day at 9:30 an old steam train with open carriages leaves Port Douglas and travels across to Mossman where passengers can inspect the mill if it is in operation.

2 MOSSMAN GORGE

Return to the town centre. From the Post Office head south along Front St and take the second right into Johnston Rd. The high school is opposite the turn-off. Head west along Johnston Rd passing the bowling club on the left. Pass the District Hospital on the right and continue for another 7km to Mossman Gorge.

To the south-west of the town is the Mossman Gorge, which is part of the magnificent Daintree National Park. The park officers have constructed a series of walkways through the rainforest which allow visitors to inspect the fauna and flora of the region.

3 HIGH FALLS FARM

Return along the same road to Mossman. Once at Front St (the highway) head north through the town centre and cross the Mossman River. The traveller leaving the town heading north will pass under a row of immense raintrees. These natives of South-East Asia were planted on the outskirts of the town over 80 years ago. Remain on the highway and continue heading north to the intersection of Daintree Rd (the highway) and Whyanbeel Rd. The intersection is marked by a service station and the direction to High Falls Farm is signposted. Follow Whyanbeel Rd for about 7km to High Falls Farm.

Further to the north of the town is High Falls Farm, the only place in all Australia where plantains (a kind of giant banana used as a vegetable in South America and

the Caribbean) are grown commercially. It has a tropical restaurant where the visitor can taste plantains cooked in a number of different recipes. The farm is also an orchard where exotic tropical fruits are grown.

4 CAPE TRIBULATION

Return east along Whyanbeel Rd to reach Daintree Rd (the highway.) Take Daintree north to the Cape Tribulation–Ferry Crossing turn-off. Take the turn-off and continue for 5km to the Daintree River crossing. After crossing the river, head north for another 2km until you see the turn-off to Cape Kimberley on the right. Do not take this turn-off, but proceed for another 29km to Cape Tribulation.

The 16 965ha Cape Tribulation National Park is an area of breathtaking beauty with rugged mountain ranges rising sharply behind the narrow coastal strip, dense rainforest tumbling down the mountains to the beaches, and a bewilderingly rich variety of flora. The rainforest boasts some species of fern which have been on earth for well over 100 million years; both the beautiful

Tall fig trees near Cape Tribulation.

A beach nestled at the foot of the rainforest, Cape Tribulation.

flowering *Idiospermum australiense* and the *Angiopteris*, the world's largest fern, are plants of great antiquity.

At Cape Tribulation, the National Parks and Wildlife have made life much easier for visitors by providing a cement path and a boardwalk through the rainforest to the headland where a lookout point affords excellent views across the bay. For those people wishing to explore further there are a number of excellent rainforest walking trails. Many of the local tour operators offer walking tours into the rainforest.

The road between Daintree and Cape Tribulation is less than magnificent, mainly because of the seemingly endless number of tours which make the daily journey from Cairns and Port Douglas. It is sealed to the turn-off to Cow Bay but beyond that point it is a winding dirt road which is passable for conventional vehicles in good weather.

5 DAINTREE

From Cape Tribulation head south for 31km, passing the turn-offs to Cow Bay and Cape Kimberley. Cross the Daintree River and travel for 5km back to the Daintree township turn-off. Take the road west for 11km to the reach the township.

Daintree is a tiny township comprising a general store, the Bushman's Lodge with its huge fibreglass 'Big Barramundi', the timber museum – a woodworking shop which produces beautiful pieces of wooden furniture from the local timbers and which mounts an exhibition of carpenter's and cabinet maker's tools and techniques – a couple of restaurants, a butterfly farm, a caravan park, a school and a number of river and rainforest tour operators.

The town is perfectly located; behind it, the magnificent tropical rainforest mountains of the McDowall Ranges rise steeply while the Daintree River winds its way lazily past the town.

Historically Daintree was first settled in the late 1870s and early 1880s by timber cutters who were searching for the cedar trees in the rainforest. At the time there were large stands of cedar near the river and the loggers moved the felled timber down the river by constructing rafts from the logs. The timber cutters were followed by dairy farmers – the town's butter factory was built in 1924 – who eventually changed over to beef production, and today the mainstay of the local economy is tourism.

Daintree's great success is that it has managed to establish a tourist industry which has not overwhelmed or vulgarised it. There are a number of cruises down the Daintree River which enable visitors to see crocodiles as well as have a close inspection of the mangroves and the tropical rainforest which edge the river. A rich range of birdlife is also a feature of the area. Along the final 22km before the river meets the ocean, the diverse fish and crustacean life attracts thousands of migratory and native birds.

Of these cruises, the most popular is the M V *Spirit of Daintree*, a strange vessel which looks like a train and which, according to the owners, is environmentally designed. Bookings for tours can be made on tel: (070) 90 7676.

A nearby coffee plantation with its distinctive, turreted, castle-like homestead produces exotic fruit as well as coffee. There are conducted tours.

6 DAINTREE RAINFOREST ENVIRONMENTAL CENTRE

Follow the road out of Daintree to the west. Shortly after crossing Barrett Creek, the Daintree Rainforest Environmental Centre will be found on the left. The centre is 4km from the Daintree township.

Across the Daintree River (take the ferry turn-off to the south of the town) is the Daintree Rainforest Environmental Centre where a clever combination of displays, an audiovisual presentation and a short stroll along a 400m boardwalk provide a good introduction for visitors. There are film presentations on the local rainforest biology, the area's feral pig problem and cassowaries, as well as interactive computer displays on the evolution of rainforests.

There are also plenty of opportunities to walk in the rainforest. The Queensland rainforests are the habitat of some of the rarest flora and fauna in the world and it is worth remembering that the environmentalists who fought against the road through Cape Tribulation and the logging in Daintree were people who realised the importance of the rainforest's ecosystem and the rareness of the species found within it. Species such as Bennett's tree kangaroo, the musky rat-kangaroo, ancient ferns, and exotic rhododendrons which are of Asiatic origin, are unique to this area.

From the Daintree Rainforest Environmental Centre take the highway south for about 45km to Mossman. Proceed through Mossman for some 14km to the Port Douglas turn-off. Take Port Douglas Rd to the left and follow it north to the town centre.

A river cruise on the Daintree River.

67 THE FIRST EUROPEAN SETTLEMENT

■ DRIVING TOUR ■ 441KM ■ 2 DAYS ■ THE CHARMS OF TROPICAL, HISTORICAL COOKTOWN

The inland road to Cooktown via Lakeland is bumpy and difficult and the coastal road, although breathtakingly beautiful, is strictly for 4WD vehicles. However the journey is worth making.

1 MOUNT MOLLOY

From Port Douglas head south for 6km to the Captain Cook Highway, then head north along the highway for about 14km and cross Cassowary Creek. Shortly after crossing the creek take the left-hand turn-off to Mount Molloy and proceed south for 33km. Turn right at the Peninsula Developmental Rd and continue south for another 2km to Mount Molloy.

Mount Molloy has a huge pub, a rusting steam engine and a few shops which have been closed for decades. There is still a bakery, a general store and a petrol station but these do not hint at the thriving centre that sprang up here in the 1890s when the coppermine was at its height.

Mount Molloy is situated in a dry area where cattle grazing is now the dominant industry. The old steam engine which used to power the local sawmill stands like a sentinel at the southern entrance to the town. To the south is a small cemetery in which James (Venture) Mulligan is buried. The new inscription on his tombstone beautifully captures both the man and the spirit of Mount Molloy at its peak. The inscription

reads: 'James (Venture) Mulligan 1837–1907 Born Rothfriland, County Down. Migrated in 1860, found Palmer River gold in 1873, Hodgkinson River gold in 1875 which led to the establishment of Cairns and Port Douglas. He mined copper at Mount Molloy in the 1890s, married in 1903, bought the Mount Molloy Hotel in 1905, and died on 24-8-1907 from injuries received when he tried to break up a fight in his hotel. He had no children.'

2 COOKTOWN

Head north out of Mount Molloy for 2km back to the Peninsula Developmental Rd. Follow the road for 144km passing through Maryfarms, Mount Carbine and Maitland Downs to reach Lakeland which is not much more than a motel/ hotel and a service station. From Lakeland take the Cooktown Developmental Rd which heads north-east passing through Springvale. After 54km the road swings north at Black Mountain National Park and after another 28km, it reaches Cooktown. The Cooktown Developmental Rd becomes Hope St and leads into the town centre.

Cooktown is a quiet tourist town. It is notable for the prevalence of 4WD vehicles, being the end of the road for conventional vehicles travelling north.

It was also the site of the first white 'settlement' in Australia when Captain James Cook, having accidentally struck the Great Barrier Reef off the coast north of Cape Tribulation, struggled up the coast and beached the H M Barque *Endeavour* on the shores of the Endeavour River. Cook and his crew were to stay on the river's edge from 17 June to 4 August, 1770.

3 COOKTOWN LIGHTHOUSE

From the Cooktown Developmental Rd (Hope St) continue as far as Furneaux St. Turn left here and head north for two blocks to Charlotte St. Turn right and travel for two blocks to Webber Esplanade where Endeavour Park can be found on the left. Some of Cook's monuments are located in the park. From Endeavour Park head west along Webber Esplanade toward the centre of town, passing Banks St. Take the

next left into Green St and the second left into Hope St. Drive along Hope St for 200m and veer left into Flinders St. Veer to the right off Flinders St into Baird Rd. The curving road leads to the top of Grassy Hill. The Cooktown lighthouse is to the right off Baird Rd.

Even the town's lighthouse is dedicated to Captain Cook. A steep winding road leads to Grassy Hill which provides excellent views of the coast, the Endeavour River and Cooktown. At the top of the hill is another monument to Cook as well as the lighthouse. Cook's journals recall the first time he climbed the hill:

18 June 1770. I climbed one of the highest hills among those that overlooked the harbour, which afforded by no means a comfortable prospect; the lowland near the river is wholly overrun with mangroves, among which the saltwater flows every tide; and the high land appeared everywhere stony and barren. In the mean time, Mr Banks had also taken a walk up the country and met with the frames of several old Indian houses, and places where they had dressed shellfish.

COOKTOWN'S MANY MONUMENTS

There are no fewer than four monuments to Captain Cook in the town. There is a cairn at the place where he beached the *Endeavour*, another smaller monument a few metres away, a Bicentennial statue in the nearby Endeavour Park, and a huge civic monument further down the road.

Next to the large Cook memorial in the park there is also a memorial to Edmund Kennedy and his journey from Rockingham Bay to Escape River. Other memorials include one to Dan Seymour who established the National Riding Track from Melbourne to Cooktown in 1977, and further along the road (the only memorial listed by the National Trust), one to Mary Beatrice Watson who in 1882, with her baby and a Chinese servant, died from lack of water after escaping from Lizard Island where they had been attacked by Aborigines. Mary Watson's monument, a perfect example of Victorian Gothic, was erected in 1888 after public subscription had raised the money. There is also a cannon in the park which was provided to the town in 1889 to prevent an unlikely attack from the Russians.

4 WESTPAC BANK

From the lighthouse take the winding road down to Baird Rd and turn left into Flinders St. Follow the road round to the right into Hope St and continue past Green and Pryde sts to turn right into Furneaux St. Continue north for two blocks and turn left into Charlotte St in which the Westpac Bank is located.

The Westpac Bank, with its superb cedar joinery and its heavy masonry columns, suggests that the Queensland National Bank (which no longer exists) believed in the future prosperity of the port. In many ways the Bank's belief was justified; at the time, Cooktown was one of the busiest ports in Queensland. By 1875 it had an incredible 65 hotels, a school, a fire brigade and two churches and the main street meandered for nearly 3km.

5 JAMES COOK HISTORICAL MUSEUM

From Charlotte St proceed east to Furneaux St. Turn right and travel to the end of the block where the James Cook Museum is on the right, at the corner of Furneaux and Helen sts.

Some indication of the optimism which existed in Cooktown during the 1880s can be seen in the James Cook Historical Museum building (built in 1886) which was originally St Mary's Convent. This magnificent two-storeyed building was constructed in the belief that the town would eventually become one of the great centres of Australia. At the time Cooktown was the second-largest city in Queensland and the elaborate cast-iron columns and balustrades reflect this sense of importance.

The museum's exhibits include delights such as a recreated Chinese joss house (it was originally brought out from Canton), artefacts from the *Endeavour*, including one of the cannons jettisoned from the vessel when it ran aground on Endeavour Reef and one of the ship's anchors which was also

Grassy Hill provides a good view of Cooktown and the Reef.

recovered from the reef, a shell collection, and also lots of interesting material on Cooktown's early history.

6 COOKTOWN CEMETERY

From the James Cook Museum proceed north along Furneaux St for one block and turn left into Charlotte St. Travel west for four blocks to where Endeavour Valley Rd branches off to the right. Follow Endeavour Valley north-west for about 500m, passing the caravan park; the cemetery is on the right.

The Cooktown Cemetery may well be the best-presented cemetery in Australia. At the entrance is a large map indicating the graves of interest which include a Chinese shrine (over 20 000 Chinese passed through the town on their way to the goldfields and at one time the town had a separate Chinatown with a permanent population of nearly 3000 people – interestingly there is only one

Chinese grave in the cemetery), the graves of the son of William Hovell, the hapless Mrs Watson, the mysterious Normanby woman – a white woman who was found living with Aborigines in unexplained circumstances – the victims of at least two shipwrecks in the area, and a special section for non-believers and Aborigines.

7 BLACK MOUNTAIN NATIONAL PARK

Follow Hope St out of town where it becomes the Cooktown Developmental Rd. Follow this road south for 28km; the Black Mountain National Park lies on the east side of the road.

Black Mountain National Park is one of three parks in the Cooktown region which contain areas of environmental significance.

The park gets its name from the strange mountains of huge granite boulders which are blackened by lichens formed on the surface. They are of special significance to the local Aborigines who tell the legend of Kalcajagga, which recounts a feud between two brothers for the love of a girl.

The park is also the main habitat of the Godmans rock wallaby.

The other Cooktown national parks are the Endeavour River, which features mangroves, mudflats and sand dunes, and the Mount Cook National Park on the outskirts of Cooktown where you can walk to the forested summit of Mount Cook.

From the Black Mountain National Park head to the south along the road which leads off the Cooktown Developmental Rd. After 4km pass through Helenvale. Continue heading south for another 9km to Rossville. The Aboriginal community of Wujal Wujal is 33km south of Rossville on the same road.

From Wujal Wujal follow the road through Cape Tribulation National Park for some 32km. From Cape Tribulation (see also Tour 66) proceed south, passing through Thornton Beach after 14km. About 20km further on lies the Daintree River ferry crossing. Cross the river and continue south for 5km to the junction with the highway and the road to the Daintree township. Take the highway south for 25km to Mossman; Port Douglas is 20km further on.

The Endeavour River, Cooktown.

Black Mountain National Park.

Some of Cooktown's oldest buildings.

James Cook Historical Museum, Cooktown.

68 SUGARCANE AND ABORIGINAL LEGENDS

■ DRIVING TOUR ■ 441KM ■ 2 DAYS ■ EXPLORING SOUTH OF CAIRNS

While Cairns is a major tourist centre, each town in the region has its own low-level activities designed to lure visitors south, but the appeal of each place is really its simplicity and its history.

1 EDMONTON

Leave Cairns (see Tour 63) via The Esplanade, heading north to Florence St. Turn left into Florence St, which becomes the Bruce Highway. Follow the Bruce Highway out of Cairns heading west and then veering south to Edmonton which is 17km from Cairns.

Edmonton is fast becoming a suburb of Cairns. Established originally as a sugar-milling town (ideally located to serve the surrounding sugar plantations and with direct access to the port facilities at Cairns) it was first called Hambledon Junction because of its proximity to the Hambledon plantation and mill.

Hambledon was established in October 1881 when Thomas H Swallow took up land which would eventually be a plantation of 6000 acres (including 900 acres for sugarcane, 100 for bananas, 20 for pineapples and 20 for citrus trees) with its own sugar mill which cost over £33 000 to build.

By 1888 the plantation employed 32 whites, 29 Chinese, six Javanese and 176 Kanakas. At this time it was producing at least 1100 tons of sugar each year.

Swallow built a huge bungalow which a contemporary described: 'situated on a gentle rise about a mile from the mill was the residence of Mr Swallow, senior. It was an ideal tropical bungalow … surrounded by fine broad verandahs, one would always enjoy some nice cool shady spot.'

In 1898 the sugar company CSR bought the mill that Swallow had sold to a relative in 1891, and in 1911 the Queensland Railways Department changed the name of the settlement from Hambledon Junction to Edmonton – after a village in Middlesex, England. The irony is that even today the name Hambledon persists. The local school is 'Hambledon State School', the hotel is 'Hambledon Hotel' and the mill is still 'Hambledon Mill'.

2 SUGARWORLD

Entering Edmonton on the Bruce Highway, cross the bridge over Blackfellows Creek and turn to the right at Mill Rd. Continue along this road for 500m to a round-about. Veer to the right onto Isabella Rd and drive

some 500m to Store Rd, the Sugarworld carpark. Sugarworld is open on weekends, public holidays and during Queensland school holidays. It is open during the week for group bookings.

Sugarworld is an innovative leisure park that includes Hambledon Mill as part of its attractions. There is also an exotic fruits orchard, a water slide, a restaurant, and a train which runs around the perimeter of the park.

3 GORDONVALE

Return to the centre of town and turn right onto the Bruce Highway. Travel along the highway for approximately 9km. After crossing Maher Rd, turn left into Draper Rd which becomes Cairns Rd. Follow the road alongside the railway line into the centre of Gordonvale.

This sugar-milling town has a special charm. Unlike most sugar towns, it is built around a park and most of the buildings date back 70 or 80 years. It can also lay claim to the rather dubious privilege of being the place where the dreaded cane toad was first introduced to Australia. Apparently, on 22 June 1935, 102 cane toads were released near Gordonvale in the misguided belief that they would wipe out pests which were damaging the sugarcane crops.

Behind the town stands The Pyramid, or Pyramid Hill, a volcanic core which is shaped as its name suggests. Each year there is a competition to see who can get to the top in the shortest possible time. The record currently stands at 1 hour 20 minutes.

4 MULGRAVE RAMBLER

From Cairns Rd, which becomes Thumm St as it veers sharply south, turn left into Gordon St. The Mulgrave Central Sugar Mill is located on the right. The Mulgrave Rambler departs from near the Mulgrave Mill.

The town offers a number of attractions of which the most appealing is 'The Mulgrave Rambler', a journey on a steam-driven sugar train along a railway which takes passengers from the town, crosses the Mulgrave River

several times and passes through rainforest before reaching its destination at Orchid Valley, a substantial orchid nursery.

The trip includes a visit to the Mulgrave Sugar Mill which started operations in November 1896. The first mill in the area was the privately owned Pyramid Mill on the upper Mulgrave River which started crushing in 1885; it failed within a decade. The Gordonvale Mill replaced it as the main sugar mill in the district. By early 1898 a railway line had been constructed between the town and the port at Cairns.

5 DEERAL ABORIGINAL AND TORRES STRAIT ISLANDERS CORPORATION

From the mill travel back along Gordon St, crossing the railway tracks and turning left into Mill St. Follow Mill

Munro Street, Babinda.

St for 1km to the Bruce Highway. Turn left onto the Bruce Highway and drive south to Babinda. The Deeral Aboriginal and Torres Strait Islanders Corporation is located just north of the town. Turn right into Nelson St at the cemetery before you enter Babinda.

Babinda is the location of one of the most successful experiments in Aboriginal self-management in Australia. The local Deeral Aboriginal and Torres Strait Islanders Corporation has established a business manufacturing artefacts which has become so successful that it not only attracts tourists but also sells locally and overseas. A wide range of products, from didgeridoos and boomerangs to bark paintings, is made in the workshops which are open to visitors.

6 BABINDA

Return to the Bruce Highway and continue towards Babinda. After crossing Weinerts Creek turn right across the railway lines into Munro St.

Babinda's name is probably a corruption of the word 'binda' which meant 'waterfall' in the dialect of the local Aborigines. One wonders whether the Aborigines were actually referring to the waterfalls in the nearby Wooroonooran National Park or the annual rainfall which is a huge 4218mm.

The town's most unusual building is the Babinda Hotel (once known as the State Hotel) in Munro Street, the main street. It looks like just another north Queensland pub but it is the only hotel in Queensland (and probably in Australia) which was built by a State Government.

The unusual landlord was the brunt of many jokes and unintentional ironies. The State Government tried to justify the building of the hotel on the grounds that it had been constructed to encourage controlled drinking and stamp out sly grog shops. It also claimed that the hotel would offer reasonably priced lodgings for the hundreds of itinerant workers who came to Babinda during the cane-cutting season.

The hotel was opened on 29 May 1917 by the Home Secretary, Mr Huxham, who, after delivering an opening address which attacked the sly grog industry, invited his audience into the pub for a free drink.

An aerial view of Cairns and the hinterland.

7 JOSEPHINE FALLS

Head out of Babinda travelling west on Munro St which veers to the left and becomes the Boulders Rd. Drive 10km to The Boulders picnic and swimming area. After visiting The Boulders, return to Babinda and turn right onto the Bruce Highway. Travel 9km south to the turn-off to Bartle Frere. The Josephine Falls are well signposted; there is a 800m walk from the car park to the falls and the swimming area.

The Josephine Falls are regarded by many as the most beautiful falls in north Queensland. Certainly their beauty was enough to attract the advertising world – they were the setting for a TV advertisement for Lifesavers.

8 EUBENANGEE SWAMP NATIONAL PARK

Return to the Bruce Highway and head north to Bramston Beach Rd. Travel east for 8km, across the Russell River. Turn to the right at a fork in the road onto Cartwright Rd. The entry to Eubenangee Swamp National Park is located on the right.

The Eubenangee Swamp National Park with its 1.5km walk allows visitors to experience the variety of the flora and fauna which inhabit tropical coastal wetlands.

Return to the Bruce Highway and go back to Babinda. Return to Cairns heading north on the Bruce Highway.

THE BOULDERS

Legend has it that a very beautiful girl named Oolana from the Yidinji people married an old and respected elder, whose name was Waroonoo, from her tribe. Some time after their marriage another tribe arrived in the area. In the group was a handsome young man named Dyga. When they saw each other Oolana and Dyga fell in love. Realising the crime they were committing the young lovers fled into the valleys. Both tribes followed them. When they were finally captured Oolana broke free and threw herself into the still waters of the nearby creek calling for Dyga to follow her. As she hit the waters her cries for her lost lover turned to rushing water and the land shook with sorrow. Huge boulders were thrown up and the crying Oolana disappeared among them. It is said that her spirit still guards the boulders and that her cries can still be heard as she calls for her lost lover. Travellers should beware of her siren calls.

A series of large rocks in the river, The Boulders, have been worn smooth by rains. They are a dramatic sight but one which is given greater significance by the Aboriginal legend and the modern tragedies which have surrounded them. Since 1959 over 15 people have drowned in this dangerous stretch of water.

At the beginning of the path to The Boulders is a simple monument which reads 'Pray for the soul of Patrick McGann he came for a visit and stayed forever'. The easy walking path then moves through tropical rainforest which echoes with the incessant sound of the birds. The roots of the trees have been twisted into fantastic shapes, and the canopy from the tall trees offers a cool covering even on the hottest days.

Cutting sugarcane, Gordonvale.

69 THE ATHERTON TABLELAND

■ DRIVING TOUR ■ 174KM ■ 1 DAY ■ A WORLD OF CATTLE AND TROPICAL GREENERY

The Tableland was originally settled by gold prospectors and cattlemen who discovered rich deposits and excellent pastures. Today it combines its historic past with a sense of quietness and simplicity.

1 MAREEBA

From The Esplanade in Cairns (see Tour 63) drive south. Turn right into Florence St and drive four blocks. Turn right into Sheridan St which becomes the Captain Cook Highway. Follow the highway to Smithfield. Turn to the north-west at the roundabout onto the Kennedy Highway to reach Kuranda (see also Tour 63). Leave Kuranda on the Kennedy Highway travelling south-west for about 34km to Mareeba.

The largest town on the Atherton Tableland, Mareeba is a service town which is only partly ameliorated by the bright displays of flowers and flowering trees which adorn the central island in the town's main street.

Mareeba, first settled by John Atherton in 1880, is the centre for a number of agricultural activities including coffee plantations, mango and avocado farms, and, most importantly, tobacco growing.

The town of Mareeba is the centre of the Atherton Tableland's tobacco industry and consequently is home to the Tobacco Leaf Marketing Board. Tobacco was first grown in the area in 1928 and the crop did much to bring prosperity to a centre which had previously been nothing more than just a stopping point. Today there are over 400 tobacco farms in the area around the town. The Tinaroo Falls dam supplies the industry with most of its water requirements.

Mareeba is supposedly a local Aboriginal term meaning 'meeting of the waters' or 'place to meet'.

2 JOHN ATHERTON MONUMENT

The monument to John Atherton is located at the northern end of Byrnes St, just before Granite Creek.

Fascinating Facets Crystal Caves, Atherton.

A monument located at the northern end of the town declares: 'John Atherton (1837–1917). Pioneer of the Tableland. Founder of Mareeba. Settled at Emerald End Station on the "Barron" 1876. Discovered tin and named locality Tinaroo. Led party to Wild River (Herberton) where he had previously discovered tin. Erected Mareeba's first house near this site 1880'.

His house became a kind of inn. Atherton was by nature a generous man and his house, the only one in the region, was a popular stopping-off point for the miners, teamsters and Cobb & Co coaches on their way from Port Douglas to the tinfields at Herberton and the Hodgkinson River goldfields. Mareeba eventually became the first town to be established on the Atherton Tableland.

The town grew rapidly with the arrival of the railway in 1893. The mining activities at Chillagoe led to the creation of a private branch line which ran out through Dimbulah to the Chillagoe copper smelters. The railway line was built in 1899 and eventually taken over by the government.

3 ATHERTON MOSQUE

Return south along Byrnes St to Lloyd St, just past the Rotary Park. Turn left into Lloyd St. The mosque is located on the corner of Lloyd and Walsh sts.

One of the town's most fascinating landmarks is a mosque. Built by the town's Albanian community it shows a religious dimension of the town which would otherwise go unnoticed.

4 GRANITE GORGE

To reach Granite Gorge turn back into Byrnes St and drive south to the roundabout. Turn right into Rankin St. Cross the railway line and take the fourth turn-off left into Stewart St. At the end of the street turn right into Morrow St, which becomes Chewko Rd. Travel west for about 12km to reach the gorge.

The town's major tourist attraction is the Granite Gorge. As it is situated on privately

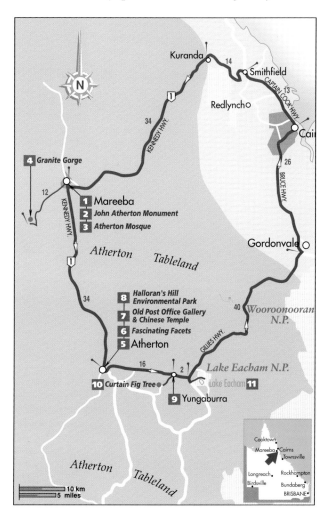

owned land, there is a nominal charge to enter. The huge granite boulders were formed by relatively recent volcanic activity. They are a dramatic and unusual anomaly in the surrounding landscape. The boulders slump across the terrain looking like Dali watches and a stream (which obviously becomes a torrent during the wet season – look for the flood debris in the nearby trees) winds through the area.

5 ATHERTON

Return to Mareeba along Chewko Rd. Turn left into Stewart St and right into Rankin St. Turn right at the roundabout into Byrnes St, which becomes the Kennedy Highway. Travel 34km south to Atherton.

Atherton, at the heart of the Atherton Tableland, is a typical country service town and was named after John Atherton. It was first settled in the early 1880s when it became a camp for cedar cutters. Initially called Prior's Pocket after the Priors, a family of cedar cutters who settled near the present site of the town, it was surveyed in 1885 and renamed Atherton. The town became a stopover point on the roads from the coast to the Herberton tinfields.

A substantial Chinese population (at its peak it probably numbered around 1100 people) lived around the town working for the timber cutters and setting up businesses. They also worked the rich soils producing vegetables for the miners. The Chinese began to leave the area after 1907 and much of their land was taken over by soldier settlers after World War I.

Over the years Atherton has been the centre for a number of industries on the Tableland. The rich red volcanic soils of the area (estimated to be over 30m deep) have been used to produce maize, potatoes, peanuts, macadamia nuts and avocados. The town has also been important to the local dairy industry with a butter factory opening in 1909 and a large dairy co-operative being established in 1914.

6 FASCINATING FACETS
Head into Atherton on the Kennedy Highway, which becomes Tolga Rd. Cross the railway line to reach Anzac Place. Turn right into Main St. Fascinating Facets is located between Jack and Vernon sts.

The town's major 'tourist attraction' is the much publicised Fascinating Facets. This gem shop has a gallery of very high-quality gems and valuable rocks and a basement area which has been constructed like a cave with a variety of crystals (quartz, amethyst and topaz among others) on display in a carefully lit area.

7 OLD POST OFFICE GALLERY AND CHINESE TEMPLE
Head south along Main St towards Herberton. The Old Post Office Gallery and the Chinese Temple are located on the left just past the caravan park.

Located at the southern end of town on the Herberton Road is the Old Post Office Gallery. The town's post office was moved to this site and is now used as a gallery and museum. It contains a range of work by local artists and potters.

The Chinese Temple to the Emperor Ho Wong (known as the Chinese Joss House) situated next to the Old Post Office Gallery is a rare combination of traditional Chinese architecture and local corrugated iron. The prominent local Fong On family is currently rebuilding the old temple and its adjacent kitchen annex and community hall. The ornate interior with its subtle pink shading and cedar lining is truly remarkable.

8 HALLORAN'S HILL ENVIRONMENTAL PARK
Return along the Atherton–Herberton Rd to the Kennedy Highway. Turn right and drive to Louise St, just after the bowling green. Turn left into Louise St. After crossing Priors Creek turn right into Maher St.

The Halloran's Hill Environmental Park is a very interesting reminder of the Atherton Tableland's volcanic past. A path leads the visitor to the edge of a crater which was formed from an extinct volcano. It was once

Tobacco farming, Mareeba.

possible to go down into the crater but it is now fenced off. The crater hole is densely vegetated with rainforest and offers superb views of the Atherton Tableland.

9 YUNGABURRA
Return along Maher St to Louise St and turn right. This road becomes the Gordonvale–Atherton Rd. At the end of the road turn to the right into Maunds St. Drive about 16km to Yungaburra.

Yungaburra is an attractive little township on the Atherton Tableland which came into existence as a direct result of John Atherton's discoveries of tin and gold at Tinaroo Creek in 1878. The gold and tin fossickers who moved into the area sought a new route to the coast, arguing that the existing routes to Cairns and Port Douglas were unnecessarily long. John Robson, who had been with Atherton when he found the tin, cut a track from the Tableland to the coast which became known as Robson's track. The settlement of Allumbah Pocket, which grew up on this track, eventually became known as Yungaburra.

For some time the town of Yungaburra operated as a staging post for people moving to and from the coast. There was some timber cutting, particularly cedar, in the early days but the town's primary function was as a service centre.

The town now has a large number of interesting buildings all built from local timber. No fewer than 23 have been listed by the National Trust. The boom period for the town seems to have occurred shortly after the arrival of the railway in 1910, and between 1910 and 1920 some of the town's most attractive buildings were constructed. St Mark's Anglican Church on Eacham Road was built in 1913 at a cost of £250. The same year St Patrick's Catholic Church at the top of Eacham Road was completed. The buildings along Cedar Street, the narrow street at the side of the Lake Eacham Hotel, all belong to this period. The former Bank of New South Wales is on the corner directly opposite the Lake Eacham Hotel.

10 CURTAIN FIG TREE
Head west on the Gillies Highway out of Yungaburra. The turn-off to the Curtain Fig Tree is on the left after leaving the town.

Yungaburra's great tourist attraction is the deservedly famous Curtain Fig Tree, located only 3km from the town on the Malanda road. This huge tree has, by an accident of

Granite Gorge, Mareeba.

nature, created a vast curtain of roots which drop some 15m from the main body of the tree to the ground.

11 LAKE EACHAM
Return to Yungaburra and head east on the Gillies Highway for 2km to the turn-off to Malanda. Turn right and travel 2km to the turn-off to the Lake Eacham National Park.

Nearby is Lake Eacham, a huge crater lake which was probably formed as recently as 10 000 years ago. The local Aborigines, the Ngadyan people, explain the origin of the lake in a way that seems to blend myth with reality. Apparently two newly initiated men broke a taboo and the Rainbow Serpent punished them by destroying their camp with a combination of winds like a cyclone, a red cloud in the sky and the earth shaking. The men tried to escape but were consumed by a hole which opened in the earth.

Lake Eacham is now a place of remarkable beauty and peacefulness. The walks around its foreshores are quite superb and the swimming facilities are excellent. Over 100 bird species have been recorded in the surrounding rainforest which is also home to the musky rat-kangaroo.

Return to the Gillies Highway and turn right, heading north-west for 40km to Gordonvale (see Tour 68). From Gordonvale head north on the Bruce Highway for about 26km to Cairns.

Monument to John Atherton, Mareeba.

70 DAIRY CATTLE AND FIG TREES

■ DRIVING TOUR ■ 290KM ■ 1 DAY ■ TEA, CHEESE, GIANT FIG TREES AND WATERFALLS

The Atherton Tableland is an area of dairy cattle, sleepy villages, interesting volcanic formations, lakes surrounded by forests, and huge fig trees. The driving is pleasant and the sites are memorable.

1 CATHEDRAL FIG AND LAKE TINAROO

Leave Gordonvale (see Tour 68) via George St and head south onto Riverstone Rd which crosses the Bruce Highway and becomes the Gillies Highway after the roundabout. Continue along the Gillies Highway towards Yungaburra. Before reaching Yungaburra turn right onto Boar Pocket Rd, also known as the Danbulla Forest Dve. Travel along this road to the Cathedral Fig.

Tinaroo, Tinaroo Falls, Tinaroo Falls Dam and Lake Tinaroo all refer to the small settlement which has sprung up on the shores of the huge artificial lake which lies to the north of Yungaburra. The town takes its name from a creek where John Atherton found tin and gold in 1878. Atherton is credited with naming the creek Tinaroo.

Construction on Tinaroo Dam began in 1953 and was completed in 1958. It is now one of the three largest water storages in Queensland and has dammed the Barron River to supply water for local tobacco farming and to supplement the water moving through the Barron Gorge Hydro-Electricity Station.

Tinaroo is an ideal place to stay while exploring the 31km Danbulla Forest Road. This road, which runs from the Gillies Highway to the village, is partly sealed and partly dirt. It winds through a variety of vegetational zones, from rainforest where the spectacular Cathedral Fig Tree (not to be confused with the Curtain Fig Tree near Yungaburra) can be seen to the precisely planted pine forests which are administered by the Atherton Forestry Office.

2 LAKE EURAMOO

From the Cathedral Fig continue along the Danbulla Forest Dve to Lake Euramoo.

Halfway along the route is the beautiful crater lake, Lake Euramoo which, like so many lakes on the tableland, is volcanic in origin. Contained in a double-explosion volcanic crater, it is recognised as one of the youngest geological features on the Atherton Tableland – little more than 10 000 years old. It is a popular haunt for birdwatchers and an ideal place for a relaxing bushwalk.

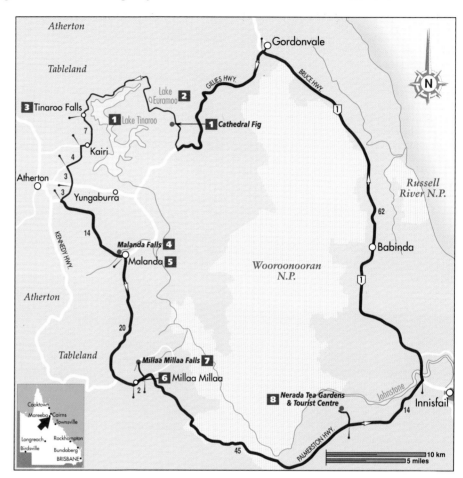

A tea plantation near Millaa Millaa.

The old cheese factory, Millaa Millaa.

3 TINAROO FALLS

Continue along the Danbulla Forest Dve to reach Tinaroo Falls.

The town of Tinaroo Falls has grown over the years so that now it offers a pleasant escape from the heat of the coast. Its setting on the shores of the artificial lake is exceptionally beautiful and the locals, aware that there is a passing tourist trade, have attempted to cater for the tourists' differing needs. There is a very peaceful caravan park nestled in the trees, the Lake Tinaroo Orchard Gardens and Nursery, and facilities for boating and windsurfing on the lake.

Since 1986 the favourite fish of the north, barramundi, have been breeding in the lake. They have now reached a size where it is legal to fish for them.

4 MALANDA FALLS

Continue out of Tinaroo Falls on Tinaroo Falls Rd to Kairi. About 1km out of Kairi turn left on the road to Atherton. Drive along this road for 4km and then turn left, heading south to the Atherton–Gordonvale Rd. Cross this road and continue south for 3km. Turn left onto the road to Malanda. Drive 14km to Malanda.

The northern entrance to the town passes the Malanda Falls. In comparison to the spectacular gorges of the escarpment these humble falls are something of a let-down. They fall no more than a few metres and the town's swimming pool lies at the bottom. The name 'Malanda', according to some sources, is the local Aboriginal word for 'waterfalls'.

The Malanda Environmental Park (just opposite the Malanda Falls) offers a short walk through the rainforest and a wonderful opportunity to see a wide range of tropical rainforest trees.

5 MALANDA

Continue into the township.

The name of Malanda is synonymous throughout north Queensland with milk. There are even some places where 'Malanda' milk is slightly more expensive than 'common' milk; it is, in the opinion of the locals, the best milk in the world. Tourist promoters have seized upon the fact that Malanda milk is sold in the Northern Territory and as far north as Weipa, and have declared Malanda to be 'the headquarters for one of the largest and longest milk runs in the world'. In fact, the milk is also exported to Indonesia and Malaysia.

A small and pleasant town on the Atherton Tableland, Malanda was first developed in the 1880s when the discovery of tin in the Herberton district saw a steady stream of miners moving over the mountains from the coast.

In 1886 a decision was made to bring the railway into the area but the problems of construction were enormous. By 1890 the railway had reached Kuranda. It pushed on to Mareeba in 1893 and Atherton in 1903 but didn't reach Malanda until 1911. The line was closed in 1964.

In 1908, James English (later the publican of the Malanda Hotel) and James Emerson moved into the area. Both saw the district's dairy potential; English brought cattle from Kiama and the Richmond River areas in New South Wales and Emerson had a herd of 1026 cattle overlanded from Lismore. They took about 16 months to reach Malanda and only 560 survived the journey. The industry grew and by 1919 Malanda had its own butter factory. In 1973 this amalgamated with the factory in Millaa Millaa to form the Atherton Tableland Co-operative Dairy Association.

In 1910, in response to a developing local industry, John Prince established a saw mill in Malanda. It was from this mill that the boards for the Malanda Hotel (built in 1911) were sawn.

6 MILLAA MILLAA

From James St turn right into Patrick St, which becomes the Millaa Millaa–Malanda Rd. Follow this road for 20km to Millaa Millaa.

Millaa Millaa lies on the southern edge of the Atherton Tableland. It is a tiny, attractive settlement; the wide and uncluttered main street has a vivid display of flowering trees and bushes running down one side of it.

Like most of the towns on the Atherton Tableland, Millaa Millaa is economically one-dimensional – it is essentially a town servicing the local dairy industry. The hills around the town are dotted with the black and white of numerous Holstein Fresian cattle, including a number of stud herds.

The name Millaa Millaa is said to mean 'waterfalls' in the language of the local Aborigines. There is a story which suggests that it was Christie Palmerston who gave the town its name. In 1884 Palmerston, an expert at constructing routes leading from the Tableland to the sea, created a track from Innisfail through Millaa Millaa to the mining settlement at Herberton.

Land in the area was settled after 1910. In 1921 the railway, which had been working its way slowly south from Cairns for over 30 years, finally reached Millaa Millaa. The town was the terminus for the line until it closed in 1964. During its time as a railhead Millaa Millaa saw a boom in the local timber industry.

In the centre of the main street is the Eacham Historical Museum. It is usually only open on Sundays but if you contact the news agency next door they can arrange for it to be opened at other times. The museum has some Aboriginal artefacts and some very well-presented displays of photographs and old pieces of equipment from the area. There are some particularly interesting pieces from the local butter factory which opened in 1930 and was amalgamated with the larger factory at Malanda in the 1970s.

7 MILLAA MILLAA FALLS

Drive out of Millaa Millaa on the Palmerston Highway. About 2km out of town turn left to the falls.

A couple of kilometres out of town are the Millaa Millaa Falls. The car park is the viewing area, so lazy visitors can sit in their cars and watch the falls!

The circuit road runs for about 15km and rejoins the Palmerston Highway. The falls are the first in a series of three on what is known as 'The Waterfalls Circuit', a circular trip of less than an hour which also encompasses the Zillie Falls and the Ellinjaa Falls. There are at least five more sets of falls within this rich farming and rainforest area for people who never tire of watching water cascade from great heights.

8 NERADA TEA GARDENS AND TOURIST CENTRE

Continue eastward along the Palmerston Highway for about 45km until the turn-off north to the Nerada Tea Gardens and Tourist Centre.

The Cathedral Fig, near Tinaroo Falls Dam.

Nestled into the foothills below Mount Bartle Frere (Queenland's highest mountain) are 250ha of tea plantation. Started in 1959, Nerada prides itself on being the only commercially productive tea plantation in Australia. Specially designed machinery and labour-saving techniques were implemented and it is projected that Nerada will be able to produce 5 million kilograms of tea annually before the year 2000. It is open from 9:00 to 16:30 each day and visitors are shown the process from withering to crushing, oxidising, drying, sorting and packing.

Innisfail has a long association with tea production. It is widely believed that the very first tea in Australia was planted in 1884 at nearby Bingil Bay.

Return to the Palmerston Highway and travel about 14km to the Bruce Highway. Turn left, heading north on the Bruce Highway through Babinda. It is about 62km to Gordonvale.

Millaa Millaa Falls on 'The Waterfalls Circuit'.

71 THE UNDARA LAVA TUBES

■ DRIVING TOUR ■ 536KM ■ 2 DAYS ■ WALKING INSIDE A VOLCANO FLOW

The Undara Lava Tubes are reputedly the largest in the world. They can be inspected only by taking conducted tours organised by an eco-tourism organisation known as the Undara Experience.

1 RAVENSHOE

Leave Cairns (see Tour 63) and head south along the Bruce Highway for 24km, passing through Edmonton until you reach the Gordonvale turn-off. From here turn onto the Gillies Highway, headed south-west. About 43km along this route is Yurraburra and it is an additional 13km to Atherton. Turn off the Gillies Highway onto the Kennedy Highway in Atherton and follow it south for 53km to Ravenshoe.

Ravenshoe is the highest town in Queensland. The temperature is typically mild, rarely exceeding 26°C, which means that it attracts people wanting to escape the heat and humidity of the coast.

The first European settlement in the area gave an indication of the town's future. In 1881 William Mazlin discovered substantial stands of cedar in the area and named the local river (later to become the settlement) Cedar Creek. The first sawmill was built in 1899 but the town wasn't settled to any significant extent until 1910, mainly because of the difficulties involved in getting timber from the Tableland down to the coast. By this time, the railway line had reached Millaa Millaa and bullock teams could haul the timber to the railhead.

For 70 years Ravenshoe relied on timber for its economic survival and its sawmills produced high-quality rainforest timbers for markets in Australia and overseas.

Ravenshoe is the access point for both the Tully Falls (signposted off the Kennedy Highway) and the Millstream Falls which, when they are in flood, are supposed to be the widest falls in Australia.

2 WARRUMA SWAMP

A further 44km west of Ravenshoe along the Kennedy Highway is Mount Garnet. Just before entering the town from the north there is a dirt road which heads east to Warruma Swamp.

Although little-known, this is one of the wonders of the Mount Garnet area. The swamp retains water long after the other

Large ant-hills near Ravenshoe.

wetlands in the area have dried up and consequently draws an amazing range of birdlife from the surrounding region. Edged by lilies and with dozens of varieties of birds, the swamp is something special. At certain times of the year there are literally thousands of black swans here.

3 MOUNT GARNET

Return to the main road and drive to Mount Garnet.

Mount Garnet is one of those towns that is easy to pass through without stopping. To the traveller it looks like nothing more than a couple of pubs and service stations, and a few shops and houses in the middle of nowhere. The miners who first settled the town hardly slowed down as they moved through. It is said that when, in about 1904, a rumour went round that the original copper mine was going to close down, half the men didn't wait for their notice to quit. They simply packed up their few belongings and were gone by lunchtime.

Mount Garnet was first settled in the late 1890s and early 1900s when copper was found in the area. Within months, the Mount Garnet Freehold Copper and Silver Mining Company Ltd had built a smelter and was busy hiring hundreds of men to dig the valuable mineral out of the ground.

At first the smelted copper was shipped out by camel (there are some interesting photographs of the camel teams on the walls of the Norwestgate Cafe), but by 1902 a branch line connecting the town to the line from Mareeba to Chillagoe had been built and the copper was being railed out to Lappa Junction and then to the coast.

A few remnants of the mine are still in evidence. Take the road opposite Norwestgate Motel and follow it south on a dirt road; this leads to the old Assay House (which is currently being restored) and beyond it is evidence of the mining operations. Little is left but there is enough to show the scale of the operation at the turn of the century.

Today the town has a reputation as an excellent starting place for gold prospectors and gem collectors, with fields of topaz nearby. Tin is also an important source of income for the area.

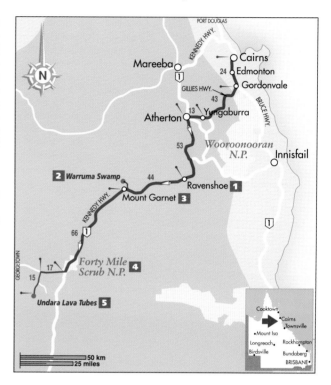

4 FORTY MILE SCRUB NATIONAL PARK

Continue south along the Kennedy Highway for some 66km until you reach the fork at the southern end of Forty Mile Scrub National Park.

This is a most unassuming area with only small signs on the side of the road indicating that it is anything special. There are no roads into the park and no signs to clarify why the area has been declared a National Park. The first indication the traveller receives is an awareness that the vegetation on either side of the road has changed – there is a density and richness to it which is not characteristic of the region. Forty Mile Scrub National Park is a relic of an ancient rainforest which has remained virtually untouched for millions of years. It has a bewilderingly rich variety of flora species – some say it is the greatest concentration anywhere in Australia – and is also an area which is used to support the theory of continental drift. The rainforest has parallels with similar rainforests in India and Burma, suggesting that at one time the Australian and Asian continents were linked and that over millions of years they have gradually drifted apart.

5 UNDARA LAVA TUBES

From here, head west along the Gulf Developmental Rd. After 17km turn left off this road heading south. After a further 6km there is a fork in the road to the right. The Undara Lava Tubes lie 9km along this road.

172

This is one of Queensland's most wonderful natural phenomena. The Undara Lava Tubes were formed when 23km^3 of lava from a volcano spilled out over the land and travelled along a river bed. It is estimated that the whole process took two to three weeks with the lava flowing at a rate of around 500m per hour. The water in the river ensured that the lava formed a vast cylindrical tunnel. It is believed that 'The Wall', the name of a section of the lava tube near Mount Surprise, is similar to the lunar ridges on the moon.

There are two branches to the Undara Lava Tubes – one runs for about 16km and the other for possibly as much as 28km. At various points the tubes have collapsed and these can be seen from the air as dark, heavily vegetated depressions.

The tubes are vast with a maximum width of 21.2m and heights of up to 10m. They tend to be relatively straight and are only interrupted where the roof has caved in.

Nearby is the Undara Crater but it is inaccessible by vehicle and involves a considerable walk. The huge crater, some 340m across and 48m deep, has steep inner slopes. It is estimated that the volcano erupted about 190 000 years ago.

The Undara Tubes are open to the public but they can only be explored by joining an organised tour which leaves from the Undara Lava Lodge. It is absolutely essential to book a trip in advance before travelling to the site. People are turned away if a tour is full and it is silly to drive hundreds of kilometres to see nothing more than a camping site, a restaurant and cabins made from old Queensland Railways rolling stock in the middle of the bush. There is no vantage point near the Lava Lodge where you can see the tubes. Contact tel: (070) 31 7933 or fax (070) 31 7939 for bookings.

A number of tours are available but the main tours are a half-day and one-day tour which visit a number of the breaks (or caves)

The ancient volcanic landscape at Undara.

One of Undara's huge lava tube formations.

The Undara Lava Lodge bush breakfast.

Vegetation around a collapsed lava tube.

in the lava tubes and actually allow participants to climb down into them. The half-day tour starts at the Lava Lodge and travels through the bush past the Hundred Mile Swamp until it reaches a rocky outcrop. Visitors climb to the top of the outcrop where they can see the remnants of the volcano which produced the lava flows. The guide gives a detailed description of how the lava tubes were formed and points out the main features of the area. There are also warnings about the number of snakes in the region and interesting comments about both the flora and fauna. The journey then continues to the first of the lava caves. It is an easy walk to the base of the cave and, once again, the guide explains the fauna of the cave as well as the geological features. The

tour then stops for morning or afternoon tea in the bush. After tea another lava cave is explored. During the afternoon, the animals start to come out and it is common to see kangaroos grazing beside the road and rock wallabies sitting quietly in the bush at the top of the entrance to the caves.

The area around the tubes is typical tropical bush country with pandanus, ironbarks, white-barked gums and cabbage gums as well as remnant rainforest – known as semi-evergreen vine thicket – in the mouths of the caves. There are spectacular views from the surrounding granite bluffs – several of the guided walks will take you there. It is common to see a wide variety of Australian wildlife – there are spiders and colonies of the eastern horseshoe bat. The guides are highly qualified and their talks are interesting. There are also opportunities to spot nocturnal animals in their natural habitat on guided night walks.

If you are disappointed that you are not making your own way around the lava tubes, just remember that a bus with about 20 people is much more environmentally friendly than 10 4WD vehicles with two people in each one. This is eco-tourism which is committed to protecting the surrounding environment.

It is worth booking accommodation at the Lava Lodge as the meals are typical Aussie bush tucker and the breakfast – held around a campfire in the bush – is a real experience. People say that it's the best bacon they've ever eaten. But then few of us eat bacon cooked over an open fire.

Return to the Gulf Developmental Rd and turn right. After 17km turn left, back onto the Kennedy Highway and follow it for 163km to Atherton. From this point head east, back along the Gillies Highway for 56km and turn onto the Bruce Highway, heading north to Cairns which lies a further 24km along this route.

Millstream Falls, Ravenshoe.

INDEX